W9-AZO-491

THE MIND OF AN ASSASSIN

Isaac Don Levine

The Mind of an Assassin

"In the Twentieth Century power wears the mask of tragedy."

ALBERT CAMUS

NEW YORK

Farrar, Straus and Cudahy

Library of Congress catalog card number 59-10190
First Printing, 1959
Manufactured in the United States of America
by H. Wolff, New York
Published simultaneously in Canada
by Ambassador Books, Ltd., Toronto

TO RUTH

who shared in this arduous effort

Acknowledgements

To Sylvia and Nathaniel Weyl, who lived in Mexico and wrote the first biography of President Cardenas, I am indebted for translating from the Spanish the voluminous official and documentary reports on the assassin and his crime, and for their collaboration in digesting the material for publication.

To Dr. Alfonso Quiroz Cuaron, who placed at my disposal altogether some 1,500 pages of minutes, questionnaires, correspondence, photographs and other manuscript material covering the psychological and medical examinations of the assassin, I owe a debt of lasting gratitude.

Without the encouragement of Clifford Forster, friend of Mexico, New York attorney, ever-ready champion of civil liberties and anti-totalitarian causes, this labor would never have been undertaken.

Special credit should be given to Murray Teigh Bloom, the enterprising journalist, who first publicized in the United States the discovery by Dr. Quiroz Cuaron of evidence that Trotsky's assassin, Jacques Mornard, was in reality Ramon Mercader.

Profound thanks are due to correspondents in Mexico City and Spain as well as to former political associates of the Mercaders, Catalonian refugees and exiles abroad, all of whom prefer to remain anonymous, for their contributions of vital biographical data to this study.

Contents

Background

It was late in the afternoon of August 20, 1940. Leon Trotsky sat at his desk in the study of his fortified villa on the outskirts of Mexico City. Within his reach was the switch to an alarm system, but at that moment a young man of twenty-seven stood between him and the switch. The young man has told, in memorable words, what then happened:

"I put my raincoat on the table on purpose so that I could take out the ice-axe which I had in the pocket. I decided not to lose the brilliant opportunity which was offered me and at the exact moment when Trotsky started to read my article, which served as my pretext, I took the *piolet* out of my raincoat, took it in my fist and, closing my eyes, I gave him a tremendous blow on the head . . .

"The man screamed in such a way that I will never forget it as long as I live. His scream was *Aaaa* . . . very long, infinitely long and it still seems to me as if that scream were piercing my brain. I saw Trotsky get up like a madman. He threw himself at me and bit my hand. —Look, you can still see the marks of his teeth. Then I pushed him, so that he fell to the floor. He lifted himself as best he could and then, running or stumbling, I don't know how, he got out of the room."

Trotsky's chief guard, who was in the next room, has described what followed: "The Old Man stumbled out of his study, blood streaming down his face. 'See what they have done to me!' he said." Shortly afterward he lapsed into unconsciousness.

"See what *they* have done to me!"

They, as Trotsky knew in the last moments of his life, were the planners whose patient, ingenious, and painstaking efforts over four years had finally achieved their goal—his murder. *They* knew that the assassin could penetrate the fortress-like home, with its high walls, its towers manned by a crew of gunners, its iron-doored entrance guarded around the clock, in one way only —as a friend. *They* knew that, by gaining friendly entrée, the young man would not only have access to Trotsky's study, but would even be able to stage a rehearsal of the murder (as the reader will find in Chapter 6) three days in advance.

They were clever planners, with all the resources of a powerful modern state to draw upon. And what was the key to their plan? Seduction. It was carefully worked out, in a reversal of the classic Mata Hari pattern. The young man would be the seducer. He would seduce Sylvia Ageloff, one of Trotsky's trusted American followers, who was innocent of complicity and who had a nervous breakdown after the murder. The assassin successfully carried out his assignment of seduction for murder for more than two years (it takes time to gain entrée into the household of a world-famous political exile) before he struck.

As a dedicated communist of the Stalinist school, the assassin disguised his identity from the start. In 1938 he was introduced to Sylvia in Paris by the friend of a friend as "Jacques Mornard," the son of a wealthy Belgian diplomat of aristocratic origin. Despite the Belgian government's official statement that there never was such a diplomat, the assassin continues to claim that he is "Jacques Mornard Vandendreschd." He followed Sylvia to Mexico via the United States on a doctored passport which had belonged to a Canadian volunteer killed in the Spanish civil war. *They* had it made out, with a curious slip in spelling, in the name of "Frank Jacson."

Since the fatal day almost nineteen years ago, the assassin has stubbornly refused to produce any evidence or witnesses as to his claimed birth, schooling, military service, past employment and other activities, or to acknowledge the members of his family, particularly his mother and sister and brother, now living in Paris, and his father, living in Barcelona.

His full name is Jaime Ramon Mercader del Rio Hernandez. Attractive in appearance, cultivated in his manners, considerate of his fellow-prisoners, with a record of exemplary conduct in jail, Ramon Mercader was denied parole by the Mexican prison authorities because of his determined refusal to admit his real identity, irrefutably proven by fingerprints.

Ramon Mercader is, of course, trapped by the logic of his situation. He cannot give up his disguise without revealing that he is a Soviet agent. To admit his true identity would lead, through his mother, to facts which prove who *they* are—to an admission that the Kremlin had plotted and carried out Trotsky's assassination on friendly foreign soil. And that is both impermissible for Moscow, and highly dangerous to the future security of Ramon Mercader and his mother.

Beneath this surface dilemma in which the assassin finds himself is the far more challenging, deeper problem of the mind of this assassin, the frightening product of a totalitarian era. In exploring this riddle of our time, this book attempts to show why, when he completes his twenty-year sentence on August 20,

1960, Ramon Mercader will walk out of prison still wearing the mask of "Jacques Mornard."

The origin of Stalin's feud with Trotsky goes back to the beginnings of the Russian Revolution. When Trotsky returned to Russia from exile abroad in 1917, he already had a national reputation as a revolutionary which he had won during the great upheaval of 1905 as the leader of the first Soviet and as a mordant pamphleteer. The trials and suffering which World War I had brought to Russia had so undermined the Czarist regime that it collapsed in consequence of bread riots which broke out in the capital. For the first time in history Russia found herself under the sway of democracy revelling in unlimited freedom amid the exhaustion of a major war.

Lenin, the chief of the Bolshevik Party, preaching immediate social revolution, formed an alliance with the independent Trotsky, a lone ranger on the multi-factional socialist front, a fiery orator and organizer of no mean ability. Stalin was at this time an obscure henchman of Lenin's. A Georgian by birth and education, Stalin spoke Russian with a heavy accent and cut an insignificant figure in the limelight of the Revolution.

While the Provisional Government was reaching a natural end after a spree of some eight months, two men with a purpose were rigging the stage for a world upset. Lenin, in the role of inspirer and exhorter, Trotsky in the capacity of insurrectionary leader, set out boldly to capture power. Among their followers was Stalin, one of those who played it safe. Although the capture of power had been hatched in a secret gathering convoked by Lenin, it was the kind of conspiracy which was the talk of the capital. The power which once held Russia in a vise was now lying helpless in the gutter. In an almost bloodless coup, Lenin and Trotsky picked it up and with ruthless hands established the Soviet dictatorship on the remains of a disintegrated government of dreamers.

Stalin left the ranks of the waverers and enlisted in Lenin's entourage for life. While Trotsky organized the Red Army out of rag, tag and bobtail and led it to victory in a bloody civil war over the various White armies commanded by professional generals, Stalin was quietly organizing the political machine back home. And when Lenin died in 1924, Stalin as the top bureaucrat maneuvered with consummate intrigue an alliance now with one and now with another political faction, until he was able to isolate Trotsky politically and bring about his deportation from the Soviet Union to Turkey and his eventual excommunication from the fold of the faithful communists.

All this was but a prelude to Stalin's grand conspiracy to kill Trotsky, the threads of which ran from Moscow to Norway to Spain to the United States and to Mexico.

I.D.L.

Key Figures in the Trotsky Drama

LEON (LEV DAVIDOVICH) TROTSKY, co-founder with Lenin of the Soviet régime; organizer and leader of the Red Army; expelled from Russia by Stalin in 1929; assassinated in Mexico on August 20, 1940.

NATALIA SEDOVA, Trotsky's widow, his faithful companion since 1902.

LEON SEDOV, their son, director of the Trotskyite organization in Europe, died under mysterious circumstances in Paris on February 16, 1938 at age thirty-two.

JAIME RAMON MERCADER DEL RIO HERNANDEZ, Trotsky's assassin, born in Barcelona in 1914; in Mexican prison under the alias of Jacques Mornard, alias Frank Jacson, alias Vandendreschd; trained as communist terrorist in Moscow.

CARIDAD MERCADER, born in Cuba in 1892 and christened Eustacia Maria del Rio Hernandez, the assassin's mother; an ardent communist who fought in the Spanish civil war and served in the Soviet international underground.

LEONID EITINGON, high Soviet officer in the NKVD, Caridad's lover, the assassin's mentor, and field director of the plot against Trotsky; had served in Spain under the aliases of General Kotov and Comrade Pablo, in Mexico under the alias of General Leonov, and in Paris under the aliases of Valery, Sakhov and Lyova.

SYLVIA AGELOFF, the assassin's sweetheart and "wife," Brooklyn-born social worker, confidante of Trotsky and his entourage, through whom Ramon Mercader penetrated Trotsky's household.

JACK SOBLE, Soviet spy, now serving a prison sentence in Lewisburg Penitentiary; since 1931 Stalin's agent in Trotskyite circles; born in Lithuania as Sobolevich; alias Sobolevicius, alias Senin.

MARK ZBOROWSKI, Soviet spy, Leon Sedov's closest associate; convicted of perjury and given 5-year sentence in New York City on December 8, 1958; a native of the Ukraine, a member of Soble's spy ring in the United States; one of Stalin's most prized agents in the Trotsky organization under the alias of Etienne.

LOUIS BUDENZ, former managing editor of *The Daily Worker*; according to his own revelations, he was deeply involved in the operations of the Soviet spy ring hunting Trotsky; author of several books exposing communist espionage activities.

RUBY WEIL LEWIS, an old comrade of Budenz who was a friend of the Ageloff family; went to Paris to act as go-between in introducing Sylvia Ageloff to Mercader under the alias of Jacques Mornard.

DAVID ALFARO SIQUEIROS, Mexican painter, fought in the Spanish civil war; veteran communist and leader of a gang armed with machine-guns and bombs that carried out an unsuccessful attempt on Trotsky's life in May, 1940.

ROBERT SHELDON HARTE, son of a New York businessman, a gullible youth who served as volunteer guard at Trotsky's villa; abducted and murdered in the aftermath of the Siqueiros assault.

JOSEPH HANSEN, Utah-born social rebel; chief of Trotsky's guards and secretariat in Mexico, editor of the revolutionary *International Socialist Review*, published in New York City.

TRYGVE LIE, the first Secretary General of the United Nations; in 1936 as Minister of Justice in the Norwegian government he expelled Trotsky from Norway under pressure from Moscow.

DIEGO RIVERA, famous Mexican painter, who secured asylum for Trotsky in Mexico and acted as his host for the first years of his stay there.

DR. ALFONSO QUIROZ CUARON, chief criminologist for the Mexican government; conducted with Prof. Gomez Robleda a six-months' psychological examination of the assassin; discovered in 1950 in Madrid police files documentary evidence establishing the identity of the assassin.

THE MIND OF AN ASSASSIN

1

The Assassin and His Mother

"You are done for. All your accomplices have already begun to talk. The police have in their hands all the threads and know who sent you to Mexico. Nevertheless, you have not said a word. Your mother will be put to death."

This message, written in Russian in a large legible hand, was unobtrusively put before the mysterious assassin of Leon Trotsky in the electroencephalographic booth where he was under observation. The place was the clinic of Dr. Ramirez Moreno in Mexico City. The time, November, 1940, three months following the assassination. Present were police officers, Department of Justice officials, and members of the medical staff. Presiding over the unusual inquiry was the psychiatric criminologist of the Mexican government, Dr. Alfonso Quiroz Cuaron.

Before entering the booth, the prisoner looked around and

seeing some diathermy machines, said: "Where is the microphone?" The attending physicians reassured him that there was no such device in the clinic, after which he settled down to be tested.

The special test with the Russian note had been devised in an attempt to unmask the man who had committed what the lexicon of Mexico calls magnicide. The physicians attached electrodes to check his emotional reactions to the message in Russian. At first, he did not seem to fix his attention on it, perhaps because the lighting in the booth was subdued. Besides, the prisoner was nearsighted. After a short lapse of time, he stared fixedly at the note, turned pale, showed anger, stretched out his right arm and brought the message close to his eyes. Visibly irritated, he pushed the note away with the remark, "I do not understand."

The physicians in attendance, upon checking all the graphs and finding a definite change in the brain rhythm, concluded that the prisoner did understand Russian.

Since that test, nineteen years have passed. Serving a twenty-year sentence, the prisoner in the Mexican Federal Penitentiary has not once, not even when confronted with overwhelming evidence such as his fingerprints, allowed the mask to slip off his face and to reveal his true identity. Indeed, he has been proud of playing the part of the international *hombre enigmatico*—the man of mystery—who drove an ice-axe into the skull of Stalin's most hated rival.

Leon Trotsky had a clear prevision of his own end. On December 30, 1936, nearly four years before he was struck down by the assassin, Trotsky wrote, while en route to his exile in Mexico, after his expulsion from Norway under pressure from Stalin: "He seeks to strike not at the ideas of his opponent, but at his skull."

But Trotsky was so blind to his immediate human surroundings that, although living behind the high walls of a fortified villa in constant fear of assassination, he failed to recognize *in his own entourage* the man assigned to kill him. Yet it would have taken little time, with the aid of his network of followers, for Trotsky to expose his future murderer who had been introduced into his family circle under the alias of "Jacques Mornard."

The man who assumed this name now stands irrefutably identified as a Catalonian with a singular personal history, who was born in Barcelona in 1914. Known in his youth to his intimates as Jaime Mercader, he adopted an alias whose initials, J. M., match those of his real name. But when this external mask is ripped off, we find behind it another, inner mask, and it poses a challenge far greater than that of his physical and legal identity. It is the challenge of reading the mind of a man unique among political assassins, of the prototype of the future denizens of a totalitarian world.

In the long roll of political assassinations which mark the pages of modern history—and one can easily account for a hundred crimes of magnicide since Lincoln's assassination in 1865—there is not another case paralleling the murder of Trotsky. There are at least three aspects which distinguish it from similar acts of political terror.

In the first place, Trotsky, an undesirable refugee in a bourgeois world for which he harbored nothing but hostility, was the object of a global man-hunt conducted with unlimited resources by a powerful modern state. The crime itself took on some of the extraordinary character of the grand master of conspiracy who dictated and supervised it, the uniquely vindictive Stalin. He set up in his secret police, the NKVD, a Division of Special Tasks charged with liquidating political enemies on foreign soil, mostly so-called Trotskyites, of whom the Number One target was Trotsky himself. These gunmen, operating underground with the assistance of the local communist parties, roved the earth to carry out their bloody assignments.

Second, the stubborn refusal of Trotsky's assassin to disclose his real identity, and his trial and conviction under an admittedly false name, enabled the organizers of the crime to disavow any connection with it. Indeed, Stalin's role in the murder plot had remained a subject for dark speculation, but could not be conclusively established so long as the assassin's own history was shrouded in mystery, especially since no other participant in the plot had ever chosen to lift the veil over the crime. In his historic speech before the 20th Congress of the Communist Party of the Soviet Union, in which he exposed Stalin as an arch-criminal, Nikita Khrushchev seemed to come close to a qualified rehabilitation of Trotsky, but stopped short and soon drew back in the face of the apprehended international reverberations of the truth about Trotsky's assassination.

Third, perhaps the most striking feature of the crime is the character of the assassin. He resorted to the seduction of an innocent woman as a means of attaining the friendly confidence of his victim for his murderous design. And yet his whole defense echoes Charlotte Corday upon her assassination of Marat when she cried out to Fouquier-Tinville, Robespierre's chief prosecutor: "Oh, the monster, he takes me for an assassin!" But what a difference. Charlotte Corday killed Marat as a bloodthirsty tyrant in power, while Trotsky was a hunted and cornered man when struck down. And the killer was that new type on the political horizon, so aptly described by Albert Camus: the philosophical executioner.

A descendant of a long line of rebels, the philosophical executioner of Trotsky is no rebel himself. If on the one side his ideological forefathers were revolutionary idealists who sacrificed themselves to assassinate tyrants in the name of justice, the new type of assassin is nothing of the kind. If, on the other side, his intellectual forebears were the nihilists whose creed of revolution called for total freedom through the total destruction of the established order, he is not of that fanatical breed either. After several generations of crossbreeding of those two types of revolutionary terrorists, from Charlotte Corday in the French Revolution to Dora Kaplan in the Russian Revolution who shot Lenin in August, 1918, the new type has emerged.

This new ugly offspring is a killer without a passion for justice or for freedom. He is a trained political assassin who takes pride in his proficiency. He is a martinet of the new order, a Kamikazi in the service of the Divine Dictator. The philosophical executioner is not a mercenary killer like Herman Marks, the Milwaukee thug who carried out hundreds of executions for Fidel Castro's revolution in Cuba. For there is nothing mercenary about Ramon Mercader.

No, our philosophical executioner is a rationally indoctrinated murderer, the product of the age of reason at its dead end. He is a monument to the school which makes a religion of politics. He is, like Stalin himself, a mockery of the communist philosophy of economic determinism, that super-rational theory which negates the role of the hero in history. He is a scientist of the kind to whom all life is matter. In this philosophical executioner modern man, the bearer of a 4,000-year old spiritual heritage, has produced the pioneer of a line of soulless monsters, the harbingers of a coming race.

In August, 1936, one month after the outbreak of the civil war in Spain, the first of an infamous series of purge trials was staged by Stalin, with Trotsky as the chief defendant *in absentia*. To no one's surprise, it came to a close with the conviction of Trotsky and his son, Leon Sedov. "They were sentenced to death by the Moscow court," wrote Natalia Sedova, the wife and the mother of the two doomed men. And on a later occasion she added: "Since the first Moscow trial, i.e., for more than three years, we have been waiting, with sure inner knowledge, for the assassins."

Stalin struck his first ominous blow at Trotsky while the latter was living in great secrecy in Norway. The Kremlin's ambassador demanded Trotsky's expulsion from the country, and the Norwegian government quickly went into action. In 1936 its Minister of Justice was none other than Trygve Lie, the man who a decade later emerged as a world figure in the post of the first Secretary General of the United Nations. Incidentally, this honor came to him after the Soviet delegate had first proposed that Trygve Lie be elected President of the General Assembly by acclamation (upon waiving the secret ballot requirement).

To Trotsky, one of the founders of the Communist International, Trygve Lie was no stranger. Lie had visited Moscow in 1921 and, according to Trotsky, had been identified with the Comintern in its early days. At that time Trotsky was at the height of his glory as the victorious war lord of the Red Army. Now Trygve Lie, as Norwegian Minister of Justice, faced Trotsky at bay and presented to him, immediately upon the conclusion of the Moscow trial, a demand that he voluntarily sign a statement submitting his mail to censorship and that he stop writing on current events. Trotsky saw in Lie's proposal a scheme of Stalin's to gag him, and proposed that he be given an open trial in Norway to establish his innocence and to expose Stalin's judicial frame-up.

On August 26, two days after the Moscow announcement of the verdict at the purge trial, Trotsky addressed a letter to Trygve Lie which had been suppressed in Norway but was later published in the United States.[1]

"To refrain from bringing me to trial before a Norwegian court," Trotsky wrote, "and at the same time to rob me of the possibility of appeal to public opinion on a question that con-

[1] See Sources and Notes, page 223.

cerns myself, my son, my whole political past, and my political honor, would mean to transform the right of asylum into a trap and to allow free passage to the executioners and slanderers of the GPU."

Trygve Lie insisted that Trotsky submit to being muzzled.

"If you intend to arrest me," Trotsky told Lie, "why do you want me to authorize you in that act?"

"But there is an intermediate step between arrest and full liberty," retorted Trygve Lie.

"That's either ambiguous or a trap. I prefer arrest," replied Trotsky.

The Minister of Justice obliged Trotsky at once. First Trotsky's secretary was expelled from Norway. Then Trotsky and his wife and all their belongings were transferred to a large country house at Sundby where they were installed on the second floor. The ground floor was occupied by a squad of fifteen policemen. No visitors were allowed and the Trotskys could not leave the grounds. For the first time since the summer of 1917, Trotsky found himself in prison.

This was the beginning of the drama which was to reach its criminal climax in Mexico four years later. And contributing heavily to the initial blow which Stalin inflicted upon Trotsky was the hand of a leading American communist, Louis F. Budenz, then editor of *The Daily Worker* in New York. Budenz was destined to play in other ways a key role in the backstage preparations for the assassination of Trotsky, according to his own voluntary testimony.[2] As Budenz tells the story, the ground for the Soviet pressure upon Norway was confidential information he had supplied to "Roberts," his superior in the underground, a top Soviet secret agent in the United States. Budenz reported that a former colleague of his, the prominent left-wing pacifist, the Rev. A. J. Muste, had visited Trotsky in his Norwegian hideout early in June, 1936, and that Trotsky had discussed with him plans for the violent overthrow of the Soviet solini and Stalin, and threatening to develop into a world war. Since the Spanish Republic had a Popular Front government, communist, socialist, revolutionary and other anti-fascist elements from all corners of the earth rallied to its support. Spain became a symbol of the struggle against fascism, but behind the main front another civil war was silently being waged in the Republican ranks. Stalin, whose Spanish policy was calculated to appease Hitler and Mussolini, ordered his gunmen in Spain to launch a campaign of extermination of all dissident revolutionaries and libertarians who were branded as Trotskyites. Under the protection of a government which depended upon Stalin's favors, his executioners began their purge.

Even before the Trotskys departed from Norway, a delegation of Spanish communists set sail from Barcelona bound for Mexico. The leading member of this mission traveling on the *Manuel Arnuz* to the Caribbean was a woman of striking appearance whose destiny was to be inseparable from that of Trotsky. She was Caridad Mercader, the 44-year-old mother of Ramon, the future assassin.

Among the passengers from Spain arriving at Veracruz on November 6, after changing boats in Cuba, was Ramon's reputed bride, the 19-year-old Lena Imbert, who accompanied Caridad. Slender, with intense green eyes and wavy black hair, Lena was feminine, shy and serious. The delegation included two communist schoolteachers. They all traveled on forged Mexican passports. The ostensible purpose of the mission was to mobilize public opinion in support of the Republican cause and to find homes for orphaned children.

Caridad Mercader, Lena Imbert and their companions were upon examination quickly identified as Spaniards traveling on Mexican passports to which they were not entitled. The group was detained by the immigration authorities at Veracruz. The Spanish consul soon appeared on the scene, asked that they be given the status of political refugees and offered to post bond.

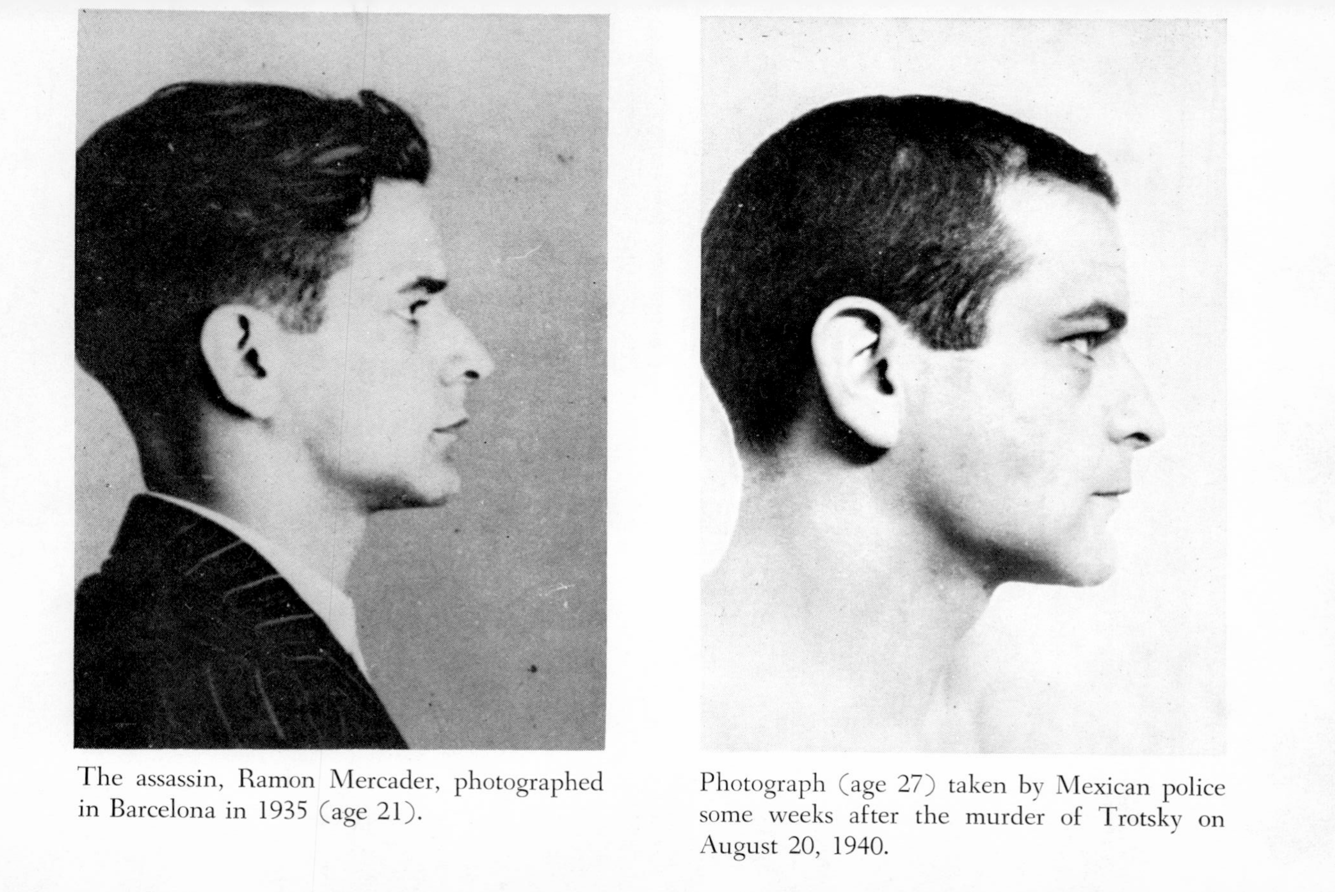

The assassin, Ramon Mercader, photographed in Barcelona in 1935 (age 21).

Photograph (age 27) taken by Mexican police some weeks after the murder of Trotsky on August 20, 1940.

An early photo of the mother, taken in the 1920's, from the Mercader family album.

A teen-age photo of Ramon taken in Barcelona, also from the family album.

Ramon, about age 19, with his grandmother. He is wearing the uniform of a junior lieutenant in the Spanish Republican Army.

Copyright by Isaac Don Levine

Copyright by Isaac Don Levine

Copyright by Isaac Don Levine

The assassin's brothers and sister: The late Pablo Mercader, top left, killed in the Spanish Civil War; his sister, Montserrat Mercader, top right; and Jorge Mercader, bottom right.

Ramon's mother, Caridad del Rio Mercader.

Trotsky and his wife, Natalia Sedova.

Leon Trotsky working at the desk at which he was murdered.

Acme

Trotsky's fortress-like villa at Coyoacan, Mexico (photograph taken in 1938).

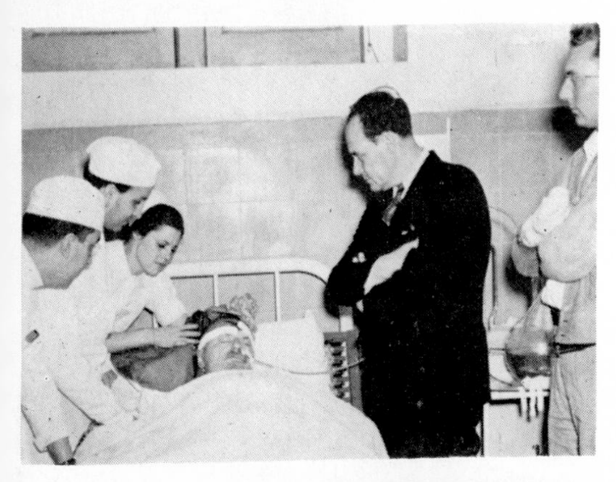

The unconscious body of Trotsky in the Green Cross Emergency Hospital, where he died.

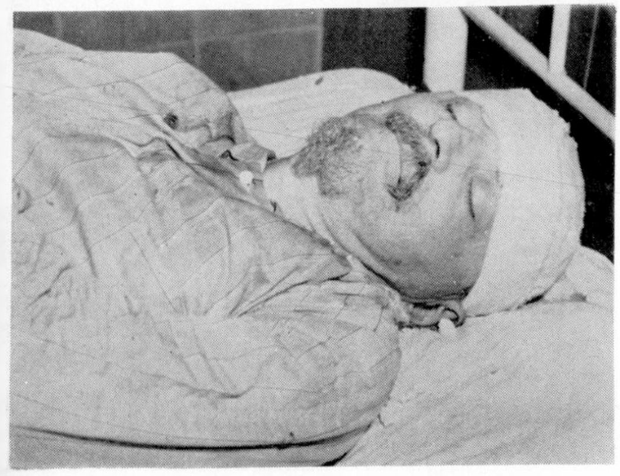

Wide World

Trotsky shortly after his death.

The assassin shortly after the murder, showing effects of the beating by Trotsky's guards.

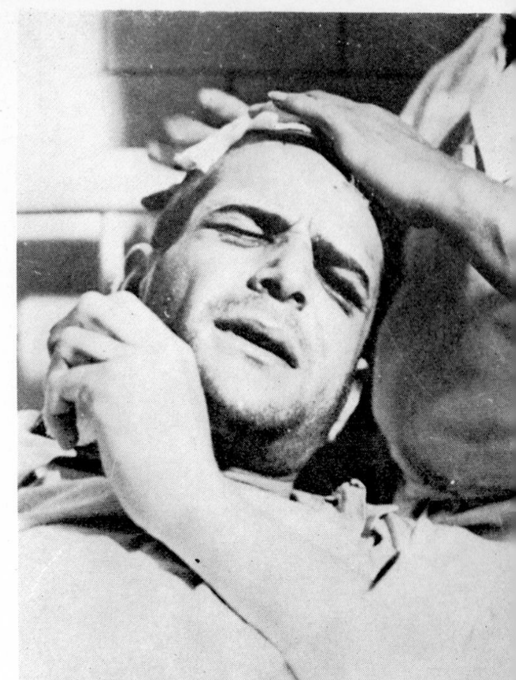

Another view of the assassin in prison after the murder.

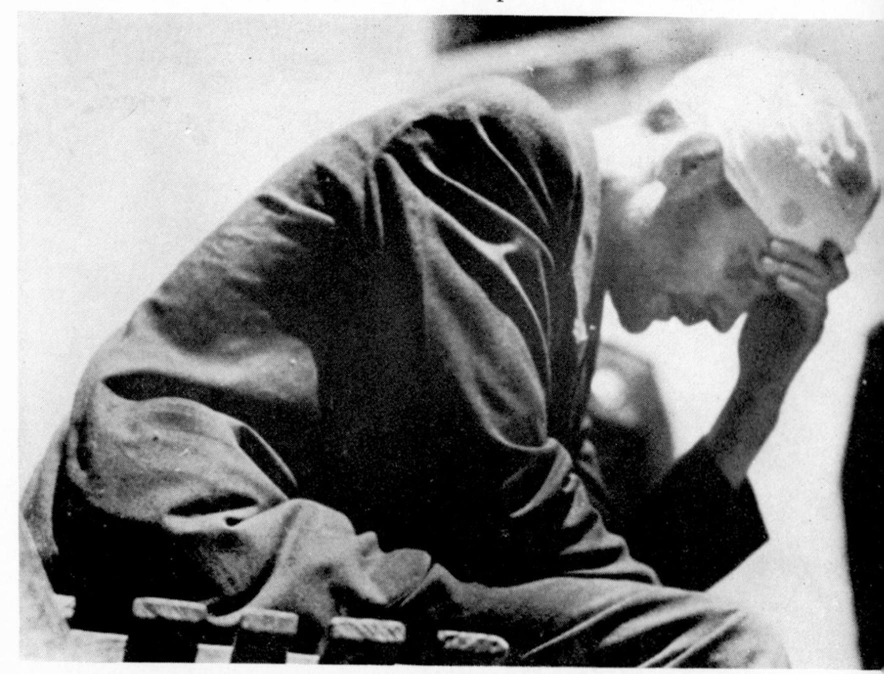

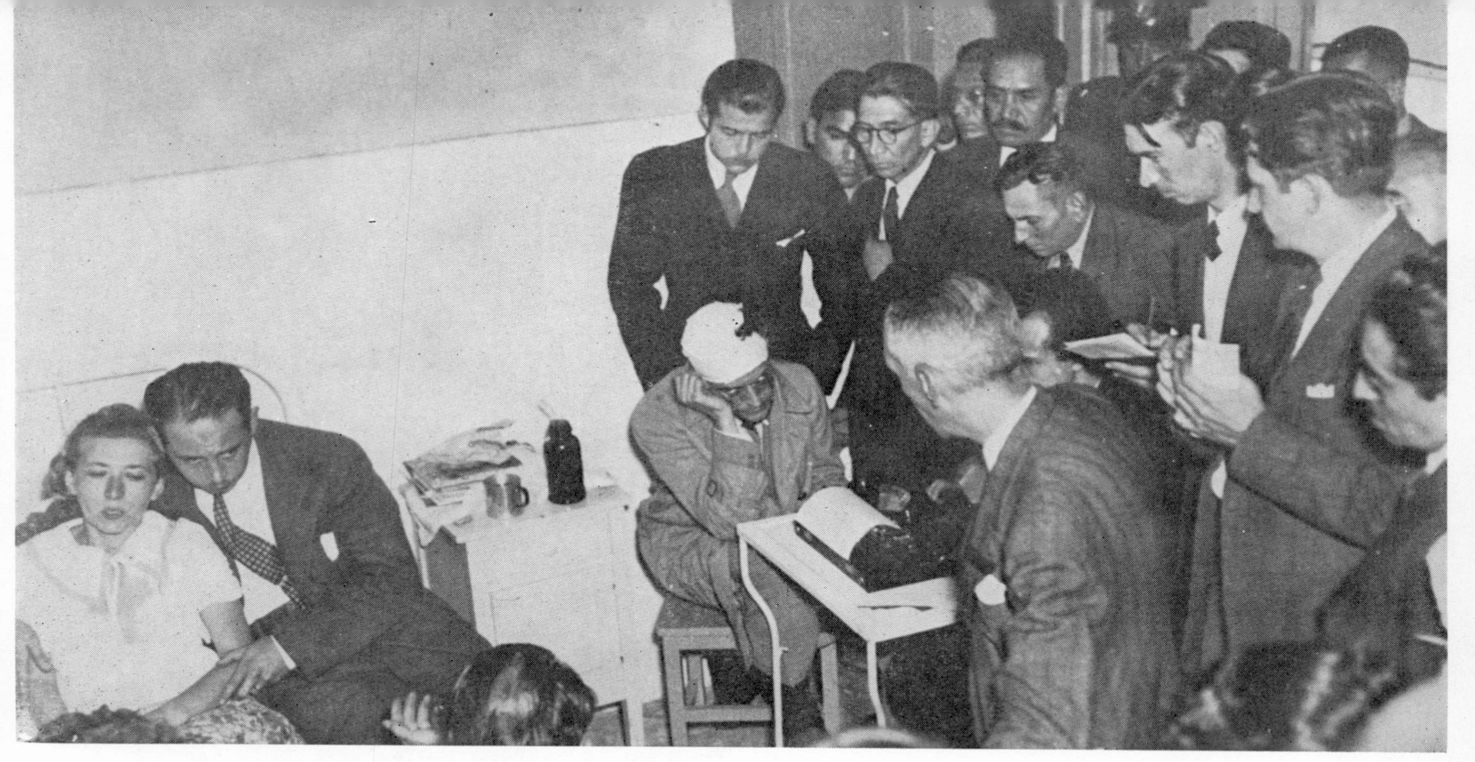

The confrontation of Sylvia Ageloff and the assassin after the murder of Trotsky (see page 146). Miss Ageloff is at the far left, her brother seated next to her. Mercader, with bandaged head, is seated next to the typewriter, surrounded by police officials and reporters.

Mexican police records, proving that Mercader's fingerprints of 1935 (Spain) and 1940 (Mexico) are identical.

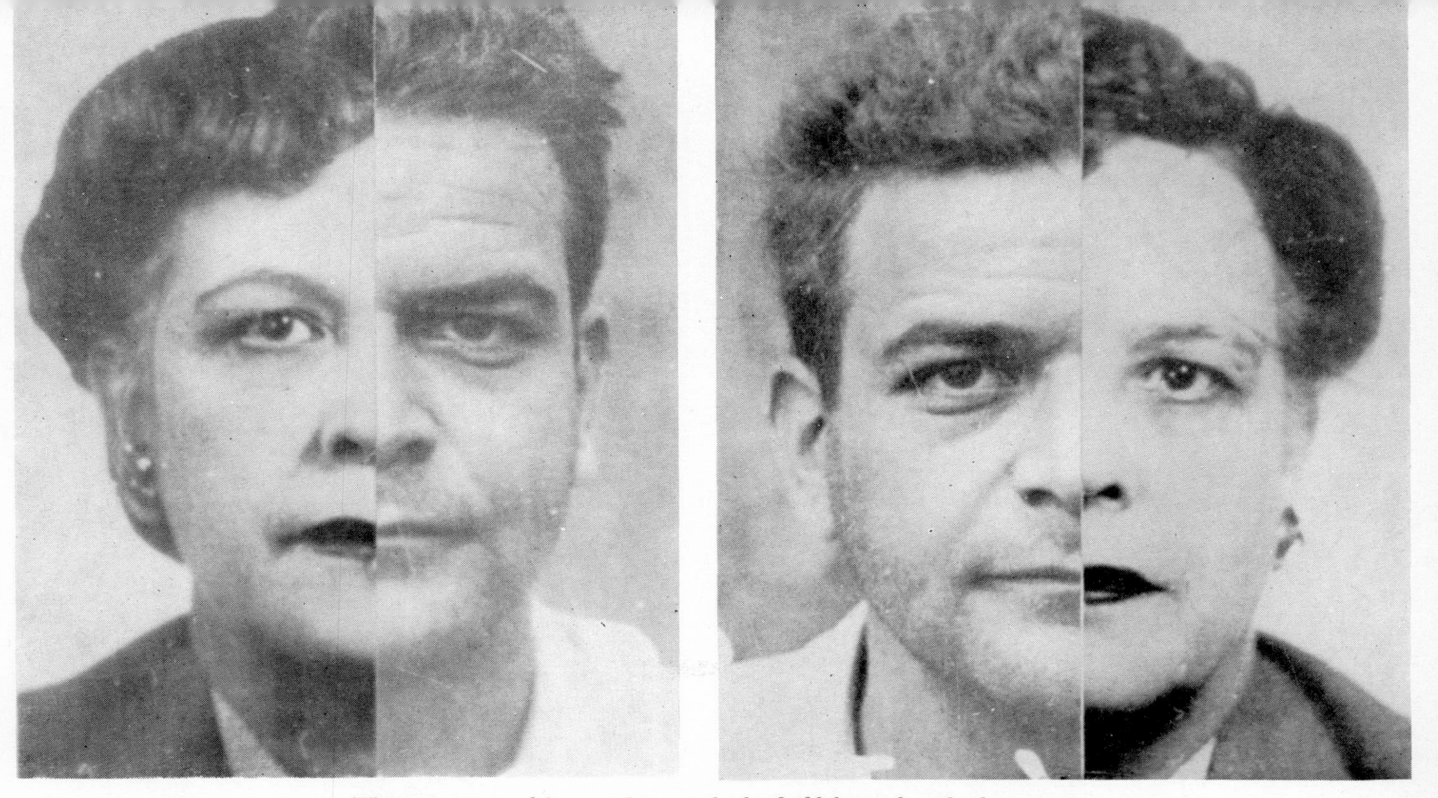

The assassin and his mother, with the half face of each shown in juxtaposition. Photographs prepared by Mexican police officials.

The assassin, seated, in a photograph taken with his medical examiner, Dr. Quiroz-

The assassin 18 years after his crime. (The photograph was taken in prison in 1958.)

The Minister of the Interior intervened with a ruling that the Spanish delegates could stay in the country as visitors. Meanwhile, on November 10th, he requested the Mexican Foreign Office to find out why the Mexican consul at Barcelona had documented these people as Mexican citizens. The Mexican authorities had no way of knowing that the handsome, impressive lady heading the group had for years been a secret agent of the Comintern and a member of the underground apparat of the NKVD abroad.

The delegation proceeded to Mexico City where it operated from Communist Party headquarters. The humanitarian part of Caridad's mission, the task of raising funds and finding homes for some 500 Spanish children, was successfully accomplished. The more important overt political task was to mobilize the Mexican Teachers' Union for active support of Loyalist Spain. The Confederation of Educational Workers had the overwhelming majority of Mexico's 50,000 teachers in its ranks and was probably then the most important trade union in the country. It was communist-controlled, and the Ministry of Education itself was under strong communist influence. The political temper of many of the rural teachers can be gauged by the fact that in Yucatan they began to tear down the Mexican flag from the schoolhouses and run up the Hammer and Sickle in its place, and to display portraits of Stalin, instead of Cardenas, in the classrooms.

Wearing her militia woman's uniform of blue overalls, Caridad Mercader addressed the Mexican Chamber of Deputies on November 18. A tall woman of great vitality, whose appearance gained distinction because of her prematurely greying hair, she was eloquent and effective. On November 21, the Day of Mexican Independence, she addressed thousands of people massed in the Zocalo, the old square of Mexico City. On this occasion, she said that the world had to choose between fascism and communism, and that the forces of international communism had come to the rescue of the Spanish Republic. She toured the provincial capitals with representatives of the Mexican Teachers' Union and of the Socorro Rojo Internacional (International Red Aid). She spoke at dozens of meetings. Many Mexicans knew her well and her photograph appeared in the Mexico City newspapers.

On December 16, 1936, the Mexican consul at Barcelona replied to the Foreign Office query. He stated that the names of the Spaniards who had been questioned at Veracruz upon their arrival did not appear in his records. This was confirmation that they had entered the country on false papers. For the next two months, nothing happened. Mexico was the leading ally of Spain in the Western hemisphere, and in the following years would become the great haven for Spanish refugees among whom there was a hard core of Soviet hatchet men.

In February, the Mexican Department of the Interior circularized the police to find and produce the irregular visitors. But by that time Caridad and Lena Imbert and their companions had left for Spain. Caridad's tour of the country and her meetings with the leaders of the Mexican Communist Party gave her opportunities to acquire knowledge of the terrain and environment where the murder of Trotsky would have to be committed and of the local forces available for the operation, a knowledge which few other NKVD agents in Europe possessed. But did she know then that it would fall to her son to carry out Stalin's supreme assignment?

Cast in the image of his mother, a woman who had plumbed all the depths of a wild and violent age, Ramon Mercader had all the qualities Stalin required. His mother, christened Eustacia Maria Caridad del Rio Hernandez, born on March 31, 1892, into a well-to-do family in Santiago de Cuba, came into the world in the last years of the rococo Spanish Empire. Forty-eight years later she was awarded in the Kremlin the highest Soviet decoration, the Order of Lenin, for her son's assassination of Trotsky.

The revolutionary movements of our epoch know many figures like Caridad, but none who mothered and raised an assassin like Ramon. Just at about the time when a young student in the Caucasus, who was to become known as Stalin, was expelled from the seminary in Tiflis for revolutionary propaganda, and when another student in the Ukraine, who was to emerge as Trotsky, was imprisoned and exiled to Siberia for fomenting strikes, the thoroughly bourgeois Hernandez family placed their daughter Caridad in a school in France run by the nuns of the Order of the Sacred Heart. At the age of 14, in 1906, Caridad was transferred to a similar school in Barcelona where she had relatives prominent in the social as well as business life of the city. After completing her education, Caridad returned to Cuba with her parents. It was not until October 23, 1910, that the Hernandez family moved back to Spain to take up permanent residence in Barcelona. Caridad, a strikingly attractive girl of 18, is remembered by her kinsfolk as quick-tempered, nervous, unpredictable in her behavior, and given to mysticism. One day she announced that she wished to join a feminine religious order. For a brief spell she served a novitiate as a sister in the Order of the Carmelite Descalzas (the shoeless).

A match was arranged for Caridad and her betrothal to the twenty-six-year-old Don Pablo Mercader Marina took place about this time. The scion of a well-known though not too prosperous Catalonian family, Pablo, born in Barcelona August 26, 1884, was of a retiring and conservative disposition, the very antithesis of his bride. Caridad married him on January 7, 1911, when she was not yet nineteen. The newlyweds took an apartment on the fourth floor of 8 Sarria Street, Barcelona, where they lived until the middle of 1912. Although dates and full addresses make dull reading, they seem unavoidable in pinpointing all the facts of Ramon's identity.

Since Ramon has made every effort to confuse both the authorities and the psychiatrists about his origin, age and birthplace, it is also necessary to record here that he was Caridad's second child, and that he was born on February 7, 1914, at 24 Illas y Vidal Street, Barcelona. He attended first the English Institute and later the school of the Escolapian Fathers on Corcega Street in the same city. In addition to Ramon, Caridad had three other sons, Jorge, Pablo and Luis and a daughter, Montserrat. Their dates and places of birth are given elsewhere.[3]

As a spirited young society matron, Caridad was noted for her fluent French and English and the ease with which she had acquired the Catalonian dialect. When she reached the dangerous age of thirty-three, she began to show unconventional interests. She took up painting under the tutelage of the well-known Borras Abella. And she continued to reach out towards larger horizons. She developed associations with intellectuals and Bohemians, with people of advanced ideas who were bent upon changing the world and were leading exciting lives.

When she compared these new friends with her husband Pablo, who disliked, distrusted and disapproved of them, he appeared, according to the strongly biased recollections of Ramon, as an insignificant provincial figure with authoritarian manners. The image of his father which Ramon, who idolized his mother, carried away from his childhood, an image which crops up in the various examinations to which he was subjected since the crime, is that of a fat, sluggish and physically dull man, who was harried by petty phobias and who accepted without questioning the prevailing religious, political and sexual standards of a past era.

The political climate of Catalonia in which Ramon was raised had singular elements, but in some respects it paralleled that of Russia in the early years of the century. During 1918, when Ramon was four, 200 bombs were exploded in Barcelona alone by anarchist terrorists and by *agents provocateurs* in the employ of the police. Like Russia, a hotbed of violent revolutionary idealism, Catalonia had its own distinct character: here the anarchist disciples of Bakunin and the syndicalist followers of Sorel predominated over the socialist and communist partisans of Marx. Strikes in Barcelona were invariably bloody, as their leaders were out to foment class war, and every strike was accompanied by rioting and bomb throwing. The most important revolutionary labor organization in Catalonia was the FAI (Federation of Iberian Anarchists).

A citadel of radicalism, Catalonia lacked a nationalist bond with Spain, and had in fact a strong separatist movement which aimed at autonomous government. The energetic, forward-looking industrialists of Barcelona were contemptuous of Spanish backwardness. They were of two minds about the apostles of class war and revolution. For the progressive elements in Catalonia were themselves revolutionaries of a sort: they were opposed to the rule of Madrid and to the established church with its strong medieval traditions.

This was reflected in the home environment in which Ramon grew up, in an atmosphere charged with the bitter strife of a foundering marriage, unusual in the Spain of those days among members of the cloistered upper middle class to which the Mercaders belonged. From his very childhood, Ramon displayed the marks of a broken personality which was riven beyond mending during his adolescence under the influence of his mother.

In 1925 Caridad, having made life unbearable for her husband with her frivolities and hysteria—as their relatives now describe it—left home and took all their children with her to France. There are hints that Pablo's economic condition contributed to the domestic crisis, for he was none too successful a businessman. Caridad settled first in Toulouse, then moved to Dax and thence to Bordeaux. During the next four years there were several attempts at reconciliation. Pablo followed his wife and children to Toulouse where he remained from September,

1925, until March, 1926. He found employment there with Air France.

Communism now came to Caridad through a love affair. She was in her prime, bursting with vitality and compulsion to adventure. "It is known that after her arrival in France," writes a correspondent in Barcelona, "she became very friendly with a certain individual, a prominent French aviator who was a communist. This friendship grew into a very intimate relationship. It was this person who initiated her into communist doctrine."

The final break with her husband, who from time to time visited her and the children in France, did not occur until 1929. During this period of great emotional stress, Caridad twice attempted to commit suicide. One of these attempts nearly succeeded. She had taken a strong dose of poison, and spent a long time in a Bordeaux hospital recovering from the effects.

The children lived now with their mother in France and now with their father in Spain. Ramon had been sent off to Lyons at the age of 14 to attend a school for apprentices in the hotel business. He returned to Barcelona and took a job as messenger at the Goya Centennial Exhibition then held there. In 1929, he went to work in a hotel at the Plaza de Espana. He then secured employment as an assistant to the chef at the Ritz, Barcelona's most fashionable hotel. His training there was responsible for the deep impression he made some years later on several Trotskyites in Paris when he displayed his prowess as an expert carver at dinner parties.

His mother had moved to Paris. Here Caridad emerged in that sprawling area on the Left Bank, the 15th Arrondissement, as an active communist. She carried on underground work and served as a courier between Paris and Belgium, and later Spain. This was the period of the reorganization and consolidation of Stalin's apparats in the Comintern and the secret police. It was not unusual for an operative of the latter service to assume the duties of the undercover representative of the Communist International, as Caridad did, at the headquarters of the French Communist Party.

Caridad's numerous and promiscuous love affairs with the French communist leaders became in later years a subject with which she herself regaled her intimates in Moscow. To one of these, a former top figure in the Spanish Communist Party, whose reputation for reliability is recognized by his political friends and enemies alike, she confided tantalizing and unforgettable details. She described how Maurice Thorez, Jacques Duclos and other Red mandarins looked in the nude, and made pungent remarks about their behavior in the privacy of the bedroom.

When Ramon was 18, he found himself embroiled in the revolutionary turmoil. The Spanish Revolution had exploded in the spring of 1931. King Alfonso XIII fled Spain, and later that year he was declared guilty of treason by the republican-socialist coalition which took over supreme power. Before he was due to be called for obligatory military service, Ramon joined in July, 1932, the Jaen Infantry Regiment as a volunteer, rose to the rank of corporal, was recommended for that of sergeant, remaining in the army until 1934.

His conservative relatives had now noticed a profound change in the youth. He visited them seldom. He was reserved in their presence about his activities and embittered in his occasional comments on events. They began to suspect that he was participating in the frequent terrorist outbreaks of the time. The country was torn by insurrections of royalist officers on the one hand and uprisings of revolutionary extremists on the other. On January 8, 1933, the anarcho-syndicalists took up arms in Barcelona, but were put down by federal troops. In December of that year, barricades again blocked the streets and for ten days the greatest city in Spain was a bloody battleground.

In October, 1934, a general strike broke out in Catalonia, and it gradually developed into a separatist armed rising against the Federal Government in Madrid. The revolt was backed by the simultaneous insurrection of the dynamite-throwing miners of Asturias, in the Basque province which had its own separatist movement. Ramon had taken part in the bloody fighting as a full-fledged member of the communist units.

The defeat of the revolts led to the indefinite suspension of Catalan autonomy and to the rise of an anti-radical government in Madrid which resorted to severe repressive measures. Ramon helped organize, under difficult conditions of an alert police, the Cervantes Artistic Recreational Circle, which was a front for an underground communist cell of Barcelona youths. He lived in a boarding house above a shoe repair shop at 7 Calle Ancha, and the group met in a bar at 11 Calle Wilfredo where its secretary worked as bartender.

The police raided the bar and on June 12, 1935, Jaime Ramon was arrested together with seventeen other members of the group. He is described in the police records as a writer and bachelor, a native of Barcelona. As a member of the executive committee of the organization, Ramon attracted the attention of the central authorities in Madrid. He spent three months in the Barcelona jail, and was then transferred to the prison of San Miguel de los Reyes in Valencia. In accordance with the Law of Public Order, he was to remain in custody at the disposition of the central government after serving whatever sentence the judge imposed.

Ramon did not remain long in custody. In February, 1936, a Popular Front government took over the helm in Madrid, and the anarchists, socialists and communists were once more given free rein. Ramon was briefly prominent during this period in the organization of a schoolteachers' strike in Barcelona.

On July 17, 1936, General Franco, in command of the army in Spanish Morocco, raised the banner of revolt against the Popular Front government, having secured assurances of support from

Fascist Italy and Nazi Germany. Nearly all of the regular army garrisons on the mainland answered Franco's call to establish an authoritarian regime, and began to sweep eastward toward Madrid and Barcelona.

Caridad was in Barcelona when General Franco struck. On July 18 one of the main plazas of the city was occupied by some military units loyal to Franco. Crowds of armed workers, lacking leadership, milled around the edges of the plaza and in the adjoining arcades, prepared to offer resistance to the troops. Caridad took charge of the situation and called upon the mass to advance from all directions on the machine-gun positions held by the army. She was seen leading the attack. The operation cost many lives, but the gun positions were snuffed out with home-made grenades and rifle fire, and the units manning them annihilated. The spine of the pro-Franco military element in Barcelona was broken before it could be consolidated for a full-scale offensive in an effort to capture Catalonia. Shortly afterwards Caridad took charge openly of the Union of Communist Women with offices at the party headquarters in the Hotel Colon.

The government in Madrid called for volunteers to form a people's militia to fight Franco. Caridad and her adult sons were among the first to enlist in the republican forces. While on her way to the front, Caridad was wounded in the shoulder when her column was strafed. She was evacuated to Lerida and from there was moved to the Montserrat Clinic at Calle 22 Septimana. The wound was not serious, and upon her recovery she was dispatched by the government early in October at the head of the mission to Mexico.

Ramon, with the rank of a lieutenant, became a political commissar in the 27th Division on the Aragon front. From now on his tragic path would be set for him by the power to which he had surrendered his own will, a path which led to his ultimate crime, the murder in Mexico.

2

Agents of Death

On December 19, 1936, the Trotskys were "deposited" on the oil tanker *Ruth* in the port of Oslo and, in the company of a high Norwegian police official, set out on a three-weeks' voyage to the port of Tampico. The only ominous note was sounded in the December 17 issue of the Kremlin's mouthpiece, *Pravda*, for all faithful communists to heed:

"As for Catalonia, the purging of the Trotskyists and the anarcho-syndicalists has begun; it will be conducted with the same energy with which it was conducted in the USSR."

When the Norwegian tanker reached the shores of Mexico on January 9, 1937, Diego Rivera's beautiful wife, Frida Kahlo, an artist in her own right, was there with a group of Trotsky's followers to welcome him and his wife ashore. The Mexican government provided a special train to take the Trotsky party to Mexico City. Trotsky cabled President Cardenas a message of gratitude for Mexico's hospitality and pledged himself not to interfere in the internal affairs of the country, a pledge to which he adhered rigorously during the four remaining years of his life.

At Mexico City Trotsky was installed by Diego Rivera in the house where his wife Frida had been born, located in the residential suburb of Coyoacan, not too far from the Rivera residence in San Angel. For almost three years, until the political break between Rivera and Trotsky following the Stalin-Hitler pact in 1939, the two families dined together occasionally and took trips jointly in the country. Rivera painted Trotsky in his murals as the leader of the revolutionary working class of the world and Trotsky hailed Rivera as the "greatest interpreter" of the Russian Revolution in the medium of art.

Subsequently, when Diego Rivera aligned himself with the Stalin camp and tried hard to rejoin the Mexican Communist Party, he boasted that he had lured Trotsky to Mexico to enable Stalin to settle accounts with his archenemy. This boast was, of course, a figment of Diego's devious and unbridled imagination, and was obviously designed to reinstate him as a Stalinist hero in the good graces of the communist apparat. For if Diego had really been a loyal servitor of the Kremlin, Trotsky would have been liquidated early and soon after his arrival in Mexico, as no one was in a better position than Diego to provide inside tips and leads on Trotsky's habits and movements to Stalin's murder ring.

But Diego did have many unbroken contacts with the leading Stalinist members of the Communist Party, and Caridad Mercader thus had unusual opportunities for several weeks to acquire valuable data about Trotsky's mode of life and associations, to be added to the enormous Trotsky file accumulated at headquarters in Moscow. The vast size of this dossier has come to light only after the death of Stalin and the liquidation of his chief executioner Beria. Since then there has emerged a whole galaxy of material witnesses each of whom possesses some vital evidence bearing upon the hunt and assassination of Trotsky. All of the witnesses, as we shall see, had held high positions in the super-secret underground apparat. Some of these former operatives in the Soviet punitive organs have come to the surface voluntarily by defecting to the West, and gave testimony in public. Others were exposed and delivered to Western justice as a result of disclosures made by the defectors.

When the various pieces of evidence, produced at different times and places, are assembled in their natural sequence, there appears fully outlined the web of espionage with which Stalin had enveloped Trotsky in the decade preceding his murder, from 1931 in his exile in Turkey to his last day in Mexico. And nothing is left of the elaborate mystery with which Moscow had cloaked the closing link in the human net, Ramon Mercader.

At the Lewisburg Penitentiary in the State of Pennsylvania there is a prisoner who can justly be called the veteran of Stalin's net around Trotsky. He is Jack Soble, whose case made front-page news when he was arrested in New York after more than a quarter of a century of secret service for the Kremlin. It was before dawn, at 6:30 A.M. on January 25, 1957, that the doorbell rang at the Manhattan apartment of Soble, a seemingly respectable 53-year-old importer of bristles, who lived there quietly with his wife Myra and their 17-year-old son. Mr. Soble opened the door, and found himself facing seven wide-awake men, all agents of the FBI.

"Jack Soble, you are under arrest," the leader of the group announced. When Jack and Myra Soble were arraigned on charges of espionage and held in bail of $100,000 each, the public had no suspicion of a connection with the Trotsky affair. Although he and his wife Myra had been charged with spying in wartime on U. S. defenses and faced death sentences, they were given prison terms of only 7½ years because of "valuable assistance" to the government, in the words of the federal judge who tried them.

Since his arrest, Soble has twice attempted suicide. His second attempt in February, 1958, took place, significantly enough, months after his conviction, when he was about to be taken for further questioning before the grand jury in New York. Soble had swallowed one pound and nine ounces of nuts and bolts in the hardware shop at the Lewisburg Penitentiary, but was saved from death by surgery in New York at Bellevue Hospital. He could not escape testifying in the case of another key figure in the ring which Stalin forged around Trotsky.

The son of a wealthy businessman, Soble had joined the Communist Party at the age of 17 in his native Lithuania, had been a student at Leipzig in the twenties, and blossomed out as the leader of the Trotskyist group in Berlin in 1931. As such, under the alias of Senin, he was welcomed by Trotsky when he visited him in his place of exile at Prinkipo, Turkey.

"My services for the Soviet secret police went back to 1931," Soble himself confessed.[4] "The job was to spy on Leon Trotsky for Joseph Stalin, who was obsessed with the idea of knowing everything his hated rival was doing and thinking even in exile. . . . For two years, in 1931 and 1932, I spied on Trotsky and the men around him. Trotsky, suspecting nothing, invited me to his heavily guarded home at Prinkipo, Turkey. I duly reported back to the Kremlin everything Trotsky told me in confidence, including his pungent remarks about Stalin."

Trotsky did not then know that Stalin had a spy planted in his inner circle, but soon enough reports reached him of a planned attempt on his life. Whereupon he addressed a scorching letter on January 4, 1932, from his exile in Turkey to the Political Bureau of the Communist Party in Moscow, charging that "Stalin has come to the conclusion that it was a mistake" to have exiled him abroad, that "the bureaucrat" Stalin had not realized that Trotsky without any resources was not helpless since "ideas have a power of their own," and that Stalin had concluded: "It is necessary to rectify the mistake."

Stalin's initial step in rectifying his mistake followed promptly. On February 20, 1932, the Soviet government published a decree depriving Trotsky, his wife Natalia, his son Leon Sedov and his daughter Zinaida of Soviet citizenship, thus barring them from returning to Russia and, in effect, condemning Trotsky to the precarious existence of a wanderer seeking refuge while living in fear of assassination from White Russians as well as Red.

Jack Soble met Trotsky for the last time in Copenhagen in December, 1932, when Trotsky was permitted to come there on a brief lecture tour. This Copenhagen meeting was fated to become an international bone of contention.

"I had the suspicion, as other friends who worked in the German organization," Trotsky testified about Soble's Copenhagen visit, "that the so-called Trotskyite was more or less an agent of the Stalinists. He came to assure me that it was not true—that is, Senin came, and we had a conversation for one hour or a bit more." [5] Soble's own account of the visit is more graphic: "Trotsky called me in and in a fit of rage told me he had discovered what I was up to. He said: 'You will one day regret what you are doing. I never want to see you again.' "

Stalin made use of Soble's report on that meeting to incorporate it, in doctored form, as a crucial item in the indictment of Trotsky presented at the first purge trial, the verdict of which put Trotsky under death sentence. But since Soble was too valuable to the Soviet apparat to be dispensed with through public exposure, another undercover agent, Berman-Yurin, was wheeled out by Prosecutor Vyshinsky as a witness to recite in court an account of his meeting with Trotsky in Copenhagen. That substitute actor testified that Trotsky was plotting the overthrow of Soviet rule.

This sleight-of-hand operation was calculated to confuse Trotsky and to impair his defense. He could not deny certain points establishing that there actually had been a meeting in Copenhagen, although he could claim, as he did, that he had never seen or known the new witness. But, then, it was common knowledge that secret agents operated under various aliases.

Trotsky's gullibility about people around him stands out in this affair. Although he had already suspected in Copenhagen that Soble might be a Stalinist, Trotsky died believing him to have been formerly a follower of his. In his testimony on the Copenhagen incident, he declared that Soble "was at that time a comrade but has since become an agent of the GPU." Trotsky simply would not admit the thought that Soble, when he first appeared as the leader of the Trotskyite group in Berlin, had been infiltrated by the Kremlin as a spy into his organization at its very inception.

Soble, having aroused Trotsky's suspicions, had to be withdrawn from the front stage of the operation, but there was no break in Stalin's net covering his quarry. In the deep recesses of the Moscow headquarters Soble was put in charge of espionage in the Trotsky camp, and another link in the ring, Mark Zborowski, replaced him in the field, in Western Europe. Zborowski, exposed as a spy while serving as an anthropologist associated with Columbia and Harvard universities, turned out to be a more suave and astute operative when planted in the Trotsky entourage, and left behind him a trail of duplicity and blood worthy of a Shakespearean villain.

If the world crisis had not driven both Soble and Zborowski to the United States where their paths converged, the record of Zborowski's performance would still be buried in the Kremlin archives, and he would have escaped discovery.

It was not long after Trotsky's return from Copenhagen that he was able to leave Turkey for good. After Hitler's rise to power in 1933, the government of France granted permission for Trotsky to take up residence there, on condition that he live strictly *incognito* in some provincial spot. In the greatest of secrecy, after unusual preparations, the Trotskys landed in July, 1933, in

Marseilles and proceeded to the vicinity of Royan, a popular beach resort at the mouth of the Gironde on the Atlantic Ocean, not far from Bordeaux. Trotsky's friends in charge of the arrangements had been warned by the *Sûreté Générale* against the selection of Royan as it was "very near the island of Oleron where there was a colony of communist children" and therefore an unsafe haven for him.

It was indeed an ironic coincidence that Trotsky's first hideout in France should have been located in the very vicinity of Bordeaux where Ramon and his mother had lived for several years. In the course of his examination in prison by the psychiatrists, Ramon dropped a clue, which has remained an enigma until now, in the form of a dream he claimed to have had. That dream as written up by him—which is cited and analyzed later—gives an account of a sailing accident off the harbor of Royan.

A modest villa, "Spray of the Sea" (Les Embruns), on a remote point of the seashore at Saint-Palais had been rented for the Trotskys who attempted upon their arrival to pass themselves off as Americans. Yet before they had time to remove the baggage from the automobiles which brought them out, a mysterious fire broke out, threatening the villa. And the secret of the identity of Trotsky leaked out at once. During the eleven weeks of his sojourn at Royan, it became a mecca for his "comrades and sympathizers," among whom was Jennie Lee, M.P. (the wife of Aneurin Bevan) and André Malraux, now one of General de Gaulle's chief advisers. Only Moscow knows how many of the fifty-odd visitors from all over the world to Royan were agents of Stalin.

We do know that Mark Zborowski had already embarked on his bizarre career in Stalin's secret service when Trotsky came to France where he remained until May, 1934. Born in the Ukraine in January, 1908, raised in Poland after the revolution, Zborowski had become a communist at an early age. He was arrested by the Polish authorities on suspicion of being a Soviet agent. After a few months in prison, he went to France in 1928 where he attended the University of Paris and later studied medicine and philosophy at Rouen and Grenoble. His first known job was that of secretary of the Union for Repatriation to Russia, a disguised offshoot of the Soviet secret police designed to lure former Imperial officers back home so as to promote the disintegration of the anti-communist emigres. This organization "served as a reservoir of Soviet agents for many tasks, including kidnapping and murder." [6]

Zborowski, the "masterful infiltrator," in the phrase of the well-known author of *Soviet Espionage,* David J. Dallin, who was his friend and victim for many years, gradually penetrated the inner sanctum of the Trotskyite movement. Its headquarters were in Paris, where Trotsky's young son, Leon Sedov, was in charge of operations of the Fourth International, set up by his father as a rival to Stalin's Communist International. Sedov was also the editor of the organization's chief organ, the *Bulletin of the Opposition* to which Zborowski contributed under the pseudonym of Etienne. Trotsky himself lived at Barbizon, not far from Paris, and was in close touch with his headquarters.

Zborowski had met, cultivated and become the right-hand man of Sedov, with access to all the important Trotskyite documents, including underground information from the Soviet Union. Stalin himself perused the reports from his spy Etienne in Paris. Zborowski was such a superb dissimulator that, as an ardent Trotskyite, he was presented with an autographed picture and acknowledged the gift with a worshipful note to Trotsky. All of this was very much to the taste of the dictator in the Kremlin, who was personally accumulating the "evidence" for the series of show trials in the great purge he was scheming to unleash.

Upon the outbreak of the Spanish civil war, in July, 1936, Trotsky's Fourth International held an underground conference in Paris. At this moment Trotsky himself, expelled from France, was living in Norway. The man who was commissioned by his son Sedov to escort the visiting delegates to their secret quarters and to usher them to the clandestine meeting place so that the Stalinists would not learn of the conference and its participants, was none other than Stalin's own man, Zborowski.

On the eve of the anniversary celebration of the Soviet revolution in 1936, the NKVD cell in Paris decided to make a special present to Stalin. What gift would be more appreciated by their great leader in the Kremlin than Trotsky's archives? The NKVD had been tipped off by Zborowski that these had been transferred for safety's sake from Sedov's office to the quarters of the International Institute of Social History at 7 rue Michelet, headed by Boris Nicolaevsky, the anti-communist Russian socialist writer. Zborowski was employed at the Institute. One of the associates there was the present Mrs. Lilia Dallin, who was a close friend of Leon Sedov. Indeed, it was Sedov who had introduced her to Zborowski. And as Mrs. Dallin has herself revealed,[7] she and Zborowski had packed the Trotsky archives in fifteen bulky bundles and moved them in a taxi to their new depository.

During the night of November 7 the premises of the Institute were broken into and thoroughly ransacked. But the burglars took no money or other valuable documents. They helped themselves only to the fifteen packages of the Trotsky files. Zborowski, as he later confessed, had an anxious time over this assignment, as he feared that it would lead to his exposure as a spy for Stalin, but everybody's confidence in him remained unshaken. (The Dallins became such intimate friends of Zborowski and trusted him so implicitly as a rock-ribbed opponent of Moscow that they even sponsored his immigration to the United States, but subsequently had an honorable share in delivering him to justice.)

From now on terror and violent death began mysteriously to stalk the Trotsky household and political camp where Zborowski had left his footprints. But still he remained above suspicion. He was next assigned to lure Leon Sedov to a place where Soviet agents could kidnap him and take him to Russia. Something upset the NKVD plans on this occasion, although Zborowski claimed that it was his failure to cooperate which frustrated the plot. Yet the next attempt was successful. Zborowski was no killer himself but a wizard as a finger man, David Dallin observes.[8] He discerned Zborowski's hand "in the case of the high-ranking NKVD man Ignace Reiss" who defected in July, 1937, and sought to affiliate himself with the Trotskyite group.

"Moscow decided to liquidate Reiss at once," Dallin reports. "According to Swiss and French police reports, two gangs of assassins were dispatched to meet Reiss—one on September 4, 1937, in Lausanne, Switzerland and, should that fail, another the next day in Reims, France. Zborowski was the only person who could have told the NKVD about Reiss's plans to go to Reims, for a meeting between Reiss and Sedov had been scheduled there on that date."

The bullet-riddled body of Ignace Reiss was found sprawled on the highway near Lausanne in the early morning of September 4. A ticket to Reims was in the dead man's pocket.

Another high NKVD officer, General Walter Krivitsky, had the narrowest of escapes from a band of Stalin's assassins put on his track by Zborowski. Krivitsky, with whom this writer collaborated in preparing his memoirs, was later found shot to death under mysterious circumstances in February, 1941, in a Washington hotel room. Late in the summer of 1937 Krivitsky decided not to heed a call to go back to Moscow, and turned to Sedov in Paris for help in escaping from Stalin's network. Sedov appointed Zborowski as Krivitsky's bodyguard!

"Zborowski now admits he was reporting to the NKVD on where Krivitsky spent his time, whom he was seeing, and so on," Dallin records. Krivitsky, however, was able to get police protection from the French government. Accompanied by an officer of the Sûreté, he went to Marseilles to look for safe quarters for his family. At the station he spotted and recognized four Soviet underground operatives standing in wait for him, and raised an alarm. His guard attempted pursuit without success. Only Sedov and Zborowski knew his destination. Krivitsky was baffled, but never suspected Zborowski. "To this day I do not know how the Ogpu found out my route and schedule," he wrote not long before his violent death.

Zborowski's long arm reached into Spain to turn over to the NKVD executioners Trotsky's secretary, Erwin Wolf, who had been expelled from Norway before his master had set sail for Mexico. Upon his arrival in Spain, Wolf was promptly murdered in cold blood by agents of the Division of Special Tasks, newly set up by Stalin. In command of the Spanish branch of this special apparat, under the alias of General Kotov, was Leonid Eitingon, who had come to Stalin's attention through his cloak-and-dagger operations in France during the years of Zborowski's espionage within the Trotsky camp.

It was Eitingon who had organized the sensational abduction of General Alexander Kutepov in broad daylight on a street in Paris, an event which rocked Europe early in 1930. Kutepov was the head of the powerful Federation of Imperial Army Veterans, the leading body of White Russians abroad. Directing Stalin's subversive operations in France at that time was the up-and-coming GPU officer, Eitingon, who was attached under a cover name of Sakhov to the Soviet Embassy and operated under the aliases of Valery and Lyova. Zborowski was then one of the operatives in his network. It was not until fifteen years later that Eitingon's role in the Kutepov affair, which has never been solved by the French police, became known. Both Zborowski and Eitingon were deeply enmeshed in the mystery of Trotsky's assassination.

Eitingon subsequently emerged in Mexico as the man who masterminded and organized the assassination of Trotsky. His capital share in the plot was interwoven with a love relationship with Ramon's mother which brought him close to the assassin whose career as an underground terrorist he had molded. Although officially known in Spain as General Kotov, he was also disguised in Communist Party circles there under the cover name of Comrade Pablo. Of medium height and stocky build, with small piercing eyes under beetle brows, Eitingon grew a beard and mustache to conceal a scar on his chin left after an automobile accident in Spain. His resemblance then to Campesino, the notorious peasant guerrilla leader, became so striking that he was frequently taken for the Spaniard. This annoyed him so much that he would fly into a temper whenever it occurred.

For years students of the Trotsky murder have sought in vain to identify on the basis of fragmentary reports the man behind the scenes of the crime, normally an impossible task in the case of an inside conspirator of a secret service such as Stalin's. However, a chain of fortuitous events in different parts of the world has made it possible to establish the facts about Eitingon. Late in 1936 Stalin had dispatched a top secret NKVD mission to Spain headed by General Alexander Orlov who, according to his own account, was charged with "matters pertaining to intelligence, counter-intelligence and guerrilla warfare behind enemy lines," to be carried out by "my former assistant, Kotov." The duties of the latter were to pick men for commando and sabotage operations, train them and organize detachments for diversionary and terrorist acts.

General Orlov, who later fled to the United States and wrote the revealing *Secret History of Stalin's Crimes,* has testified [9] that "at the head of that business stood a man by the name of Eitingon—his other name was Kotov." Together they had organized six schools for saboteurs, mostly recruited of Spanish communists. Orlov himself had attended in Barcelona the opening of one such school with some 600 students.

Bursting upon the world horizon in April, 1954, in Bonn, Germany, was one of Eitingon's Russian underlings, Captain Nikolai Khokhlov of the Soviet secret service who confessed at a news conference arranged by United States officials that he had been sent from Moscow to carry out the assassination of a leader of a militant Russian emigre organization. To substantiate his disclosure, he produced an assortment of extraordinary lethal weapons, such as poisoned bullets and noiseless revolvers in camouflaged forms, which unmistakably came from Soviet laboratories for murder. In his subsequent sworn testimony,[10] Khokhlov revealed that "Trotsky's assassination was organized by Major General Eitingon, the same general who was in Spain under the name of General Kotov," and who "recruited Spaniards for diversionary activities of the Soviet Intelligence." And then Khokhlov added:

"*And that is where he recruited a Spaniard who was brought to the Soviet Union, and who was briefed in detail, and who was later sent to Mexico under the name of Mornard.*"

At the same time another world sensation, emanating from the opposite end of the globe, from Canberra, Australia, provided information in support of the evidence produced by General Orlov and Captain Khokhlov. The case of Colonel Vladimir Petrov and his wife Captain Evdokia of the Soviet secret service, who sought and found asylum in Australia after they were rescued from a plane bound to end in their delivery to Soviet hands, led to a rupture of diplomatic relations with Moscow. Petrov offered supplementary testimony on the minute preparations at Moscow headquarters for the assassination of Trotsky, and backed up Khokhlov's evidence as to Eitingon's part in the affair.

In his Russian autobiography published in Frankfurt two years ago, Captain Khokhlov devotes much space to Eitingon and discloses how he had pressed him in Moscow to take up the career of a terrorist and assassin in Stalin's service.

Upon the return of Caridad Mercader from her mission to Mexico, her underground activities brought her into close contact with Eitingon. The relationship developed into an intimate affair which lasted for years. They were later seen in close company in Moscow by Spanish refugees high in the councils of the Comintern. Caridad had even confided to one of these comrades that Eitingon had once hinted at marriage to her. She had fallen deeply in love with him and hoped to share his life. She had found him a delightful companion, for Leonid Eitingon was a gourmet who enjoyed high living, and who could turn on considerable charm when needed. But in Russia Caridad discovered that Eitingon had a wife and family, and had never been serious about marrying her.

Ramon was given special training in guerrilla warfare in Barcelona under the supervision of Eitingon. As a member of a commando unit, he learned how to penetrate deep into enemy territory, ambush officers there, derail trains, blow up ammunition dumps and commit acts of sabotage. He was brought back from the front with a wound in the elbow, and was placed in the improvised hospital in the Pension Bank Building at Montjuich. While under treatment for this wound, he suffered an attack of jaundice. His mother visited him frequently there. But when his father once came to see him, the son in a fit of temper told him that he wanted no truck with bourgeois elements.

No wonder that after the assassination of Trotsky he was able to create for the authorities during his examination the convincing image of a fictitious father who had died in 1926. And what a seismic shock it would be to Ramon's whole being now if his father were to be brought unexpectedly into his cell. For Don Pablo Mercader Marino, aged 74, is still very much alive in his home in Barcelona as this is being written.

The hospital room next to Ramon's was occupied by another

convalescent patient, a tall, blonde Dutch girl, Fani Castedo, prominent in the communist movement. Ramon had an affair with her. His room became a meeting place for some of the most notorious communists in Barcelona as well as Soviet NKVD operatives hospitalized in the establishment. The attending nurses remember him for his fanaticism, and describe him as a neurotic, like his mother, who dreamed of performing great deeds.

One such deed has left the stigma of Cain upon Ramon among those who knew him in Barcelona. His brother, Pablo Mercader, also served as a junior officer in a communist military unit. He was in love with a girl known to be a member of an anarchist group, which put Pablo under suspicion. When he was ordered to break his relations with her, he refused. He was put in command of a squad assigned to execute three political prisoners rounded up in the course of the numerous raids then common in Catalonia. It is an unwritten communist law that such an execution must be carried out in a back yard or basement, out of sight. Pablo had his men shoot the victims in the open and leave their bodies sprawled in the street. For this breach of the communist code he was attached to a penal shock battalion which was sent to the advance line of the active front. This was a Soviet practice which was considered as tantamount to a death sentence.

Ramon and his mother did not intercede for Pablo. And shortly afterwards when Pablo was killed in action, Ramon openly hinted that his brother had received his just desserts.

Together with his mother, Ramon served as commandant of the barracks remembered in Barcelona to this day as the Russian headquarters. It is more than likely that this was the place where General Orlov witnessed the opening of the school for training saboteurs and terrorists, which was established by Eitingon. But Caridad and Ramon are also remembered for less important items. Some of their highly respectable relatives, fleeing from

Barcelona for fear of persecution by the revolutionaries, had turned over their house to Caridad and her son. When these owners returned at the end of the civil war, they found the interior of their house completely dismantled by its former communist occupants.

In December, 1937, Ramon paid a farewell visit to the nurse who had attended him in the hospital. He told her that he was leaving Spain on an important mission, but did not indicate the nature or place of his assignment. This was the last time he saw Spain. He turned up next in Moscow, as a protégé of Eitingon, and was given highly specialized extra training in the arts of terror. Already the plans for the great assassination were being laid at No. 2 Djerzhinsky Street, Moscow, the headquarters of the NKVD, where Ramon had occasion to study the voluminous files assembled with the aid of Soble and Zborowski, dealing with Trotsky, his mode of living, his physical surroundings, his associates and his guards.

While Ramon Mercader was settling down in Moscow to learn the fine crafts of dissembling and assassination as taught by Stalin's foremost technicians, Trotsky was wrestling in Mexico with the problem of defense against attacks by local Stalinist hotheads. The Mexican communist press was in a rage over the asylum granted to Trotsky and was inciting its followers to violence against him.

"In Mexico the first attempt at assassination was made in January, 1938, by an unknown man who appeared in my house with a forged message from a Mexican political figure," Trotsky wrote in an article finished a few days before his murder and published posthumously. "It was precisely after this incident, which alarmed my friends," Trotsky continued, "that more serious defense measures were adopted." As examples, he cited the establishment of a 24-hour guard and the installation of an alarm system in his villa at Coyoacan.

The following month Diego Rivera noticed strange comings and goings by suspicious characters in a house near Trotsky's villa. Alarmed, he insisted that Trotsky stay away from his home for a while, apparently to gain time to check on the suspect neighbors. Trotsky went to stay for a few days with a Mexican friend, Antonio Hidalgo, who lived in the vicinity of the restful Chapultepec Park.

On February 16, 1938, Diego suddenly burst into Trotsky's room in Hidalgo's villa. Without any preliminaries, in a state of obvious excitement, he blurted out:

"Leon Sedov is dead!"

"What? What are you saying?" Trotsky asked as if awakened from slumber. Diego showed him the evening newspaper with the despatch from Paris.

"Go away!" Trotsky cried out, and begged to be left alone to pull himself together. For quite a while, he remained in his room, stunned by this totally unexpected blow. Natalia Trotsky, the mother of Sedov, was not with her husband at the time.

"An hour later," wrote Trotsky in his moving tribute to his favorite child, "I brought to Natalia the news of the death of our son—in the same month, February, in which Natalia 32 years before had communicated to me in prison the news of his birth. Thus ended for us the day of February 16, the blackest day in our personal life."

"I was in Coyoacan arranging old photos of our children," Natalia Trotsky narrated much later. "The bell rang and I was surprised to see Lev Davidovitch come in. I went towards him. He entered bent over in a way I had never seen him before, his face ashen-gray, suddenly turned into an old man."

"What's the matter? Are you sick?" she asked, upset.

"Liova is sick, our little Liova. . . ." Trotsky answered. Liova was the diminutive Russian name by which the Trotskys referred to their son Leon.

"It began to dawn on me," Natalia recalled the event. "I

feared so much for Lev Davidovitch that the idea of misfortune befalling Liova had never entered my mind."

What happened in Paris on that February 16 is one of those innumerable pages from the book of Stalin's life on which history has put its stamp: "Unsolved." Mrs. Lilia Dallin and Mark Zborowski, Sedov's closest associates during the critical time, have left their testimony. The Trotskys have their accounts, on the basis of information which reached them from Paris.

Leon Sedov was taken ill with abdominal pains, and had to be rushed to a hospital for an appendectomy. Mrs. Dallin and her good friend Zborowski took elaborate precautions to prevent the NKVD from finding out where Sedov was going to be operated upon. Zborowski ordered an ambulance and accompanied Trotsky's stricken son to a small hospital in Auteuil, the head of which was a Russian emigré physician. To protect the patient from Stalin's killers, Zborowski had him register under the name of Martin, posing as a French engineer. The operation was successful and there was steady improvement thereafter, so that the special attending hospital nurse was removed.

Then, suddenly, Sedov died. Immediately before his death he was found pajama-clad and in delirium wandering around the corridors of the hospital. The surgeon who had operated upon him was so puzzled by his death that he asked Mrs. Sedov whether her husband had ever tried to commit suicide. His mother, Natalia, subsequently added what she called bizarre details: that the hospital was frequented by pro-Stalinist Russians, that her son had been addressed in Russian by a physician, and that he had been given something to eat in the hours between regular meals.

The man who had taken Sedov in the ambulance, Zborowski, asserted under oath that his hands were clean of blood, because he had always informed on those who trusted him too late for the NKVD to murder them.

Trotsky, in his obituary of his son, also dealt with the mystery of his death. He wrote:

"The first and natural assumption: he was poisoned. To gain access to Leon, to his clothes, his food, presented no great difficulty for Stalin's agents. . . . In connection with chemical warfare, the art of poisoning has been developed to an exceptional degree. It is true, the secrets of this art are beyond the reach of ordinary mortals. But the poisoners of the GPU have access to everything. It is fully possible that there now exists a poison which cannot be traced after death even by the most thorough analysis. And where is the guarantee of such thoroughness?

"Or did they kill him without the aid of chemistry? . . ."

Zborowski was tried and convicted on charges of perjury in New York early in December, 1958, receiving the maximum sentence of five years. Although the United States Attorney accused Zborowski of having served the cause of Soviet Russia and international communism from the very beginning of his adult life, the defendant could not be brought to justice here for his criminal acts committed in France in connection with Stalin's operations against Trotsky.

The first break in the far-flung espionage web around Trotsky, leading to the downfall of Soble and Zborowski, was made by Alexander Orlov who confided his suspicions to the Dallins. Orlov had learned in Moscow of the reports of the mysterious Etienne, which Stalin cherished, on the inside doings in the Trotsky camp.

"Before I left Russia in 1936," runs Orlov's own account,[11] "I learned that the NKVD had succeeded in planting a spy in the entourage of Trotsky and his son, Leon Sedov, and that Stalin himself knew about that agent and used to read his reports about Trotsky and Trotsky's son. I understood very well what that meant. I understood that Stalin was doing his best in order to corner Trotsky and assassinate him, and I understood that through this man Stalin might introduce, under the guise of a guard or secretary, an assassin into Trotsky's household. . . .

"While working in Spain during the civil war, I used to come on business to France, and there I did my best to find out the identity of this agent from the chief of the NKVD in Paris, in France. I found out that this agent had become the closest friend of Trotsky's son, Leon Sedov, and that he was in correspondence with Trotsky himself. . . . I found out that his first name was Mark. . . . I did not know at that time that his name was Zborowski."

Orlov had also picked up some information about Zborowski's age and family and his place of employment. After Orlov's revelations, the FBI caught up with Zborowski. He was questioned, and word of this gave the chief of his ring, Jack Soble, a case of extreme and lasting jitters. For although this was 1954, some fourteen years after the assassination of Trotsky, Soble continued to spy on the Trotskyite groups, in addition to his other and perhaps more important special assignments.

For an insight into the ways of the Kremlin, it should be recorded that Soble was enabled to save all the members of his large family—literally an entire clan—to bring them out of Russia and get with them to the United States via Japan on the eve of Pearl Harbor, all because of a decade of signal service in the hunt and kill of Trotsky. Lavrenti Beria, the chief of the Stalin terror machine, had called in Soble to reward him with the new espionage assignment in the United States, and announced: "Comrade Stalin remembers your name and the services you performed regarding that dastardly enemy of the state, Trotsky."

Soble arrived in the United States from the Far East a few weeks ahead of his old collaborator Zborowski who fled from Europe when the Hitler tide was at its height. For the next thirteen years the two spies who made their secret careers in Stalin's service as Trotsky-hunters built successful careers in the life of the America which had given them refuge, until their unanticipated downfall and the collapse of their underground network.

The unmasking of Zborowski led to Soble's apprehension, breakdown and confession. And that in turn resulted in Zborowski's arrest. Soble was able to cast authoritative light on the mystery of Sedov's sudden death. Ramon Mercader had, perhaps inadvertently, already made his contribution to its solution. During his examination by Judge Trujillo after Trotsky's assassination, he was asked at a preliminary hearing:

"What is your opinion about the death of Sedov?"

The assassin hesitated, fumbled for words, replied sullenly: "Only what is printed on the case."

"Was it the GPU?"

"Yes. The GPU killed Leon Sedov."

And in New York, eighteen years later, Jack Soble, under examination as a witness at the trial of his former deputy, Mark Zborowski, was asked the same question. His answer was, "Yes, it was a GPU job."

Natalia Trotsky, the stricken mother, put the tragedy in its proper historical frame when she wrote about the death sentences passed upon her husband and son:

"Both . . . knew that the verdict of the Moscow court was not platonic in character and that it would be carried out in one way or another."

The executioners had done half their job.

3

Seduction for Murder

The master plan called for the introduction of Ramon Mercader into the very bosom of Trotsky's fortified household in Mexico. Moscow improved upon the classic pattern of seduction for murder. Instead of employing an attractive young woman to exert her charms in the pursuit of the victim, the NKVD high command reversed the old pattern and picked Ramon for the role of the seducer of a woman who had ready access to Trotsky.

Ramon had all the prerequisites for such a masquerade. He was tall, handsome, well-bred, spoke French and Spanish perfectly, and English well enough to pass for an American. He was only 25, but looked a bit older. He could don the mask of a well-to-do, glamorous aristocrat. The young woman chosen as the gull in the imposture was Sylvia Ageloff, a 28-year-old social worker who lacked glamour. Because of her communist proclivities and associations, she was listed in the NKVD records as a Trotskyite courier and she may, indeed, have carried some messages from or for Trotsky on occasion in her travels across the Atlantic.

The devious arrangements to bring about a meeting of the two principals in the staged romance were plotted in the United States and France. Louis Budenz, a native of Indiana with a typical small-town face that nobody was likely to distrust, was then playing a large part in the wolf-in-sheep's-clothing spectacle of the American Communist Party which at the time was being exhibited in public under the slogan, "Communism is twentieth-century Americanism." Very early in his career as a communist, Budenz found himself taking orders from Russian agents of the NKVD, and soon was deeply enmeshed in the web of Stalin's international underground. His Soviet superiors thought so well of him, Budenz later revealed, that they considered firing Jack Stachel, the shrewd labor boss of the American Communist Party, and giving Budenz his seat on the Political Bureau.

Budenz was the unwitting matchmaker in the preliminary arrangements that eventuated in the murder of Trotsky. He lent himself to this purpose because his bosses in the underground had told him it was necessary to check on the Trotskyites and their movement, according to his own account, "to offset any plots against the life of Stalin and against the Soviet Union that might be planned." He elaborated in his testimony: "This was the period of the great purge trials and I agreed to help. . . . I therefore collected and took them all the available information I could obtain in regard to the movements of secret Trotskyites, Trotskyite couriers, and their relations to the left-wing socialists. At that time, I had a number of agents for the Stalinist group planted in the Trotskyite camp, that being one of my first assignments with the Communist Party, and from them I obtained this information." [12]

There was good reason for involving Budenz in this highly secret operation even though he was a fledgling communist. The Conference for Progressive Labor Action, the left-wing organization which Budenz had just left after serving as its national secretary, was filled with Trotskyites. Budenz, therefore, knew a great deal about the personnel, organization and methods of the group. He was able to find the sort of American communist who, when placed inside Trotsky's Fourth International, would infiltrate effectively. He made it possible for the NKVD to steam open and pilfer Trotsky's mail to his New York followers. He got a Communist Party girl, a Chicago social worker, to move to New York and volunteer her services to James Cannon, the American Trotskyite leader: "She had the full run of the Trotskyite offices, became Cannon's secretary, and made available to the Soviet secret police all the correspondence with Trotsky in Mexico City and with other Trotskyites throughout the world," he testified.

Budenz was invaluable to Stalin's apparat. In 1937, he relates, two of his Soviet underground chiefs introduced him to another "and clearly more important agent who went by the name of Robert or Roberts." This Roberts was a specialist in Trotskyism. He was a "very intelligent person, fatherly in his manner, alert and fanatical," but also persistent and infinitely inquisitive.

Roberts began to show Budenz photographs of people he said were Trotskyite couriers to see whether he could identify them. One of these suspected international couriers was Sylvia Ageloff.

Roberts was in reality Dr. Gregory Rabinowitz, officially the representative of the Soviet Red Cross in the United States, Budenz discloses in his testimony. He tells of seeing Roberts sign a Chicago hotel register as Rabinowitz. He describes how he had made this extremely important identification "after five years' investigation on my part, and after examining hundreds of photographs of men connected with Soviet espionage."

Roberts got Budenz to bring them together at dinner with selected persons from the communist hard core. He would question them, size them up, and decide whether or not they were suitable for NKVD infiltration work.

One day Roberts startled Budenz by asking that he bring to dinner Miss Ruby Weil, a young woman who, he had learned, was a friend of Sylvia Ageloff, "the Trotskyite courier." Roberts had apparently checked on Ruby Weil and seemed confident that she was "loyal," though she had never done undercover work before, Budenz reports, adding that she had been "a family friend before either she or I had joined the Communist Party. . . ." He goes on to say: "The man in charge of secret work in the New York district, Comrade Chester, had selected her as a young woman with the requisite conservative background to act as a courier and in other secret capacities . . . Accordingly, he had drafted her for a secret training school for those who were to be called on to perform underground service."

Budenz approached her on behalf of Roberts while she was in that school, he reveals. He goes on to say that the main reason Ruby Weil had been "chosen by the secret police out of the party's rank and file, and was coerced into becoming a leading figure in a great tragedy" was that she had been a friend of the three Ageloff sisters—Ruth, Hilda and Sylvia—before she joined the Communist Party.

Hilda Ageloff, Ruby Weil's particular friend, had met Trotsky and was an adherent of the Fourth International. Ruth had done secretarial work briefly for the John Dewey Commission which had investigated in Mexico the Moscow trial charges against Trotsky, and acquitted him. Sylvia Ageloff was a social worker, employed by New York City. She had studied philosophy under Dr. Sydney Hook and had taken a master's degree in psychology at Columbia University. She belonged to the Trotskyite group—the American Workers' Party—of which Ruby Weil had been a fellow-member before 1938.

During her summer vacations, Sylvia sometimes travelled to Canada, Europe and Mexico. A secret world conference of the Fourth International was scheduled in Paris for the summer of 1938, and the NKVD headquarters in Moscow, tipped off early of the coming event, assumed that Sylvia Ageloff would go to Europe to attend it. She later testified that she had not even known of the meeting in advance, and had decided to go abroad on her own, solely for pleasure. A key factor in these preparations for the Trotsky murder was that the Soviet secret service overestimated Sylvia Ageloff's participation in the Trotsky movement and her importance in it.

The problem now was to arrange a politically impeccable introduction of Sylvia to the agent designated to seduce her. It was also desirable that she be accompanied to Europe by a loyal communist who was a party to the conspiracy and who was familiar with her habits and character—essential information which had to be communicated to the seducer in advance.

Ruby Weil who was picked as Sylvia's traveling companion, had to be persuaded to go along with the plan, Budenz testified, with the argument that "we were engaged in stopping Trotskyite plottings against Stalin's life."

It was necessary to finance her. Budenz gave her "a considerable sum of money" supplied by Roberts "for the specific purpose of enabling her to be dressed well, and to keep up telephone and other connections. She was reluctant to take the money, but upon learning its purposes, agreed to do so," Budenz states.

Ruby had to re-establish her neglected relationship with the Ageloff girls. "Then we didn't see her too much," Sylvia Ageloff recollected. "She disappeared. The rumors were that she was joining the Communist Party, or was interested in it, and we didn't see her much at all, except that we had been personally friendly in the sense that we met her sometimes to go to the movies.

"A few weeks before I went to Europe, she said her sister, who lived in England, had sent her money for passage, and since she had free time or was unemployed, wasn't it wonderful, and she would go along. I said that was all right with me. That was in June, 1938."

While cultivating Sylvia Ageloff in New York, Ruby was observed by Stalinist party members. Association with Trotskyites was regarded as a counter-revolutionary act. Since the open members of the Communist Party naturally knew nothing of Ruby's underground role, she fell under suspicion. This disturbed her immensely and she tried to get out of her sinister arrangement. Budenz used all his powers of persuasion and managed to prevent this.

Roberts now drifted out of the picture and Ruby Weil was put in contact with an agent known as Gertrude, whose identity has been the subject of much speculation. According to Budenz, this Gertrude, a resident of Greenwich Village, instructed Ruby in New York, then preceded her across the Atlantic and gave her further instructions in Paris.

Sylvia and Ruby landed at Southampton and went to London, where Corinne, the English sister who was supposedly paying for Ruby's trip, met them. Ruby Weil announced her intention of going on to Paris. Of course, she would travel with her friend, Sylvia.

The two girls went on a boat train together to Paris and put up at the same hotel. According to Sylvia's own account, Ruby had told her that she knew a comrade in Paris named Gertrude.[13] And this Gertrude, as Sylvia recollected on the stand, "knew somebody in Paris that she had been friendly with, who was a young student and used to visit Gertrude at her house in Paris, and she was going to get in touch with him.

"So she called him and he came around to the hotel," Sylvia continued. There followed some days of sightseeing, and then

Ruby left Paris. "I never saw Ruby after that," Sylvia concluded her story.

Ruby, in her account of the staged episode, spelled out in her own way that the "young student" whom she had introduced to Sylvia was none other than "Jacques Mornard."

"How did you meet Mr. Mornard?" she was asked.

"I met him in Paris," Ruby answered.

"Do you recall who introduced you?"

"I had known a woman in New York, had met her, and she was a friend of his. When he called me, he said he was a friend of hers."

"What was her name?"

"Her first name was Gertrude."

"Do you recall her last name?"

"I am not absolutely certain of her last name. I think it was Sauzea."

"Where did Gertrude reside?"

"In Paris."

"You saw her before you went to Paris, didn't you?"

"Not for some time. . . . I had seen her in New York."

"Did you introduce Sylvia Ageloff to Mr. Mornard in Paris?"

"Yes."

The assassin himself, Ramon Mercader, betrayed the essential facts of this critical episode when he told Dr. Quiroz in the course of an examination in prison:

"In my swimming exercises, I got to know a young North American woman named Gertrude, who came from London or New York, and in our talks, she said that she had a friend, Ruby Weil, who was looking for an apartment . . ."

Unlike Ruby Weil, who left a deep trail when she departed from the stage she had set, Gertrude went as elusively as she came. Who was Gertrude? The best evidence points to small, inconspicuous-looking Gertrude Allison, of the radical "Jimmy Higgins Bookshop" in Greenwich Village, who later in Mexico married Eduardo Machado, one of two Venezuelan brothers, glorified by *The Daily Worker* as "Venezuela's Fabulous Machados." Gertrude's husband, Eduardo, active in the communist-sponsored Anti-Imperialist League in New York, had been twice deported from the United States. With his wife he went to the Soviet Union where she arrived in 1932, and they remained for several years in the underground there. Gertrude made several trips back home. She also traveled widely as an underground courier for the Comintern. The French police records show that she lived in Paris in 1937–38. Then the Machados took up residence in Mexico, where they lived before and during the assassination of Trotsky. They returned to Venezuela during the recent resurgence of revolutionary activity there, and have figured prominently as the recognized communist leaders in the last presidential election campaign there.

The Paris honeymoon of Sylvia Ageloff and "Jacques Mornard" began shortly after their meeting in July. The well-tailored and rather distinguished-looking beau took Sylvia on automobile rides, to galleries, on sightseeing trips. He had plenty of money and he never seemed to have work to do to interfere with his romance. He knew Paris well, where to eat, what to drink and which cabarets were amusing. In fact, he was an ideal guide and companion for an American girl on vacation.

Sylvia had travelled widely, spoke French, Spanish and Russian, and had been identified with the Trotskyite movement for years. Yet her escort showed no interest in either communism or Trotskyism. In fact, Sylvia marvelled at his apparent total indifference to politics of any sort. He displayed a boredom with the subject so acute that "he never even read ordinary news articles." [14] He talked to her about music, the theatre, other cultural subjects or else personalities and sports. All the while, he posed as the scion of a wealthy aristocratic Belgian family.

One of the ironies of the affair is that, during the months they were together in Paris, Sylvia apparently never revealed to him that she was a Trotskyite. She undoubtedly feared that she would seem less desirable to this indolent member of the leisure class if he associated her in his mind with being a member of a revolutionary sect. And there was obviously nothing in her academic training as a psychologist to give her insight into the fact that the trait which her lover found most irresistible was precisely her political affiliation. Ramon's studied disinterest in politics of any variety shows that the NKVD plan was to have him approach Trotsky as Sylvia's non-political husband.

One of the other incongruities of the affair in Paris was that Ramon had told his mistress that he was combining studies of journalism at the Sorbonne with free lance sports writing. The proceeds from the sale of articles, together with whatever his family contributed, supposedly were the sources of his income. Yet Sylvia never saw him writing. He did not take her to the big sports events. They did not go to the places where leading people in the sports world congregate. They did not entertain athletes, trainers, managers. In short, if he did any of the things that a reportorial writer must do to survive in a highly competitive business, he apparently did it secretly and never allowed his work to interfere with his love-making.

In the second half of July, i.e., within a couple of weeks of their meeting, Ramon announced he had to go to Belgium because of a serious accident in his family.

There was an "accident," a frightful one, which shocked all Paris at that very time. It involved a young German political refugee, Rudolf Klement, a retiring and studious person who as secretary of the Fourth International was just then making preparations for the world conference of the Trotskyite following. The arrival of Ruby Weil and Sylvia Ageloff in Paris, and the commencement of the affair with Ramon, coincided with the event. Since the previous such conclave, Sedov had met a strange death. But his right-hand man, Zborowski, was still as active as ever, handling all the arrangements, such as assigning the delegates to their clandestine quarters and picking safe places for the sessions. Needless to add, Stalin's apparat was kept informed by Zborowski of every move by the arriving revolutionaries.

One of these had come from across the Atlantic carrying in his locked suitcase a file of highly secret documents. He checked his baggage at the railroad station, and went off to locate his comrades. Only Zborowski knew of his scheduled arrival. When the valise was retrieved from the baggage room, it was found that the lock had been broken open and all the precious papers gone.

Sylvia Ageloff was not a delegate to the conference, but she did attend some sessions in the capacity of an interpreter. Her "non-political" lover was hovering somewhere on the fringes of the gathering and "casually" met a number of the important delegates, including James Cannon, the American militant Trotskyite leader, and the Alfred Rosmers, prominent French literary figures in the Fourth International.

On July 16, a headless body was found floating in the Seine at Paris. It had been decapitated and its arms and legs cut off by someone possessed of a knowledge of anatomy, according to the authorities. The body was believed to be that of Klement. The investigation established that he had been abducted the morning of July 13, just as he was about to sit down to his breakfast which remained untouched on the table.

"The GPU mowed down Klement," Trotsky declared to Natalia. And his chief secretary in Mexico, Joseph Hansen, in answer to the question, "Why was Klement killed?" wrote:

"It was Trotsky's opinion that Klement stumbled upon some information of utmost importance concerning the GPU, the identity of a *provocateur*—perhaps proof that the GPU murdered Leon Sedov, was preparing the assassination of Trotsky."

Up to this time Zborowski had not been under suspicion. It was years later that Dallin declared that "Zborowski was probably involved also in the disappearance of the former German Communist Rudolf Klement."

Was Ramon Mercader implicated in either the death of Sedov or the murder of Klement? Dr. Quiroz, the examining psychologist, noted the remarkable manual skill of Ramon and stated that he had all the gifts necessary for a first-class surgeon. Ramon had, of course, taken care to suppress any mention of his training as a hotel chef in order to cover up clues to his past. In his discussion with Dr. Quiroz in prison, Ramon observed that he had been fascinated by surgery and used to accompany doctors, when he was in Paris, to watch them perform operations. A man with such natural gifts for surgery could easily have picked up anatomical knowledge to dismember a corpse. He would proudly show off his skill at the dinner table. "With a sharp knife," wrote Hansen, "a roast chicken under his hands seemed to fall apart almost by itself."

In Coyoacan, at Trotsky's residence, a letter arrived in the mail postmarked Perpignan, a border town in southern France. It was addressed to "Mr. Trotsky," and purported to come from Klement, stating the reasons for his alleged defection. Signed by an old alias of Klement, one which he had long discarded, the handwritten letter was quickly discovered to be a clumsy forgery. The contents of the letter, however, acquired capital importance after the assassination of Trotsky. The bogus writer expressed his "disillusionment" over the fact that Trotsky was negotiating a deal with Hitler. (Ironically enough, two years later Stalin concluded his pact with Hitler.) The false Klement announced his break with the Trotskyite organization because of its "objective collaboration with the fascists." A reference in the letter to Mr. "Bills," clearly intended to denote the American writer Carleton Beals who had resigned as a member of the Dewey Commission of Inquiry in Mexico, betrayed a Russian hand in spelling an Anglo-Saxon name phonetically, a mistake which Klement who knew English well would never have made. The striking feature about the character of this letter appeared upon the arrest of Ramon Mercader after his attack on Trotsky when it was discovered to be very similar in content to the written "confession," giving the alleged reason for his crime, which the assassin had in his possession.

After the assassination, one of Trotsky's guards, Jake Cooper, recalled chatting weeks earlier with Ramon when the latter dropped intimations of his friendship with Trotskyite leaders abroad. The name of Rudolf Klement came up. Ramon remarked that he had known him, and added that he—Ramon—was in Paris when "the GPU had foully murdered Klement."

While the gruesome details of the Klement affair were being unraveled on the pages of the Paris press, Ramon found it advisable to concoct the yarn of an "accident" which had befallen his fictional family, and to give it as the reason for breaking off his honeymoon. He left Paris suddenly, supposedly bound for Belgium.

On July 26, 1938, Sylvia received the following letter from "Mornard," postmarked Brussels:

"Sylvia darling, as I told you, my brother had given me a very bad version of my mother's accident. The thing happened like this: my father and mother were coming from Ostend to spend a day in Brussels. They were in a car driven by a chauffeur and just before getting to Brussels, my father had the car stopped for a necessary reason, and it was then that the car was hit by a ten-ton truck, killing the chauffeur and very seriously injuring my mother. My father, not having been in the car, was unhurt. My mother was operated on again yesterday (the second operation in three days) and the doctors say the greatest danger is past but they cannot be sure for a few days."

This elaborate composition, made out of the whole cloth, could not fail to be convincing to Sylvia. Its purpose became clear only after the crime: Ramon either had to go into hiding until the Klement scandal had blown over or the NKVD had other and more pressing business for him than wooing Sylvia.

During his absence, she took a trip to Prague and returned via Brussels, where she was scheduled to meet her lover and return to France with him. Instead, a woman met her at the designated address to say that "Mornard" had suddenly been called to England.

She returned to Paris. Here she received letters from him. Early in September, he appeared in person with the explanation that he had actually been in Brussels all the time, but had been under military arrest for refusal to serve in the army.

She accepted these confused and contradictory stories, perhaps because she wanted to believe in him and was afraid of the truth. When Sylvia spoke about being introduced to his family, "Mornard" refused, stating that neither his father nor his mother would consider her acceptable as a daughter-in-law. Sylvia, however, introduced "Jacques Mornard" to several American friends. They recalled afterwards his story that he was of a noble Belgian family, and that his father had been an important Belgian diplomat.

As preoccupied with the NKVD terror and espionage as the Trotskyites were during 1938, it never occurred to Sylvia or her friends to check as to whether there was a Belgian diplomat named Mornard. She did not take the trouble to scan the Belgian papers for July to see whether a fatal accident of the sort Mercader described had in fact befallen this distinguished and noble family on the Brussels-Ostend road. Nor did she find out whether her lover had really been in military prison for desertion or even whether it was the practice in Belgium to imprison young men for failing to perform their military service, and then allow them to go abroad without actually completing it.

The lovers spent months together, and when the first spell of the romance was over, Sylvia announced she would have to return to America to look for work as she had resigned her job before leaving for Europe.

At this point, "Mornard" said he wanted to stay with her permanently, but he did not suggest marriage against his parents' wishes.

The Argus Publishing Company, the syndicate which was supposedly supporting Ramon by buying his articles on sports, now turned up as the *deus ex machina.* He announced that he had talked to the Argus people and they were prepared to pay Sylvia 3,000 francs a month provided she would furnish them a weekly article on "psychology."

There were a few other conditions. The Argus Company apparently paid writers but refused to have any direct contact with them. It would also have to be understood that she would never know which papers printed her articles. If she found out, "Mornard" explained, she could short-circuit Argus and make a direct deal.

Sylvia Ageloff wishfully swallowed this preposterous story. She knew that she had no reputation in her field and that her name was unknown in France. She was not a professional writer. As the Argus people had not seen any of her stuff, they had no reason to assume it would be competent. Yet they were willing to pay her more than eminent French psychologists could get for newspaper articles; they were prepared to put her on a monthly salary instead of the usual "string" basis, and they didn't care what she wrote about provided it was "psychology." Only a person totally blinded by love could make herself believe in a syndicate which refuses to meet its writers and therefore refuses to supervise them. Finally, the secrecy about where her articles were appearing was tenuous because she could have penetrated it at any time by hiring a clipping service.

Instead, Sylvia Ageloff obviously preferred to think that the Argus story was simply a proof of her lover's delicacy and *savoir faire*. He wanted her to stay with him in Paris, but he didn't want her to feel she was a kept woman.

From Ramon's standpoint, the arrangement had advantages. It gave him time to consolidate his affair with Sylvia, and to take it out of the category of just a tourist's romance. On the other hand, it enabled him to avoid a legal marriage which would have been cumbersome.

Early in the following winter, after they had been together intermittently for more than half a year, Ramon cut the Gordian knot. He announced that he had a job lined up as American correspondent for a Belgian newspaper. Sylvia was to go home to New York, and he would follow in a very few weeks.

As the year 1938 was drawing to a close, the hunted Trotsky received both a reprieve and a warning. The reprieve came as a result of the breakdown of the worldwide Soviet secret service due to the purge which was decimating its elite. Stalin's chief of the terror machine, Yezhov, after the big show trials and the executions of the Red Army high command, went on a bloody rampage which threatened to disintegrate his own apparat. In Spain, Stalin's NKVD envoy, Alexander Orlov, defected and fled secretly to the United States where he remained in hiding for 15 years. In the Far East, General H. S. Lushkov, in charge of NKVD operations on the borders of Japan, fled to Tokyo where he published his confessions. Yezhov was suddenly removed by Stalin and liquidated as a "traitor and imperialist agent." Beria took over, a brief "thaw" ensued, and a period of reorganization of the underground agencies set in. Contributing to this reprieve was the handwriting on the wall in Spain where Franco's forces were advancing rapidly to victory over the dispirited Republicans who were chained to Moscow's chariot.

The warning of Stalin's coming vengeance came directly to

Trotsky from General Orlov in the form of a letter dated December 27, 1938. Living in dread of being discovered and liquidated by Stalin's roving killers, Orlov wrote to Trotsky in the name of an alleged American relative of General Lushkov who had just returned from visiting the latter in Japan. In the guise of a message from Lushkov, Orlov revealed to Trotsky that his Paris organization harbored a most dangerous *agent provocateur*. The reference was, of course, to Zborowski.

"In spite of the fact that Lushkov forgot the name of the *provocateur*, he supplied enough details to enable you to establish without any error who that man is," Orlov wrote. "This *agent provocateur* had for a long time assisted your son, L. Sedov, in editing your Russian *Bulletin of the Opposition* in Paris, and collaborated with him until the very death of Sedov.

"Lushkov is almost sure that the *provocateur's* name is 'Mark.' He was literally the shadow of L. Sedov. . . . This *provocateur* wormed himself into the complete confidence of your son and knew as much about the activities of your organization as Sedov himself. . . . This *agent provocateur* is about 32–35 years old . . . Lushkov had seen his photograph. This *provocateur* wears glasses. He is married and has a baby."

Orlov added that Zborowski was responsible for the theft of Trotsky's archives and that Trotsky knew about him indirectly from Sedov's letters, but had never met him personally. He said that Zborowski had regular meetings with officials of the Soviet Embassy, and asked Trotsky to have his trusted comrade in Paris check on his past and see whom he meets.

"There is no doubt, that before long your comrades will see him meet officers from the Soviet Embassy," added Orlov. "You have all the right in the world to check on members of your organization, even when you have no information that they are traitors. And besides, you are not obliged to believe me.

"The main thing: be on your guard. Do not trust any person,

man or woman, who may come to you with recommendations from this *provocateur*."

And then came the unmistakable warning, the importance of which he emphasized by underlining it:

"Lushkov expressed the apprehension that now the *assassination of Trotsky was on the agenda and that Moscow would try to plant assassins with the help of this* agent provocateur *or through* agents provocateurs *from Spain under the guise of Spanish Trotskyites.*"

Orlov thought that this weighty letter would automatically result in the exposure of Mark while keeping his own identity secret. Surely Trotsky would take the steps suggested in the letter, the only steps that could be expected from a man of ordinary prudence—namely, to check on Mark's antecedents and to have him under observation.

The only fear Orlov had was that GPU agents in Mexico might intercept the letter. Accordingly, he sent two copies, one addressed to Natalia Sedova, and requested Trotsky to acknowledge receipt by publishing in the New York *Socialist Appeal* a personal notice that the editorial office had received the letter from a Mr. Stein.

Instead, Trotsky inserted in the small socialist sheet a frantic ad:

"I insist, Mr. Stein, I insist that you go immediately to the editorial offices of the *Socialist Appeal* and talk to Comrade Martin."

Orlov testified: "I went there without disclosing my identity. I took just a side look at that Martin, and he did not inspire too much confidence in me, so that was all. . . . After that, I tried to call up Trotsky by phone. His secretary talked to me. Trotsky did not want to come to the phone. He was afraid I was a journalist who just wanted to exploit him. . . ."

How Trotsky had bungled this graphic warning was divulged by Lilia Dallin in her testimony:

"The first rumor that I heard about it, was in the summer of 1939, when I visited Mr. Leon Trotsky in Mexico. He had received an unsigned letter from a man who told him that the closest friend of his son, not mentioning his name, saying only 'Mark,' is an agent of the NKVD.

"And when Mr. Trotsky showed me this letter and asked my opinion about him, I felt a little bit uncomfortable, because the details were very unpleasant. Too many of them were in the letter. And when I thought it over and I talked it over with him, and I said, 'That is certainly a definitely dirty job of the NKVD, who want to deprive you of your few collaborators that you have in France.'

"And, at the same time, he had another letter from another unnamed agent, telling him that a woman, meaning me, is coming to visit him, and will poison him.

"So we both decided, 'See how they work? They want that you shall break with the only people that are left!' . . . And we decided that it isn't to be taken seriously, but it was a hoax of the NKVD. . . . And when I came back to Paris, the first thing I did, I told Mr. Zborowski. . . . Oh, he laughed it off. He said, 'You know how the NKVD works. They are trying to smear you. They are trying to smear you.' And it was very convincing. I trusted him, you see."

Sylvia left Paris in February, 1939, and returned to New York. Instead of being followed by "Mornard" in the flesh, she received a cable stating that he was unable to come. Later, he explained in a letter that the reason he was staying in Europe was that he could not get an American visa. His story about visa trouble was implausible. There was no reason whatever why the United States government should have refused a visa to the son of a Belgian diplomat, interested in sports and not politics, independently well-to-do, and possessing the credentials of a foreign correspondent in New York. As for passport trouble, that was a different story. If Sylvia had believed he had been actually imprisoned for evasion of military service during the previous summer, then she might well have also believed that Belgium would refuse to validate his passport for travel to the United States. Together with these excuses for the delays in joining her, "Mornard" kept embroidering the fabrication about his alleged father who was supposed to have served before World War I as Belgian minister in Teheran. He reported to Sylvia many things that his imaginary father was doing.

At this time, early in 1939, the civil war in Spain had come to an end with the defeat of the Republican forces. There was a mass flight to France and to Mexico, led by thousands of communists. Moscow was busily engaged in saving its underground cohort of spies, executioners and propagandists. Hundreds of these operatives found their way to Mexico, where the Spanish government-in-exile had moved. Many others managed to reach and tarry in Russia before crossing the Atlantic. Moscow became the secret headquarters of the Spanish Communist Party, with the fiery La Pasionaria, the embattled Campesino and other leaders being shepherded there by Georgi Dimitrov, of the Reichstag Fire fame, who was the head of the Communist International.

Caridad Mercader belonged to the top echelon of the Spanish refugees. Stopping over in France, on the way to Moscow with her other two sons, she had opportunities to learn from Ramon something about the game he was playing with Sylvia in the conspiracy to encircle and liquidate Trotsky. Caridad herself had won laurels in the Spanish civil war as a ruthless destroyer of Trotskyites. According to her own confidential admission, she had personally carried out some twenty "executions" of Trotskyites and other counter-revolutionary elements. Among the Spanish refugees in Moscow, it was known that Caridad Mercader was a crack shot who could hit a target with a gun or knife at a distance of over 30 feet. But only the elite knew that

Caridad was intimate with General Kotov-Eitingon, and enjoyed the special status of a protégé of Stalin's all-powerful Division of Special Tasks in the NKVD.

Early in September, a few days after the outbreak of World War II, Ramon Mercader arrived unexpectedly in New York on the *Ile de France*. Upon the conclusion of the pact with Hitler on August 24, 1939, in the knowledge that it would unleash war, Stalin took measures to have the death sentence pronounced on Trotsky carried out as soon as possible. Stalin expected the Western powers, the "two imperialist camps," to exhaust each other. Like Trotsky, he was sure that the war would be followed by a new tidal wave of revolution sweeping Western Europe.

Although the struggle for power at home had been waged and won by Stalin a decade earlier, his eye was now on the future international front. To ride the coming revolutionary tide in triumph, he would have to eliminate his only potential post-war rival, Trotsky. True, Stalin was the unchallenged caliph of a great empire while his quarry Trotsky was a man without a country armed only with a pen. But Stalin knew that a pen can be mightier than the sword. He had respect for Trotsky's razor-sharp pen, of which George Bernard Shaw had written: "When he cuts off his opponent's head, he holds it up to show that there are no brains in it." And Stalin remembered that Lenin's reputation and organization at the outbreak of World War I were far feebler than those of Trotsky and his Fourth International.

Ramon no longer used the name of "Jacques Mornard" when he appeared at Sylvia's home, 50 Livingstone Avenue, Brooklyn. He told the Ageloff girls that he had fled Europe on a false passport to avoid service in the war. This, he knew, would be acceptable to Trotskyites who approved such conduct with respect to the defense of a capitalist country. Sylvia and Ramon moved to an apartment in Greenwich Village put at their disposal by a Trotskyite friend, Miss M.G., now a literary associate of an anti-communist labor publication.

For his highly sensitive assignment, the NKVD had to supply him with an American or Canadian passport to avoid applying for a U.S. visa and thus submitting his document to consular scrutiny. His passport was in the name of "Frank Jacson" and, from then on until the murder, he would be known under this name. This extraordinary misspelling of Jackson was another telltale clue to the fact that the NKVD was pulling the strings. Ramon needed an inconspicuous last name, but he drew a most unusual one because the slovenly Russian police agents who doctored the passport didn't know that the surname, Jackson, is spelled with a "k." This clumsy mistake was paralleled in the reference to Carleton Beals as "Bills" in the forged valedictory letter of the murdered Klement.)

The passport he was given was Canadian. It had been issued by the Foreign Office in Ottawa on March 22, 1937 to one Tony Babich, a Yugoslav-Canadian, born on June 13, 1905, at Lovinac, Yugoslavia, and naturalized as a Canadian in 1929. Babich had applied for this passport on the pretext that he wanted to visit his family in Yugoslavia. Actually, he had gone to Spain, enrolled in the International Brigade and been killed in action, according to a Loyalist government announcement, in the early phases of the civil war.

It was the rule of the NKVD to take up the passports of all International Brigade volunteers on their arrival in Spain. The passports of those killed in action were utilized by Soviet intelligence, the procedure being simply to substitute the photograph, assumed name and signature of the Soviet agent for what had originally been on the document, and to retain the original physical description and date and place of birth.

"Jacson" told members of the Ageloff family that he had bought his passport from dealers in forged documents for $3,500. He said that his mother had given him $10,000 and that he had prospects of getting a position with the World's Fair in New York. Later he announced he had a job waiting for him in Mexico City to purchase materials needed by France and England. He told Sylvia that he would be working at $50 a week for Peter Lubeck, the manager of a big firm of British importers. He spent a month with Sylvia, giving her $3,000 to keep for him before his departure. To the Moscow staff in charge of Operation Trotsky that "advance" was a guarantee that Sylvia would join Ramon in Mexico.

If there were small discrepancies in the story he told about his job, the Ageloff girls were too little interested in the bourgeois world of making money to pay much attention to them. As Hilda Ageloff put it in her testimony: "He said he had a job in Mexico with a purchasing commission, import-export, something like that, with a Belgian importer. I don't know the details of that. I didn't pay too much attention to it."

Even less attention to details was paid by her love-struck sister Sylvia. In her testimony about her fiancé's arrival in New York, Sylvia related this episode:

"He told me that on the boat he was telling everybody what was Lower Manhattan, and so forth, and I said, 'How could you tell them, how did you know?' He said he had been so interested he had studied pictures and everything. When I thought it over I figured he must have been in New York before, although he said he had not."

Ramon left New York on a tourist card issued by the Mexican consul general on October 6 and entered Mexico at Laredo on October 12. He signed his name "F. Jacson," gave his occupation as a mechanical engineer, and his home address as 1269 St. Denis Street, Montreal, Canada. From Mexico City he wrote Sylvia that he was waiting for the "boss" of the firm employing him. She was unable to join him at once because she had but recently secured a position with the city home relief bureau which could not be abandoned without ample notice.

In Mexico, he found awaiting him a large contingent of veteran terrorists from Stalin's special corps in Spain. And he learned that his patron, Leonid Eitingon, would soon be coming to Mexico, to be joined by Ramon's own mother, to take over the direction of Operation Trotsky.

4

The Abortive Assault

Even before Ramon arrived in the United States, the underground railway between Mexico and New York went into high speed. Trotsky had signed a contract with an American publisher to write a biography of Stalin. Haunted by fear of having his monstrous crimes exposed before the world, Stalin dreaded Trotsky's pen as well as his uncompromising revolutionary ideology. With the coming of World War II, Stalin envisaged in his postwar planning another cycle of revolutions in the capitalist countries. And he saw in Trotsky a future rival for leadership on the international arena, particularly in those critical areas, from China to France, where Trotsky's role in the Soviet Revolution was still fresh in the memory of the communist and socialist masses believed ripe for revolt.

For years Stalin had promoted and supervised the methodical rewriting of the history of the Russian Revolution. To him—the

Mephisto of our age—who sprang from the mythological Caucasus, history was but a web of myths ever in the process of being refashioned by a new weaver. Other rulers lived for posterity, to be glorified by future generations. Not so Stalin, who was determined to be enshrined as a divinity in his own lifetime. As soon as he reached the pinnacle of power, he commenced to build his own grand cult in history, a cult of deification the like of which has never been known. But first the road had to be cleared: he had to hack his way through a legion of veteran revolutionaries into history's hall of fame before being enthroned as the supreme organizer of the greatest insurrection of all time—the October Revolution.

In his climb to a preeminent place in the sun of history, Stalin had finally to contend only with the two who had designed and fathered that social explosion, Lenin the prophet, Trotsky the engineer. Lenin was securely embalmed under glass. Trotsky was abroad, an active literary volcano, erupting articles, interviews, pamphlets, books, a living challenge to the thousand myths which Stalin was himself writing into history. As Trotsky's widow, Natalia Sedova, was to put it: "Stalin feared most the revelations of the leader of the October Revolution and, therefore, wanted to silence him at all costs."

Louis Budenz, the *Daily Worker* editor, was charged by Roberts, his superior in the underground, with finding the answer to this question: "Where does Trotsky's mail, concerning his book, go?" He easily obtained the information from a source in the publishing field that Trotsky's mail was being sent to one of his former secretaries living in New Jersey. Roberts then found his own means of extracting that correspondence from the mails. Every detail relating to Trotsky's announced book was of vital interest to Stalin who feared that it might contain documentary evidence of his iniquities, which were in part exposed by Khrushchev only sixteen years later.

The link in New York between Roberts and Budenz was that

well-known figure of the communist underground, Jacob Golos, the fiancé of Elizabeth Bentley, the Vassar graduate, an idealistic convert to Soviet espionage. Golos ran a travel agency, World Tourists, Inc., as a cover for his activities in the underground where he went under the names of John and Timmy. It was Golos who notified Budenz to meet Roberts for the last time before the latter departed from the United States. At this farewell meeting in the Bronx, Roberts told Budenz that Ruby Weil had done a splendid piece of work in Paris.

It was some time later that Elizabeth Bentley discovered that Comrade Timmy with whom she had fallen in love was really "Yasha" Golos, a key figure in the apparat. (Not long afterwards, the Attorney General of the United States filed charges of military espionage against Jacob Golos and his World Tourists Agency, among others; the eventual result of the proceedings was a suspended sentence.)

Elizabeth Bentley describes [15] how in the summer of 1939 two Mexican communists, shuttling between Mexico and New York, appeared on her horizon: "One of them was a tall, dark, fierce-eyed young man, by the name of Leopoldo Arenal. The other was a short, excessively fat man . . . a Mexican painter. . . . They, too, had business with Timmy (Golos), and because Leopoldo always brought his wife Helena along, I was taken to lunches and dinners," continues Bentley. "What I did not know until later on was that the two of them were not just Mexican communists but part of the Russian secret police's hatchet squad. Even then they were laying plans to 'liquidate' Leon Trotsky. . . . Timmy needed a 'mail drop' where he could receive letters from the Mexicans, and he was unwilling to use my address. . . . After some thought, he decided to have the letters sent to Leopoldo's sister-in-law, Rose Arenal, a school teacher then separated from her husband and living in the Prospect Park section of Brooklyn. I was introduced to Rose, who was told only that I was 'Elizabeth,' a good and trusted comrade, and it was arranged that I go out to her house every so often to pick up whatever mail she had."

Of a cultured old Mexican family, the brothers Arenal were able artists. Their sister, Angelica, was married to David Alfaro Siqueiros, the famed Mexican painter. Soon they were all deep in Operation Trotsky.

When Ramon Mercader arrived in Mexico in the fall of 1939, his key to Stalin's underground apparat there was Siqueiros, a fanatical communist with the reputation of a swashbuckler. Siqueiros had known Caridad Mercader since her first visit to Mexico in 1936 and she had introduced her son Ramon to him in Spain where he had gone in January, 1937, to join the Loyalists. He had left with the personal blessings of President Cardenas, who had presented him with a pistol for the occasion.

Born in Chihuahua, Siqueiros had been swept up in the Mexican Revolution and at the age of seventeen had been a staff officer of Carranza. In his early twenties, he had served as a Mexican military attaché in Paris. There he began to experiment with revolutionary forms of plastic art, with new concepts and techniques. From these interests he went on to revolutionary politics. In the 1920's he made a pilgrimage to Moscow. According to information in Trotsky's possession about the Soviet secret police, Siqueiros joined the service of the NKVD as early as 1928.

In the Spanish civil war, Siqueiros was the leader of the Mexican volunteers and was known by them as "the little colonel." He had the sort of valor that made him excellently suited for raiding operations, but there is reason to doubt that he found the mud and blood of trench defensive warfare to his liking. In any event, while in Spain, Siqueiros spent a large part of his time in the Union of Revolutionary Artists in Barcelona, and had sponsored Ramon's membership in that organization. Ramon became something of a protégé of his, being fifteen years his junior. Upon his arrival in Mexico City, Ramon used for cover purposes the address of an office maintained by Siqueiros in the business center.

Siqueiros was the most prominent figure in the band of Spanish and Mexican communists who were active in the conspiracy to liquidate Trotsky. Mexico was then the scene of a portentous concentration of veteran Stalinist killers and conspirators. A leading member of this crew was Vittorio Codovila, a short, chunky and almost neckless Italian-born founder of the Argentine Communist Party. Affiliated for a quarter-century with the Soviet underground, he had risen to the top as Comintern boss in South America. In Spain, operating under General Kotov-Eitingon, he became known as a ruthless terrorist. He was linked with one of the most revolting crimes in the log of Stalin's atrocities in Spain, the torture and assassination of Andres Nin, the leader of the left socialist party, the POUM. But Codovila had also liquidated many of his opponents and dissident leaders in the Spanish Communist party as "Trotskyites" and "Franco agents."

Perhaps the most formidable Stalinist figure to reach Mexico at this time was Carlos Contreras, who under the name of General Carlos had organized the famed Fifth Regiment in Spain which had stemmed the first onrush of the Franco tide. Holding his force together by terrorism, his daily executions in his own units were the subject of dreaded talk along the front. Boasting a string of aliases, he had come under the name of Enea Sormenti to the United States where he formed communist strong-arm squads. He was deported in 1927. An old hand in Mexican communist operations, he was believed to have surreptitiously returned to the United States after taking an active part in the liquidation of Trotsky. It has been repeatedly charged in the public prints that it was Contreras-Sormenti who had planned the assassination of Carlo Tresca, the popular Italian-born anti-communist radical, who was shot to death on January 11, 1943, at Fifth Avenue and Fifteenth Street, New York City. Under the name of Vittorio Vidali, Contreras emerged after the last war as Moscow's *Gauleiter* in the critical zone of Trieste.

In charge of the Spanish Communist Party machine in Mexico was Pedro Checa, who had been the organization's secretary in Spain. A communist of the "Old Bolshevik" school, he had apparently adopted his assumed last name after the Cheka, Lenin's original organ of Red Terror, which later was renamed GPU and then NKVD. Pedro Checa's duties included picking suitable party members for transfer to the underground apparat in Operation Trotsky. After the first major but abortive attempt on Trotsky's life, Checa came to a bad end under mysterious circumstances described later.

Moscow had sent reinforcements to the gang being concentrated in Mexico. A special mission was dispatched by Stalin immediately after the Ribbentrop-Molotov talks in August to the scene of the operation against Trotsky. As revealed by Campesino,[16] once the Red hero of the Spanish civil war, in his reminiscences of his disillusionment in and flight from the Soviet Union, the special team comprised three Spanish operatives, two of them notorious for atrocities which had aroused the indignation of all of Spain. The team was assigned to Carlos Contreras, to whom they had brought from Moscow secret instructions in the handling of the organization of Trotsky's assassination.

Ramon took up again his old sport of mountain-climbing soon after his arrival in Mexico. He struck up a friendship with a Mr. Patino of the Pan-American Airways office in Mexico City, to whom he spoke of his experiences in Europe, boasting that he had scaled Mont Blanc. In November, he joined an excursion, organized by Mr. Patino, of a dozen men out to climb Popocatapetl. He carried full alpinist equipment, but tired before reaching the top, and stayed behind in a way station until the party returned. To Mr. Patino, who disclosed all this to the authorities, Mercader represented himself as "Jacson," a Canadian mining engineer, who had come to Mexico to look into mining properties, claiming to have a local bank account of $5,000. Mr. Patino stated that he had personal knowledge that Ramon made trips to Central and South America in a private plane, ostensibly on mining missions. He also knew that Mercader had purchased a Buick in December from the Hernandez Agency at the corner of Morelos and Iturbide Streets, which marked him as a person of considerable means.

Dr. Quiroz, the government criminologist, sent one of his university students, Miss Maria Ricaud, to make inquiries at the automobile agency. She reported that Mercader had bought a 1937 model Buick on December 7, 1939, giving in part payment an unsatisfactory Ford which he had purchased from the same agency immediately upon his arrival. "He said he had come from Canada and was traveling with his wife," reported Miss Ricaud. "On another occasion, he came to this same place accompanied by a woman who was over fifty whom he introduced as his mother."

Mr. Patino also recalled some remarks of a political nature made by Mercader upon the outbreak of the Russo-Finnish war when the world was filled with admiration for the heroic resistance of little Finland against the attack by the mighty Soviet Empire. Mercader spoke slightingly of the Finns and emphatically aired the view that one day the USSR would rule the world.

During these weeks, as if undergoing training, Mercader went off alone now and then to climb Ajusco and Citlaltepetl. In the course of the investigation which followed the crime, when the matter of the unusual murder weapon was raised, Mercader spoke of his mountain-climbing in Switzerland, and declared once:

"I discovered there that I had a rare ability to handle the

piolet, since two blows were sufficient for me to crack through an enormous block of ice."

The examining psychologists asked him to put down in writing something of his experiences as an alpinist. In a hand markedly different from his usual style, he penned a short story purporting to be an account of an accident in which he had been involved in the Alps:

"An Alpine accident is not the sort of thing precisely which inspires literary reflections in the style of Mann. I once had one which gives me authority to make the above statement. We left on the 5th of May at five in the afternoon for the *Aiguille du Midi* (one of the chief peaks of the Pennine Alps, near Mont Blanc, and considered dangerous climbing) against the advice of many people. The ascent was difficult and we counted on the full moon so that we would not have to stand the heat of the sun. About ten o'clock at night, when we were on the N.E. wall of the mountain, the accident occurred, terrible and unexpected. The footholds on this wall are such that the line of the rope took a direction of N.N.E. which gave us a very oblique line of ascent. The avalanche fell, therefore, on the last two men on the rope. They had to let go their grip and they fell, but the rope held so that they remained suspended over the abyss. The three of us now had to support the dead weight of these two men.

"No other solution was possible as we could not relax our grip and this was the beginning of an agonizing wait. We knew that the Alpine Club would resume its surveillance by telescope as soon as light permitted. We decided not to shout so as to save our strength because it is very probable that our cries would be lost in the night, thus all that remained for us to do was to keep our foothold and wait for help. The effort to do this was superhuman, but we had no alternative.

"About midnight we decided that in this situation we could not hold on more than another ten minutes and consequently it was necessary to consolidate the situation at no matter what price. The leading man on the rope descended to the next level and drew the rope to him; I descended to my companion who was in the third position and who was about to let everything go because the weight on the rope was cutting off his respiration. I put two *pitons* (mountaineer's cleats) into the wall of the mountain and we attached the rope to them, which relieved us of 80% of the dead weight. This was our salvation because now all we had to do was hold on until we got help.

"In any event, we had six or seven hours in which we had to hang on to the rock face. Literary reflections certainly did not press on my brain, for the needs of each second were so important that no other thought could coexist. What are these needs? They are really prosaic: The need to save one's strength; how to rest first this finger, then that one; how to change the position of one's foot on a foothold of not more than 3 or 4 square centimeters; how in such a constrained position to fight against ankylosis and cold, hunger, etc. I can assure you that, when one finds oneself in a situation like that, this is all that the mind thinks about except for an exact calculation of the seconds passed and to come."

In spite of the stilted beginning, with its superfluous reference to Thomas Mann as an apology for the impossibility of having "literary reflections" when one is fighting for one's life, the story itself is significant. Whether or not the event actually occurred is of secondary importance. The treatment is certainly revelatory of the pattern of conduct Mercader set for himself. The striking feature about it is the tremendous *esprit de corps* displayed by the author. The possibility of cutting the rope, letting the two men plunge to their deaths, but saving the other three, is never even mentioned. Yet it is an alternative that would have occurred to most men under the conditions of desperation and terror Mercader describes, if the choice were between a loss of five or two lives.

In this story Mercader places himself in a consciously heroic, yet quite impersonal, role. He is a hero as part of an heroic team. The subject of the story is a type of comradeship in which no individual stands out, but the collective entity functions with superb efficiency. Its purpose is self-preservation. The self that is to be preserved is the five-man group, tied together by the rope.

Did Mercader compose an allegory to fit the team selected by Stalin's apparat to carry out the perilous assignment, and is the rope the symbol of the link binding the conspiratorial band of assassins to Moscow—the rock of their security?

Surely, the behavior of Ramon during the many long years in prison, his determination not to break with his past, shows that he finds safety only in belonging to an iron order such as the disciplined world party of communism.

In January, Sylvia Ageloff arrived in Mexico, "anxious to see" Ramon. Although he had never before, in his relationship with Sylvia, betrayed any interest in Trotsky at all and virtually none in politics, he now adopted a slightly new course. "When I was in Mexico from January to March," Sylvia testified, "he showed a little more interest in politics as a concession to me, but nothing that would give a clue to his feelings."

Neither did she have the slightest inkling that Ramon's mother was in Mexico City. Caridad Mercader had arrived there with her lover, Leonid Eitingon, who now assumed the name of Leonov. He was Stalin's representative on the scene, in supreme command of Operation Trotsky.

One of the Catalonian communists, whom we shall call "Juan," and who had accompanied Caridad to Mexico on her first mission in 1936, ran into Ramon in a book shop. "Juan" had suspicions as to Ramon's underground affiliations during the preceding years. Ramon was at first taken aback by the encounter. True, "Juan" was a party member, but was known to hold some independent, unorthodox views. After the first meeting, Ramon arranged to get together again with "Juan."

At the next rendezvous, "Juan" was introduced to General Leonov, whom he had known in Spain as Kotov. Leonov invited him to join in the projected operation against "that arch-enemy of the Soviet power," Trotsky. "Juan" parried the efforts to enlist him. After a few more inconclusive meetings, Pedro Checa, as the Spanish party boss, took a hand in the matter. He called in "Juan" and sought to impress him into Leonov's service.

A dissenter at heart, "Juan" was now convinced more than ever of the criminal character of the Stalin regime. He managed not to get entangled in the operation and to avoid the vengeance of the apparat by keeping silent and by discreet conduct when questioned by the Mexican police after Trotsky's assassination.

While these negotiations were going on, Ramon invited Sylvia to accompany him to a public meeting under communist auspices. The featured speaker was James Ford, then the most prominent Negro communist in the United States, who was candidate for Vice President on the party ticket. Ironically enough, Ford's visit in Mexico had to do with a secret mission for Stalin in connection with the preparations for the assault on Trotsky. Sylvia went with the future assassin to hear one of Trotsky's avowed enemies in the midst of a vitriolic communist press campaign against him. It became obvious after the crime that Ramon had taken her to the meeting to show her off to his fellow-conspirators in the audience as a demonstration of the progress he was making on his assignment.

Sylvia brought Ramon together again with Alfred and Marguerite Rosmer, the French couple who had escorted Trotsky's orphaned grandson from Paris the previous summer and who were living with the Trotskys in their villa at Coyoacan. At Sylvia's invitation, the Rosmers joined her and "Jacson" at dinner parties on several occasions, and took long drives with them in Ramon's car. Sylvia had told the Rosmers that her "husband,"

Jacques Mornard, was in Mexico on a false Canadian passport under the name of "Jacson," as he was a fugitive from military service.

At different times Sylvia asked Ramon where his office was. He gave her the address as Room 820 of the Ermita Building. Sylvia's sister one day went to look for Ramon in his office, and found that there was no such room. He offered the explanation that he had mistakenly given the wrong room number, 820 instead of 620.

"Sylvia became suspicious about the nature of his work," wrote Trotsky's attorney, Albert Goldman, after the crime, "and asked Marguerite Rosmer to find out whether Jacson really had an office in Room 620. Marguerite Rosmer went to the building and actually found an office boy in this room who told her it was Jacson's office. Neither Sylvia Ageloff nor Marguerite Rosmer then had any suspicion that he was a GPU agent. They thought that he was involved in work which was not strictly legal and that he consequently refused to divulge its nature."

Sylvia told Trotsky, in the course of a visit, that her "husband" was in Mexico on a false passport and stated that she would not want to bring him along for fear of compromising Trotsky. Before leaving for New York in March, she extracted from Ramon a promise that he would not visit the Trotsky villa during her absence.

It was only some months after her departure that it was discovered that the room given by Ramon Mercader as his business address was the office of David Alfaro Siqueiros, who was shortly to be exposed as a leading man in the murderous conspiracy.

Ramon's role at this pass, Caridad Mercader had assured a close friend, was to be that of a spy only. His task was to find out the nature of the security system, the guard roster, the arrangement of phone lines, power cables, alarms and special, automatic devices which were protecting Trotsky's residence. Relying on his extraordinary visual memory, he would be able to get and retain a photographic picture of house, patio, walls and guard towers, to establish where each member of the household slept, where the police were stationed and what routes they patrolled.

To accomplish all this, it was necessary for Ramon to gain entry into the grounds of Trotsky's fortified villa and to become a trusted political sympathizer ever ready with a helping hand inside the establishment.

A sudden switch by the Kremlin in the leadership of the Mexican Communist Party was the first signal—to the initiated—of the coming attack on Trotsky. Under the generalship of Contreras, a purge commission was set up by the Comintern early in 1940 to investigate the affairs of its affiliate in Mexico. One of the leading members of the commission was James Ford. Another commanding figure was the Kremlin wire-puller in South America, Vittorio Codovila.

What transpired in Mexico was in the nature of a little palace revolution engineered from Moscow, very much like the one which toppled Browder from his leadership in the United States after World War II. The Mexican Browder had been Hernan Laborde, a poet with an anarchist background and generally recognized as a man of decent traits. In physical appearance Laborde resembled Charlie Chan as portrayed by the late Warner Oland. He affected the behavior of a revolutionary buccaneer by attending meetings of the Political Bureau armed with a pair of pistols. However, he was quick to resent Russian domination and was wont to treat the Comintern "rep"—representative—assigned to the Mexican party with brusque discourtesy.

Laborde, his aide Campa and their associates had become completely indoctrinated with the popular front ideology and strongly espoused Communist Party support of the Cardenas regime. They favored the policy of going to every length to avoid a break with the leftist Mexican revolutionary government which, incidentally, had given Trotsky asylum in Mexico.

The liquidation of Trotsky therefore called, in the view of the Kremlin, for a purge of the Laborde leadership. The purge commission excoriated that leadership for a variety of imaginary sins, but the main charge against Laborde was his "conciliatory attitude towards Trotsky." When the indictment was published in the Communist press on January 28, the insiders knew, as Trotsky himself was to put it subsequently, that "some new serious blow was in preparation, if not against 'Trotskyism,' then against Trotsky."

"What happened most probably," wrote Trotsky before his death in a lengthy analysis of Stalin's murder campaign against him, "is that the GPU encountered some opposition among the leaders of the Communist party who had become accustomed to a peaceful existence and might have feared very unpleasant political and police consequences from the assassination attempt. This is the source of the charge of 'Trotskyism' against them. Whoever objects to an attempt on Trotsky's life is, obviously, a—'Trotskyist.' "

In March, 1940, two months before the attack, a secret session of the Communist Party Convention considered the question of "The Struggle Against Trotskyism and Other Enemies of the People." The top leaders of the Party, who had held office for many years, were ousted, and new henchmen were brought in who had no scruples against the extermination of Trotsky. One of the very revealing actions of the Convention, as Trotsky pointed out in his penetrating analysis, was to appoint an "honorary presidium" of a group of international communist notables and to include among them Carlos Contreras, whose record as a master of the art of assassination was well known among Spanish civil war veterans. Trotsky deduced that the inclusion of this bloodhound as a sort of patron saint of the Mexican Communist Party was part of the "moral preparation" of Stalin's executioners for the task of murdering him.

Upon Sylvia's departure for New York, Ramon's task of gathering the needed intelligence about Trotsky's establishment was facilitated by a turn of fate. Alfred Rosmer fell ill. This gave the handy Ramon a splendid opportunity to make numerous short visits to the Trotsky house to bring Rosmer various things he needed, to drive him to the hospital and, later, to transport Rosmer to and from the hospital. Mercader was careful to write Sylvia in New York that because of his friendship with the Rosmers and because of Alfred's illness, he had been unable to keep his promise to stay away from Coyoacan.

These frequent short visits enabled him to learn what he had to know about the premises. On these occasions, he took numerous snapshots, probably with a concealed miniature camera, of the household and all its occupants. Copies, or perhaps the originals, were sent to Moscow and were placed in the special Trotsky dossier in the KI Registry of the NKVD which occupied three floors. There they were seen in 1948 by the Soviet intelligence officer, Vladimir Petrov, whose defection with his wife Evdokia from the Soviet espionage service in Australia in April, 1954, created a worldwide sensation. The Australian Royal Commission on Espionage, after questioning Petrov for 37 days and his wife for 21 days, vouched for their credibility as "highly intelligent witnesses of truth." Petrov describes what he found in the secret files:

"There were also copies of instructions sent out from NKVD headquarters in Moscow to the NKVD Residents in all the countries where Trotsky had lived at various times, including instructions to the NKVD Resident in the Soviet Consulate-General in New York, who directed the assassination operation on the American continent. There was complete photographic documentation of Trotsky's life, from the first days in the Soviet Union, before his banishment in 1928, right up to his last days in Mexico, after he had grown the pointed beard which features in his later pictures. There were numerous photographs taken inside the fortified villa, perhaps by Mornard himself, showing the guards, fences and courtyards, photos of Trotsky with his wife, Trotsky having tea with his friends, Trotsky's dog."

While Ramon was hovering on the edges of the Trotsky household, trying to befriend a couple of volunteer guards doing duty behind the heavy gates to the villa, the barrage of anti-Trotsky propaganda in the left-wing press began to reach a portentous fury. Since the original plan to incite a "mass" movement for the expulsion of Trotsky from Mexico had failed, as Trotsky himself wrote in his pre-assassination analysis, "the GPU had to resort to a terrorist act. But it was indispensable to prepare public opinion for this deed."

The communist and pro-communist papers opened a campaign which accused Trotsky of collaborating with the Dies Committee for "thirty pieces of silver"; of intervention in Latin American affairs "on the side of the imperialist powers"; of violating the pledge to Cardenas and making Mexico "a center for . . . espionage"; of collaborating with Franco in Spain and with the camp of the reactionary General Almazan in Mexico; of being an agent of the imperialistic oil companies. The campaign reached a crescendo after the May Day parade in which the Mexican communists managed to stage a march of 20,000 uniformed men and women under slogans such as these: "Throw out the most ominous and dangerous traitor Trotsky."

Long before the world became accustomed to this totalitarian technique, Trotsky analyzed the barrage against him as follows:

"This is the way people write who are preparing to change the pen for the machine-gun."

The Bartholomean night for Operation Trotsky was set for the pre-dawn of May 24.

On the day of May 23, 1940, the chauffeur of David Alfaro Siqueiros drove the two Arenal brothers around Mexico City. The car stopped at various places to pick up sub-machine guns and bundles of Mexican army and police uniforms. Some of these uniforms had been dishonestly acquired from Mexican uniformed personnel; others had been made for the occasion of the very best material by excellent tailors. In addition to the arms and uniforms, the chauffeur took an extension ladder, a rope ladder with gaffs and hooks, a rotary power saw, two explosive bombs and several hand-made incendiaries packed in thermos flasks.

The operation that was being prepared was on a lavish scale and no expense had been spared to see that the large attacking force was well equipped and heavily armed. Weeks later, Siqueiros would claim that he had financed these preparations personally by the sale of his paintings. Others would say that the funds had been furnished by the NKVD.

To be sure, Siqueiros was a successful painter. Some of his canvases are emotionally warm, tender and outgoing, at the same time strong in conception and brilliantly colored. He also did revolutionary paintings where the preoccupation is with torment and destruction or with the impassive face of the Indian, depicted as a man behind a traditional mask. It has been said that if a psychiatrist were given the works of Mexico's six greatest contemporary painters and asked to find the one who was a murderer, he would not choose Siqueiros.

That night Siqueiros put on the uniform of a major in the Mexican army, a false mustache and dark spectacles. He and the shadowy chief of the operation, the so-called "French Jew" named Felipe, drove around the city rounding up participants in the conspiracy who had been used for reconnoitering or guard duty, but who were not to be employed in the forthcoming actual attack. These people were told to get away and stay out of sight for a time. As for the "French Jew," who was so described to the police authorities later by a youthful Mexican member of the gang and who has been the subject of massive guesswork by all investigators of the Trotsky assassination, there can be little doubt that he was none other than Leonid Eitingon. Introduced to the Mexican communist elite as "General Leonov," he apparently used the sobriquet Felipe in his contacts with the large motley band gathered by Siqueiros. It is known that Felipe spoke French with a Russian accent.

Among the minor characters in the plot who were ordered by Siqueiros to get "lost" and who would all be picked up by the police in fairly short order were two Communist girl spies, Julia Barrados de Serrano and Anita Lopez. These women had been hired by the Mexican communist painter, Antonio Pujol, and set up in an apartment near the Trotsky villa. Their assignment was to seduce the Mexican police on duty around Trotsky's quarters placed there by order of President Cardenas, and to keep the conspirators supplied with current information about the guard detail.

In the evening of May 23, the girls announced to their buddies pacing the street that they were leaving the apartment and were giving a farewell party for the entire police detachment. By this stratagem Siqueiros had made sure that only a few of the policemen would have to be disarmed, as the others would abandon their posts to enjoy themselves with the girls.

One of these, Julia Barrados, was the wife of David Serrano, who had fought in Spain in the Republican forces. He had deserted Julia there and bigamously married a Spanish girl. This couple had a little daughter on whom they had inflicted the name Sovietita. David Serrano himself, a member of the Political Bureau of the Mexican Communist Party, who had been trained in Moscow and Spain in NKVD work for the preceding six years, became upon his return home the liaison between the

Party and the Soviet apparatus. In Operation Trotsky he was one of Siqueiros' top aides.

About two hours after midnight, four cars employed in the operation were sent to six prearranged assembly points where they picked up an attacking force of about twenty men and then proceeded at 50-yard intervals to Coyoacan, toward Trotsky's fortified villa which was surrounded by a high wall behind which Trotsky had his own guard of young followers. One of these was usually assigned to stand watch in the tower erected at the corner of the villa facing the street.

The members of the attacking force parked their cars one block away and converged upon the Trotsky residence on foot. Wearing police and army uniforms, the assailants, led by Siqueiros, surprised the policemen on the beat and quickly trussed them up at gun point. Some of the police detail were spending the night, after the farewell party, at the flat of Anita and Julia, the girl spies.

Siqueiros' men then cut the telephone lines running into the house and the secret electric line leading to the alarm bell at police headquarters in Coyoacan. They knew that the man standing guard at the time of the attack would be Robert Sheldon Harte, the 23-year-old American follower of Trotsky, the son of a wealthy New York businessman. The young Harte had come down to Mexico to serve as a volunteer guard only a few weeks previously. The attack was timed for the night when Harte would be on duty behind the bolted door of the entrance.

That night Trotsky worked late on his book, and his literary secretary, Fanny Yanovich, who lived some distance away in Mexico City, was not ready to leave until eleven o'clock. Harte offered to drive her home, and on the way pestered her with questions about the contents of Trotsky's forthcoming book on Stalin. Clearly, it was a matter very much on Harte's mind. It later appeared that Ramon had gone out of the way to make friends with Harte, an easygoing, gullible youth. They went on drinking parties together. Ramon knew and had many calls from women, and there was strong suspicion that they shared philandering adventures. Harte came to trust the future assassin completely. After taking Mrs. Yanovich home, Harte returned to Coyoacan to resume his guard duty inside the entrance. It was a little over four hours before the fateful moment set for the assault.

The security precautions at the villa had been carefully designed to prevent the guard from being surprised and overcome by a hostile force. The guard was supposed to draw the first bolt, opening the main door a few inches and flooding the face of the person seeking admittance with a strong light. If he then recognized and approved the visitor, he could either press the electric button to open the main door fully or could signal the guard at the tower to do so. This tower guard, who was armed with a submachinegun, was not at his post that night.

A small group of the raiders in uniform went to the entrance and pulled the bell cord. Sheldon Harte came to the door and opened it without apparent hesitation. The entire attacking force then swarmed inside and broke up into detachments. A raider with a submachinegun rushed to a big tree in the patio and took up a position behind it, firing a hail of bullets at the exit of the guards' quarters, a detached building in the rear. The five men were asleep in one room, which had but one door, where they were now immobilized. Trotsky, who had led the Red Army to victory, apparently had little experience in this kind of fighting.

One of the attackers, speaking English with an American accent, kept shouting in the direction of the guards: "Keep inside there and you won't be hurt!" Two of the guards, Charles Cornell and Otto Schuessler, had made efforts to find Trotsky or else return the fire of the raiders, but had been dissuaded by Harold Robins, captain of the guard, who warned them to keep their heads down and stay out of danger. One of them, however, had fired at an assailant, but failed to hit him. The primary function of the five guards was to defend the life of Trotsky.

The main group of raiders proceeded directly toward the two bedrooms of the house, where they knew the Trotskys and their grandson slept. With their Thompson submachineguns, they opened a murderous fire into these two rooms, shooting both through the windows and the closed bedroom doors. Trotsky and Natalia at once threw themselves on the floor and sought shelter under a bed. The fire into the room continued for several minutes. The raiders did not attempt to enter the Trotskys' bedroom, evidence that they knew that there was a device on the door which, once it was set, fired automatically on anyone who tried to cross the threshold. The bursts of submachinegun fire through the windows were partially deflected by the steel shutters. However, when the police examined the Trotsky bedroom, they found that 73 bullets had been fired into it.

As the assailants were about to leave, one of them placed an incendiary bomb at the door between the Trotskys' bedroom and that of their grandson. The door and the adjacent floor boards started to burn. It was designed to destroy the house and with it Trotsky's archives and the manuscript of his biography of Stalin. Another incendiary, hurled through a window, landed in the garden and burned a patch of grass. Just as the raiders were about to leave, one of them appeared on the threshold leading to the grandson's room to administer the *coup de grâce*. He squeezed off bursts of automatic fire into the beds, turned on his heel and hurried out. The raiders left believing that they had accomplished their mission, sure that the Trotskys could not possibly have lived through their crossfire.

And if the incendiaries failed to demolish the Trotsky house with its files of documents incriminating to Stalin, the raiders took the extra precaution of leaving behind them a powerful bomb. "Investigating magistrates later found on the premises a bomb containing one and a half kilos (more than three pounds) of dynamite," wrote Natalia Trotsky afterwards. "According to the records, there was some sort of technical defect in the bomb . . . but the investigation brought out the fact that it had sufficient power to blast the entire house to its foundation."

As the attackers were withdrawing, they picked up Sheldon Harte who did not put up any visible resistance. One of the trussed-up policemen, Ramirez Diaz, testified that Harte had his arms pinned by two of the assailants when he was marched into one of their cars. Harte's enigmatic conduct at the crucial juncture of the Siqueiros operation remained a subject of controversy even after his body was found in a shallow grave on the outskirts of Mexico City some weeks later.

The raiders took two of the cars belonging to the Trotsky household with them, using ignition keys which were left in the vehicles. These cars were abandoned not far from the scene of the attack. When the police found them, they discovered such items as a rope ladder, grappling iron, electric saw, an iron bar (of the sort known in Mexican underworld argot as a "holy child"), clothing, belts, .45 caliber cartridges, submachinegun clips, an axe and two Mausers.

The Trotskys and their ten-year-old grandson survived the terrific fusillade, an escape bordering on the miraculous. How this happened was graphically described by both of them.

"The attack came at dawn, about 4 A.M.," wrote Trotsky two weeks after the night of the assault. "I was fast asleep, having taken a sleeping drug after a hard day's work. Awakened by the rattle of gunfire but feeling very hazy, I first imagined that a national holiday was being celebrated with fireworks outside our walls. But the explosions were too close, right here within the room, next to me and overhead. The odor of gunpowder became more acrid, more penetrating. Clearly, what we had always expected was now happening: we were under attack. Where were the police stationed outside the walls? Where the guards inside?

Trussed up? Kidnapped? Killed? My wife had already jumped from her bed. The shooting continued incessantly. My wife later told me that she helped me to the floor, pushing me into the space between the bed and the wall. This was quite true. She had remained hovering over me, beside the wall, as if to shield me with her body. But by means of whispers and gestures I convinced her to lie flat on the floor. The shots came from all sides, it was difficult to tell just from where. . . . Splinters of glass from windowpanes and chips from walls flew in all directions. A little later I felt that my right leg had been slightly wounded in two places.

"As the shooting died down we heard our grandson in the neighboring room cry out: 'Grandfather!' The voice of the child in the darkness under the gunfire remains the most tragic recollection of that night. The boy—after the first shot had cut his bed diagonally as evidenced by marks left on the door and wall—threw himself under the bed. One of the assailants, apparently in a panic, fired into the bed, the bullet passed through the mattress, struck our grandson in the big toe and imbedded itself in the floor. The assailants threw two incendiary bombs and left our grandson's bedroom. . . .

"At the outcry of our grandson, my wife made her way into his already empty room. Inside, the floor, the door and a small cabinet were burning. 'They have kidnapped Seva,' I said to her. This was the most painful moment of all. Shots continued to ring out but already away from our bedroom, somewhere in the patio or immediately outside the walls. The terrorists were apparently covering their retreat. My wife hastened to smother the incendiary flames with a rug. For a week afterward she had to treat her burns."

Mrs. Trotsky jotted down her impressions of that unforgettable night in the tribute to her dead son Sedov and to her husband, Lev Davidovich, penned a year after his assassination.

"They are shooting," she wrote. "Lev Davidovich is now also

awake. I whisper in his ear: 'They are shooting here, in our room.' And pressing close to him, I push him very, very gently, and drop down together with him from the low bed onto the floor. . . .

"We are lying on the floor, beside the wall in a corner and away from the crossfire which proceeded without interruption for several minutes. . . .

"On the threshold which separated our bedroom from that of our grandson, illuminated by the flare of an incendiary bomb, a silhouette flashed: the curve of a helmet, shining buttons, an elongated face flashed by me as in a dream, and then I lost sight of the intruder. The shooting in the room stopped. We heard the sound of gunfire at a distance in the patio. . . .

"As I recounted the events of the GPU's night assault to friends who visited us during that day, I felt that I was relating this *almost* with joy. But those who listened heard me with alarm, they cast frightened glances towards the heads of the two beds, where the wall was dotted with bullet holes, and I would say to myself as if in justification: 'But after all the enemies did suffer failure.'

"The following days strengthened more and more in us the conviction that the failure suffered by our enemies on this occasion must be remedied by them; that the inspirer of this crime would not be deterred. And our joyous feeling of *salvation* was dampened by the prospect of a new visitation and the need to prepare for it."

5

"In the Next Attack, Other Methods"

While the fiasco of the May 24th attempt on Trotsky's life caused consternation in the headquarters of Stalin's murder apparat in Moscow, the chief of the Mexican secret police, Colonel Salazar, who took charge of the investigation, decided that the whole affair was a put-up job: Trotsky must have staged it all himself as a publicity show to win sympathy for his cause.

Indeed, how else was one to account, not being a believer in miracles, for the hundreds of bullet holes everywhere, which turned a door to the Trotsky bedroom into a sieve, without the loss of a single life or anyone suffering serious wounds? And there were all those other suspicious aspects, pointing to an inside job. It was obvious that the assailants must have had intimate and detailed knowledge of the physical arrangements in Trotsky's house and the security measures taken for his protection. Clearly, they had known how to cut the telephone lines and the secret power line to the alarm bell. They knew where the guards slept and where to station men with automatic weapons to immobilize them. They knew exactly where the Trotskys slept and all about the protective device which made it impossible for them to send a man into the bedroom to find them and finish them off. Finally, they were familiar with the guard roster and knew when Sheldon Harte would be on duty at the main gate.

One of the first moves of the Mexican secret service was to take into custody Trotsky's servants and two of his guards for questioning. The police now elaborated a theory of self-assault which some of the pro-communist newspapers seized upon as the best means of keeping the authorities off the tracks of the real culprits. There was an indignant outcry from the veteran revolutionary, in the form of a letter to President Cardenas, who rebuked Salazar and ordered him to release the guards with apologies to Trotsky.

The police immediately concentrated their suspicions on Sheldon Harte as an accomplice in the attack. The fact that he admitted the raiders and departed with them without a struggle seemed damning. To which Trotsky countered: "If Sheldon Harte were an agent of the GPU, he could have killed me at night and gotten away without setting in motion 20 people all of whom were subjected to a great risk."

During the period of preparation and execution of the attack of May 24, Ramon Mercader lived under the name of "Jacson" in a tourist camp owned and managed by an unusually inquisitive American named Shirley. According to statements which Shirley made to the police months later, after the Trotsky assassination, Ramon received numerous visits and telephone calls from women (Sylvia had returned to New York in March). Shirley believed that one of these women spoke with a Russian accent. The observant proprietor noticed that whenever his guest used the telephone in the office, he sat with his back to the wall watching the entrance door, trying to protect himself against eavesdropping.

Ramon took his car into the country every weekend, and would bring it back coated with dust and mud, but the inquisitive Mr. Shirley was unable to speculate where his guest had been because the latter always turned the mileage indicator back to the same reading, or else disconnected it.

Much closer to the point was Shirley's observation that Ramon had kept a trunk and two suitcases carefully locked in the office of the tourist camp. These were very heavy and Ramon had said they contained engineering instruments. In the evening of the attack, on May 23, he loaded the trunk and suitcases in his car and drove off. The police concluded that he had taken part in the plot, had secret conferences with the leading figures both at the tourist camp and in his office, that he had stored the firearms and other equipment for the attacking band, and that his car had been used in the operation.

Ramon knew and had become friendly with Sheldon Harte. This would explain, according to the Trotsky entourage, why Harte opened the door that night, since he believed he was admitting only a familiar and trusted visitor.

All this information was developed only after the assassination of Trotsky. At this time, in the days following the grand fiasco of May 24, there was not even the slightest suspicion of the share of Ramon in the conspiracy, just as the leading part played by Siqueiros in the great armed attack was still shrouded in deep secrecy.

Trotsky completely ignored the possibility of a serpent crawling in his own political bosom and failed to inquire into the irregularities in the conduct of that strange and self-effacing "Jacson"—Sylvia's "husband" and the Rosmers' hanger-on. Yet an inquiry into those weighty suspicious aspects of the crime which had led Salazar to the wrong conclusion of an inside job would have put Trotsky on the trail of the assassin as he was worming his way into his household. Such research was contrary to the nature and philosophy of Trotsky to whom history was a play of forces and not of human beings.

He did undertake at once a thorough investigation of the behavior of the communist leadership in Mexico and of the maneuvers of the NKVD underground network there, and came up with the discovery of Siqueiros' direction of the commando raid. Within the week of that abortive assault Trotsky was to point an accusing finger at Siqueiros in the public prints, suggesting his interrogation by the police. But Siqueiros and some of his top aides were nowhere to be found, as they had left Mexico City in the morning of May 24 for destinations unknown.

Exactly four days later, in the morning of May 28, Trotsky for the first time made the acquaintance of his future assassin. Only a man of iron nerve could have undertaken to carry out the assignment of that day so soon after his participation in the assault which failed. The occasion was the scheduled departure of Alfred and Marguerite Rosmer from Veracruz for the United States. The Rosmers had survived unscathed the storming of the Trotsky villa where they had been house guests for several months.

Having learned from the Rosmers of their plan to sail from Veracruz, Ramon volunteered to drive them to the Mexican port in his Buick, a distance of about 300 miles over winding mountain roads. He explained his readiness to go to all this trouble on the ground that his business took him to Veracruz twice a month anyhow. Since Natalia Trotsky had never seen that part of Mexico, she was eager to make the trip, partly as a relaxation from the inordinate tension of the preceding days. Ramon was only too glad to accommodate.

The roster of visitors which Trotsky's guards now kept meticulously shows that Ramon entered the grounds at 7:58 A.M. to take the Rosmer party, which included Riva Hansen, the wife of Trotsky's chief secretary, on the trip. The scene was described by Joseph Hansen, her husband, an observer on the spot, as follows:

"Trotsky was in the patio, and met 'Jacson' for the first time. They shook hands. Trotsky continued with his chores about the chicken yard. 'Jacson' retired and began speaking to Seva, Trotsky's grandson, to whom he gave a toy glider. Both Natalia and Trotsky noticed him in Seva's room and asked Seva what it meant. 'Jacson' then explained the working of the glider to them.

"Trotsky with his customary thoughtfulness for others asked Natalia if 'Jacson' should not be invited in. Natalia responded that he must have already had his breakfast. At the table, however, as a matter of courtesy, he was invited to come in and have a seat. He took a cup of coffee. This was the first time 'Jacson' sat down at a table with Trotsky."

The journey to Veracruz gave Ramon opportunities to exercise his charm on Natalia Trotsky, who thought him shy and likable. Upon reaching the outskirts of Veracruz, Ramon did not seem to know his way about the city and stopped to make inquiries. In the back of her mind Natalia thought this odd in a man who claimed to have made frequent trips to the place. But she dismissed the thought, and it did not recur to her until it was too late. She recollected it when searching her mind after the assassination.

On the return trip with the two women, Ramon had occasion to cultivate further the relationship with Mrs. Trotsky. They arrived at Coyoacan on May 30 and entered the villa at 3:42 P.M. The register showed that he stayed exactly thirty minutes, but there was no evidence that he had at that time seen Trotsky since it was his usual siesta hour.

After the May 24th fiasco, the Mexican Communist Party washed its hands of the whole affair, and for a while even put on a show of disowning Siqueiros and Carlos Contreras. A fairly drastic purge was carried out behind the scenes in Mexico, apparently on Moscow's orders to keep the party out of the assassination project. One of the victims of this purge was Pedro Checa, who paid dearly for his independence. Checa was moved to a house in Cuernavaca, where he was guarded by agents of one of the Soviet apparats in Mexico. He was supposedly suffering from tuberculosis. His close friends—and even his wife—were not allowed to see him. He died several months later. This death occasioned so much disturbance and suspicion among the communist veterans of the Spanish civil war in Mexico that a special meeting of the cadres was held to explain the situation. At this meeting the doctor who had attended Checa—an eminent physician closely associated with Soviet circles—stated that everything possible had been done to save the patient's life, but these explanations merely intensified suspicions of foul play in the case of Checa's death.

The Mexican secret service under Colonel Salazar cracked the case of the May 24 assault wide open on June 17, with the arrests and identification of some two dozen persons. Among those rounded up were the four chauffeurs who had brought the attacking force to Coyoacan. These men had been hired through a communist chauffeurs' union and had been picked for political reliability, but they talked. The information obtained from them put the police on the track of Siqueiros. His personal chauffeur revealed that he had been given by his master a new LaSalle with Texas plates and a driver's license bearing a false name. He testified that he drove Siqueiros regularly to the house of the two communist girl spies.

The police found their vacated apartment near the Trotsky villa, and discovered that one of them, Julia Barrados, had left behind a notebook. In it she had written that Trotsky was not to be killed, but because he stood in the way of the triumph of communism, his archives had to be stolen. This explanation was apparently fabricated for the consumption of the minor cogs and accomplices in the conspiracy, rank-and-file party members.

Among the important prisoners was David Serrano, the bigamous husband of Julia, who represented the NKVD on the Political Bureau of the Mexican Communist Party. He proclaimed his innocence, and established an alibi by producing three communist girls who swore they had been with him all night. Serrano attempted to place the responsibility for the raid on his erstwhile comrades, accused of Trotskyism, Laborde and Campa, who had been expelled from the party.

But the investigation exposed the hard-core element in the attack to be Spanish refugees and Mexicans who had fought in Spain as loyal Stalinists. Another element that Siqueiros had drawn in consisted of communist miners from the Jalisco mountains personally devoted to him. The arms used were Thompson submachineguns made in the United States. Since the arms trade is a government monopoly in Mexico, it was concluded that the weapons must have been smuggled over the border.

The fugitive Siqueiros was nowhere to be found. But the reverberations of the case compromised the Mexican and Spanish communists before world public opinion. Artists and intellectuals of great reputation who had passed as "liberal" fellow-travellers, had been caught red-handed in a gangster operation, damaging the Soviet prestige. And Leon Trotsky had won global attention in radical circles as an exiled revolutionary standing against a powerful regime of terror. The Mexican Communist Party now protested its innocence, and tried to dissociate itself from Siqueiros who was described as an "uncontrolled element who was considered half-mad."

Four days before the armed attack, it was learned, Siqueiros and his younger brother, Jesus, went to a small house that had been rented for the operation several weeks previously. This house was in Santa Rosa, near the San Angel Inn. The wife of

Siqueiros, Angelica Arenal, a sister of the Arenal brothers who were members of the conspiracy, had bought a cot and other furniture found in this house of adobe construction, which contained three rooms. In the basement, there were two storerooms and a small kitchen. Information furnished by the prisoners led Salazar's men to the hideout.

The house looked completely abandoned when the police descended upon it during the night of June 25. Inside there was a painting easel, some cans of paint, clothing and canned food. The floor, the detectives observed, had been covered with powdered lime. In the basement kitchen the floor which was of earth showed signs of recent digging. The men got some spades and a neighboring peasant to do a little probing, and were soon overwhelmed by the stench of putrefying flesh.

With the aid of gas masks and searchlights from fire engines, the diggers exhumed a body. It was that of Sheldon Harte. It had been covered with quicklime and had turned a bronze color. The position of the body was that of a man who had been killed quietly in his sleep. There were two bullet wounds: one in the temple, the other, in the base of his skull, behind the ear, the favorite method of killing by Soviet executioners. The hypothesis that Trotsky's guard had been killed while sleeping was seemingly verified when the police found the remains of the blood-stained canvas of a folding cot and a bloody quilt. The assassins had not succeeded in completely burning these items.

Before the night was over, Colonel Salazar had awakened Trotsky who identified the gruesome discovery as the corpse of Harte. Although Trotsky vigorously asserted the innocence of the dead youth, the mystery of his behavior during the night of the attack continued to agitate all the students of the crime. One of the hirelings of Siqueiros, Nestor Sanchez Hernandez, insisted that when he had asked Siqueiros about the guard on duty, he was told that there was no danger of his betraying the assailants, indicating that Harte had been bought.

Mariano Hernandez Vasquez, the unemployed lover of Ana, one of the girl spies, also testified. He had been employed to help the girls in their surveillance of the Trotsky establishment. In the evening of May 24, following the pre-dawn attack of that day, Hernandez was taken to the little house at Santa Rosa by Luis Arenal, the brother-in-law of Siqueiros, and presented to Sheldon Harte there. Was he supposed to guard the American? he asked. No, to take care of him, he was told. To be sure, the tall and strapping Harte would have required more than one guard if he had been a prisoner. Arenal made arrangements for a cleaning woman to come daily to the house, but ordered that she was not to see the American. He was to go out at that time for a walk.

Five days later, according to Vasquez' testimony to which he stuck after a third-degree grilling by the police, the Arenal brothers arrived in the evening, and engaged Harte in an amicable conversation in English. They paid off and dismissed Vasquez. The police reconstruction of the crime concluded that Harte had been killed in his sleep that night, and that the job was the handiwork of Luis and Leopoldo Arenal.

Why was Sheldon Harte murdered? It would seem logical that had he been a loyal Trotskyist he would have been shot on the spot the night of the raid without the trouble of keeping him in hiding with the benefit of witnesses. Did his "hosts" change their plans for him when they learned that Trotsky was alive and that Ramon Mercader, whom Harte knew, would now have to take over the unfinished assassination task? Such a solution to the Sheldon Harte riddle seems plausible when one considers that he was an idealistic young man who accepted the role of Trotsky guard as a romantic assignment. Not too careful about his associations, inexperienced in the ways of conspirators, he may have made friends among the Stalinists who indoctrinated him with terrible doubts about Trotsky's devotion to the cause of the revolution. Perhaps, like others, he then took part in the May 24 assault and treacherously opened the door for the raiders on the assurance that nobody would be killed, that their sole mission was to seize Trotsky's archives so as to prove to the world that he was plotting against socialism and Russia.

Trotsky had tried to teach Harte a lesson shortly after he took up guard duty. "Our place was being rebuilt," Mrs. Trotsky recalled the incident, "and it was necessary to open the gates every 15–20 minutes in order to let a worker with a wheelbarrow out into the street and then let him in back again. Bob (Harte) was so carried away by building a bird cage that in order not to tear himself away from his work he handed the gate-key to the worker. This did not escape the notice of Lev Davidovich. The latter explained to Bob that this was very careless on his part and added, 'You might prove to be the first victim of your own carelessness.' "

The Arenal brothers fled to New York where one of them, the painter Luis, was encountered by Anita Brenner, the author of several books on Mexico. Luis had also been a contributor to the communist magazine *New Masses*. His younger brother, Leopoldo, had directed communist organizational activities among the workers of the nationalized oil industry. Both men were endowed with charm and broad culture. Despite his Communist Party responsibilities, Leopoldo was a *bon vivant* and something of a Don Juan. In addition to the sister who was married to Siqueiros, there was another sister who had nothing to do with communism. The mother of the Arenals was a lady of Spanish descent of the upper classes. Their ancestral house at Calle Paris 7, in Mexico City, was filled with foreign communists, generally American, who were either artists or in Mexico on party business, and who lived there as paying guests.

The repercussions in New York of the Arenals' part in the Sheldon Harte affair were immediate. Elizabeth Bentley, the secret communist courier, was using the address of Rose Arenal, the estranged wife of Luis, as a letter drop for the espionage ring she was serving. Miss Bentley, of course, did not know that she was handling communications dealing with assassination plans. On the day the newspapers carried a despatch from Mexico City reporting the discovery of the slain Harte and that the police were looking for Luis and Leopoldo Arenal, she made a routine telephone call to Rose Arenal. The latter was in a state of near hysteria, said that something terrible had happened, and wanted Miss Bentley to come to see her that night.

Picking up an evening newspaper, Elizabeth Bentley came across an item in it from Mexico City on the Sheldon Harte case in which the murderers were named as Leopoldo and Luis Arenal. She immediately phoned her superior, Jacob Golos. An hour later they met on a park bench in Sheridan Square. She gave him the paper, pointing out the item from Mexico. He read it thoughtfully and made an instant decision, according to Elizabeth Bentley's account.

"Break off all connections with Rose immediately," he snapped, "and stay away from that neighborhood. This thing's too hot."

"But she's expecting me tonight," Miss Bentley protested, "and she's in trouble."

"We can't take a chance," he said. "She's probably under suspicion already, being Luis' wife. Maybe he's even hiding out there. I just hope she doesn't go to pieces and talk too much."

Moscow decided to organize forthwith a new attempt on the life of Trotsky which should leave him no loophole for escape. The NKVD was determined not to permit another departure from its standard rules of assassination. Siqueiros had drawn too many persons into the conspiracy for effective secrecy, and made no secure provisions for the flight and concealment of the terrorists. In the Kremlin they had good grounds to fear that the authorities would find it easy to unravel the threads of the last plot, with resultant injury to its prestige and worldwide organization.

The new attempt would be carried out by one individual. And it fell to Ramon to be the star of the next great performance. He would have to do more to gain the confidence of Trotsky's guards and secretaries. He would have to ingratiate himself further with Mrs. Trotsky, who cut a lonely figure in the establishment, through such attentions as gifts of flowers and candy. In brief, he would have to achieve the status of one of the Trotsky entourage.

Caridad, through the good offices of Eitingon, obtained assurances from Moscow providing for her son maximum safeguards and a chance to escape alive before the murder was discovered. Moscow also guaranteed that transportation facilities, comprising a getaway car with a chauffeur and a private plane waiting at the Mexico City airport, would be made available. Ramon was also to be supplied with a false passport adequately documented by the Mexican authorities—a procedure arranged by the liaison between the Soviet secret police apparatus in Mexico and the communists in the Mexican Foreign Office.

Soon after the secret departure of the Arenal brothers for the United States, Ramon Mercader left for New York by air. He appeared at the American consulate with his doctored Canadian passport bearing the name of "Jacson" and applied for a transit visa to Montreal, which would enable him to make a stopover in New York. In spite of the unprecedented spelling of his name, he obtained the visa without difficulty. Needless to add, he never had any intention of going to Canada with the forged passport.

On June 12, he came to bid good-by to Trotsky, and to tell him that he was flying to New York that day to see his boss because business was bad. He was leaving his Buick for the use of the guards, which was in keeping with his practice of rendering small services to the Trotskys and their friends. Occasionally he would take visitors in his car sight-seeing. On this day he drove Jake Cooper, one of the guards, to the airport where the car was turned over to him.

While waiting for the plane, Cooper and Ramon had lunch together. Cooper raised the question of Ramon's relationship to the Fourth International, and the latter dropped some names of Trotskyite leaders abroad with intimations of his friendship with them and his connection with the movement.

What brought Ramon to New York? According to hints dropped by his mother to a Spanish comrade, Ramon was summoned to New York to confer with "General Leonov," who had left Mexico immediately after the fiasco and had gone to New York to consult on the next round in Operation Trotsky.

There can be no doubt that Ramon met in New York the permanent Resident of the NKVD attached to the Soviet Consulate General who was the director of Operation Trotsky in the United States. The instructions to such a director were seen in 1948 in the Moscow headquarters by Colonel Vladimir Petrov, the Soviet secret service officer who defected with his wife in Australia. Now it has been authoritatively established that this Resident was Gaik Ovakimian, the chief of the Jacob Golos ring in which both Louis Budenz and Elizabeth Bentley had been entangled.

Ovakimian, an outstanding Soviet master spy, who operated in this country with impunity for nearly a decade, had been linked with the great Canadian atomic espionage network, and was finally exposed thanks to a tip from British intelligence. When he was arrested in New York on May 5, 1941, Ovakimian, officially an employe of the Soviet Amtorg Trading Corporation, claimed diplomatic immunity, and the Soviet Consulate put up bail of $25,000 to obtain his release pending trial. Under an unusual agreement between the Soviet government and the Department of State, consummated after Hitler's attack on Russia, Ovakimian was allowed to return home in exchange for a Soviet pledge to grant exit visas to six detained Americans, a pledge which, incidentally, was never fully honored.

At the time of Ramon Mercader's arrival in the United States in June, 1940, Ovakimian held in his hands all the strands of the Trotsky operation on this side of the Atlantic. Ramon stayed at a New York hotel with his "wife" Sylvia until July 1, and saw something of her sisters and even of the Rosmers. Allegedly he spent most of his time in the Wall Street office of his mythical boss, but no one bothered to check on this tale. Nor did Sylvia trouble herself about the nature of the real business her "husband" was transacting uptown in clandestine meetings with Soviet experts in the technique of assassination.

There were sealed packets which Ramon Mercader kept in the safe of the office of the hotel in which he and Sylvia were staying. Their wrappers were closed with red sealing wax. When he was getting ready to leave for Mexico, Ramon sent his baggage ahead from the hotel, but took the packets and strapped them to his wrists, inside his shirt sleeves, with heavy rubber bands.

When Sylvia Ageloff asked him what they were, he replied that they contained Mexican currency. However, he did not show her what was inside. After the murder, there was considerable guessing by the authorities on the subject. The red sealing wax seemed to confirm Ramon's version that they were, indeed, packets of banknotes, but what he had obviously failed to tell Sylvia was that they had been given to him by the NKVD to finance both the assassination and his anticipated escape from the scene of the planned crime.

Ramon left New York City on or about July 1, 1940. He was supposedly bound for New Orleans, San Antonio, then Mexico City. He telephoned Sylvia from San Antonio, to say good-bye again and tell her he was flying through to the Mexican capital. However, Sylvia did not hear from him during the next four weeks. She telegraphed several times, but received no reply. She was very worried. Toward the end of July, Ramon phoned her from Mexico City. He said that he had suddenly been taken sick in a village in Puebla, a state south of the Mexican capital. He asked her to join him in Mexico City immediately, and she did so early in August. They put up at the Hotel Montejo, a quiet centrally-located hostelry on the Paseo.

On Monday, July 29, at 2:40 in the afternoon, Ramon showed up at the Trotsky villa to pick up his Buick. He stayed for one hour and ten minutes. Since he had posed as a sympathizer and was regarded as a member of the political family, the guards asked him if he had visited the headquarters of the Trotskyist Workers' Party in New York. When he admitted that he had not done so, they were astonished and asked, "Why?" He explained that he had spent his days slaving in a Wall Street office and his evenings arguing with Sylvia and her sisters in favor of Trotsky's position that the Soviet Union, even under Stalin, should be defended against attack. On this issue, which divided the Trotskyist camp into factions, Sylvia took the minority view holding that Stalin's regime was unworthy of any support, in opposition to Trotsky's own stand. Ramon sided with the latter. In this way he ingratiated himself with Trotsky who saw in him a possible valuable recruit to his movement.

The guards, however, were upset by the odd failure of Ramon to visit their party headquarters in New York, a fact which they communicated to Trotsky.

"It is true, of course, that he is rather light-minded," Trotsky observed about his future assassin, "and will probably not become a strong member of the Fourth International. Nevertheless, he can be won closer. In order to build the party we must have confidence that people can be changed." And he added that Ramon was doing some research of a statistical nature on the situation in France which might result in a useful article.

Trotsky had been reared in the early revolutionary school and admired Lenin's practice of winning individual disciples to his cause. He now sought to demonstrate to his followers that Sylvia's "husband" was potential material that could be converted into an asset for the party. The master-minds in the NKVD in Moscow who planned this approach picked on a psychological weakness in Trotsky which Ramon found most profitable to exploit. What better chance of carrying off the assassination and escaping alive than by developing a disciple-and-master relationship? Trotsky even suggested specifically to his chief secretary, Joseph Hansen, that he should go out of the way to become friendly with Ramon so as to help bring him closer to the Fourth International.

During the following three weeks, Ramon visited the Trotsky establishment five more times. On July 31, he dropped in early in the evening to bring Mrs. Trotsky a box of chocolates. Upon Sylvia's arrival, she noticed, and Mrs. Trotsky corroborated it, that a great change had taken place in Ramon's appearance. He was pale, nervous, irritable, unable to eat. His complexion was described as ashy or green. He spent long hours during the daytime in bed, and was most uncommunicative with Sylvia. Yet she never made a serious effort to get at the cause of his despondency.

Ramon was at this time wrestling with the problem of how to commit the murder so as to be able to make a getaway. His psychic state was such that he said and did many things which should logically have led to his detection and exposure as a Soviet agent. Whether these "mistakes" were part of a deliberate strategy of failure or were slips of his unconscious, they are equally significant.

This is emphasized by the physical impression he made on Trotsky's staff, as Hansen so vividly recalled after the crime: Ramon "struck one as a nervous individual, prematurely aged, darkened as if some poison were working its way through his skin. His features twitched. He talked rapidly, but found words with difficulty, causing him occasionally to stumble in his utterances. While he was not husky, nevertheless he appeared wiry. He wore horn-rimmed glasses, dressed neatly, rarely covered his dark hair with a hat. It was impossible to carry on a sustained political conversation with him; he always wandered into another subject. He claimed to be an ardent sympathizer of the Fourth International, and especially devoted to Trotsky, of whom he said many times in an admiring tone, in the presence of the guards: 'He has the greatest intellect in the world.' "

The Trotskyites were not given to the degree of suspicion which is normal among underground totalitarian revolutionary groups. Hence, the conflicting tales which Ramon told about his occupation in Mexico were not questioned.

Ramon carried a tourist card listing him as Frank Jacson, a Canadian and a mechanical engineer. However, he registered at the Hotel Montejo as North American, which in Mexico means a citizen of the United States. As we know, he had told Sylvia and her sisters different stories about his employment. He once said to Natalia Trotsky that he was planning to bring some diamond cutters to Mexico from Belgium. He told Otto Schuessler, the guard, that he dealt in sugar and oil. In talking to Joseph Hansen, the assassin-designate stated that he worked for a European broker who had first dealt in oil purchases for the Allies and then switched to diamonds. He claimed that his salary was $50 a week—not very generous pay, even in 1940, for operations on a large scale. He identified his employer as Peter Lubeck, the manager of a large British import house. No one ever bothered to look him up.

Mr. Shirley of the tourist camp where "Jacson" had stayed during the spring of 1940 gave still another version. In talking to him, Ramon claimed to be a road engineer working on the construction of the Chiapas highway. He added that he had come to Mexico City for a while because he could do nothing in Chiapas during the rainy season. According to the Mexican press, he told other people that he was working for a manufacturer of coconut oil in Torreon.

Some of the people to whom Ramon told these incompatible stories were in close personal contact with each other. The rest might easily have met and compared notes, not unlikely in view of the small size of the American colony in Mexico City at the time. Thus Ramon was running a large risk of being exposed as an impostor before he had an opportunity to commit his crime.

These multiple stories were obviously quite unnecessary to the accomplishment of his task. His conduct in this matter may have been due to his natural tendency to take unnecessary risks, to his desire to express contempt for the people he was deceiving, or to a conscious or unconscious wish to bring about the failure of his mission.

On another occasion, Ramon was driving some Minneapolis Trotskyites visiting their chief on a sight-seeing trip to Toluca. They were on a winding mountain road. Suddenly, he turned the Buick toward the precipice, then at the last moment swerved back on the road. "In that way everything would have been finished," Ramon said. His guests thought nothing of the incident at the time it occurred.

This practice of dropping little clues became more frequent as he was drawn into closer association with the Trotsky household—wearing the mask of an admirer and disciple. The possibility that this relationship created in him a major new area of emotional disturbance is suggested by one of the statements he made after his arrest.

"Were you right or wrong to kill Trotsky?" he was asked in a written test.

Mercader became very nervous and wrote the answer with great indecision and many ink blots:

"Yes, since if I had waited and allowed myself to be convinced by him. . . ."

Was doubt in the righteousness of his mission nagging him or was the inescapability of the imminent crime wearing him down? Joseph Hansen reflected on Ramon's mental condition as follows: "Possibly the enthusiasm he may have felt at first for his assignment thinned out as he became acquainted with the victim and the guards. I have heard of cases in the American movement of undercover agents who were won over to the cause they were assigned to fight. . . . It is also difficult for me to believe that his experience with Sylvia, whatever his hardness and real aims, left no imprint."

Trotsky had become accustomed to live in the shadow of impending assassination. Every morning since the attack of May 24 he would say to his wife upon waking:

"Another lucky day. We are still alive."

Like a man awaiting his scheduled execution in a death cell, Trotsky had virtually abandoned all hope of escaping Stalin's murder machine. Knowing that the Kremlin would time its blow during a critical stage of the war so as to minimize the effect of the news upon public opinion, Trotsky even predicted correctly that the next assault upon him would occur when Hitler launched his battle against England.

Nevertheless, measures were being taken to protect Trotsky against the expected attack. His followers and sympathizers raised several thousand dollars in the United States to transform the Coyoacan villa into a virtual fortress. A military engineer was called in to plan the reconstruction. Twenty-foot walls were built. A redoubt was constructed with bomb-proof ceilings and floors. Double steel doors, controlled by electric switches, replaced the old wooden entrance. Three new bullet-proof towers were erected to dominate not only the patio but the surrounding neighborhood. Barbed wire entanglements and bomb-proof nets were being installed.

The Mexican government tripled the number of outside police guards on duty around the place. James Cannon, the militant Trotskyite leader in the United States, had been to Minneapolis and selected from the ranks of the organization in the Teamsters' Union some exceptionally tough and qualified men to reinforce the inner guard at Trotsky's house.

Trotsky consented to all these drastic changes with reluctance. He had all along been opposed to the introduction of a regime in his establishment which would subject everyone who entered it to a search for concealed weapons. He also vetoed the proposal to make it an iron rule that he should never talk to anyone alone in his study. "Trotsky could not endure either of these rules," wrote Joseph Hansen. "Either we trust the people and admit them without search, or we do not admit them at all. He could not bear having his friends submit to search. . . . Mutual suspicion in his eyes was a disintegrating force much worse than the inclusion of a spy in the organization, since such suspicions are useless anyway in uncovering a highly skilled provocateur."

While the fortification work was going on, Trotsky often walked about the patio, suggesting changes, improvements. Sometimes, as he was pacing the paths alone, he would be found talking to himself.

On one occasion, he was overheard conducting an imaginary conversation with Bukharin, Kamenev and Zinoviev, Lenin's Old Guard, who had made alliances with Stalin against Trotsky only to be betrayed and destroyed later by Stalin. Trotsky, who could never admit an error of his own, reproached the purged revolutionaries for their mistakes.

Living in a cloistered fortress preyed on Trotsky's mind. He often said to Hansen:

"It reminds me of the first prison I was in at Kherson. The doors made the same sound when they shut. It is not a home; it's a medieval prison."

Later he referred to it again and again as "the jail." In a conversation with Ramon, in which Hansen and Cornell participated, Trotsky asked his future assassin what he thought of the "fortress" under construction. Ramon replied that everything seemed well done, adding significantly:

"In the next attack, the GPU will use other methods."

"What methods?" Hansen asked.

The man with the ice-axe on his mind just shrugged his shoulders.

Trotsky himself had anticipated the other method to be employed against him when he had on a previous occasion remarked to Hansen:

"A single agent of the GPU who could pass himself off as my friend could assassinate me in my own home."

But he did not perceive that his future murderer disguised as a friend was now standing at his very side.

The Kill

In one of the top secret offices at No. 2 Djerzhinsky Square in Moscow a quiet, stooping man with a brilliant plotting brain, Colonel Serebriansky, was watching for Stalin the approaching consummation of Operation Trotsky. He had drawn up a plan based upon experience in a recent successful assassination which the Division of Special Tasks had pulled off abroad, in a Middle Eastern capital, early in 1939.

Commissar Beria needed a killer to liquidate a Soviet ambassador who was believed to be scheming to defect from the service, according to the testimony of Colonel Vladimir Petrov of the NKVD who broke away in Australia. "I believe it was either Teheran or Kabul," he stated in recalling the circumstances of the crime. A colleague of Petrov's in the code section, a veteran of the Red Navy of great physical strength, by the name of Bokov, was selected for the assignment. Bokov was summoned before Commissar Beria who told him that he had been picked to carry out an extraordinarily important task.

"Comrade, I hear that you are a man of unusual strength," Beria said. "Are you strong enough to kill a man with a single blow of an iron bar?"

"Yes, Comrade Commissar," Bokov replied.

Beria then explained that the Soviet ambassador in question was a traitor who was about to desert to the enemy. Supplied with a phony diplomatic passport, Bokov was sent off on his mission. On arrival, the local NKVD Resident gave Bokov a short iron bar which could be concealed in one's clothing, and brought him into the ambassador's office supposedly to pay his respects. Bokov stepped behind the ambassador, struck him once with the bar, splitting his skull and killing him instantly. The two callers then wrapped the corpse in a rug, so as to leave no bloodstains, bundled it into a waiting jeep and disposed of it. The ambassador's wife was told that her husband had to leave for Moscow suddenly on a matter of the greatest urgency, and arrangements had been made for her to follow him there.

As Bokov later told it all to Petrov, this was a model assassination which left no traces. True, the lethal weapon was crude, but the execution was skillful. Ramon undertook to use an ice-axe rather than a bar of iron, but he too thought, as he himself subsequently admitted, that "a single blow would suffice to kill Mr. Trotsky." This plan was adopted to enable Ramon to fulfill his murderous mission behind the closed door of Trotsky's study with very little noise and then to walk out of the gate of the fortified villa, as Petrov put it, "quietly and unmolested."

On Thursday, August 8, at 5:55 P.M. Ramon and Sylvia came to take tea with the Trotskys. This was the first time that such an invitation had been extended to the couple. There was a political discussion at the table, revolving around the issue of the defense of the Soviet Union, which Trotsky favored, but Sylvia heatedly questioned. Ramon took little part in the argument, although he clearly showed that he was on the side of Trotsky.

On Saturday, August 10, at 3:25 P.M., Ramon was checked in at the entrance to the Trotsky villa. He stayed 37 minutes. By this time his relationship with most members of the staff of the Trotsky establishment had been cemented into something approaching acceptance. "The fact that he was Sylvia's husband not only gave him entrance, but screened him from suspicion," Joseph Hansen stated afterwards. This was true of the guards and secretaries. The Trotskys themselves would now and then be disturbed by flashes of doubt of the man.

There was, for instance, the occasion when Natalia casually mentioned to him a walk which she had taken with her husband in the mountainous country outside Mexico City when Trotsky developed a passion for collecting cactus plants. Apparently this came as startling news to Ramon, who had never heard of Trotsky's penchant for long walks. "I was struck hard by his strong reaction," she recalled afterwards. "What! A walk?" he ejaculated, and offered to escort the Trotskys on their next expedition. Although his reaction made an impression on Mrs. Trotsky, she did not stop to analyze the incident as a possible clue to what was on his mind.

"I did not understand until later why he wanted to accompany Lev Davidovich into the mountains," she observed.

Then there was the matter of Ramon's boasted involvement in shady speculations for his mythical "boss" who, he casually remarked, had made fantastic profits. He even hinted that if the Trotskyist organization would put up a few thousand dollars, his "boss" could make a fortune with the sum for the Fourth International. Trotsky, who disliked people obsessed with money-making and who always spent all his royalties on his party's political activities, felt that there was something wrong about these advances of Sylvia's friend. One time, he said to Natalia, who did not like these references to financial deals: "What about this very rich boss of his? One must find out. After all, he may be some kind of a fascist trader. And we would do better if we did not receive Sylvia's husband any more."

But Trotsky failed to follow up on the suspicion that had been aroused in him. When Ramon asked him for an appointment to go over the draft of an article he was writing, Trotsky readily agreed to see him for a few minutes. In the light of the subsequent events, it became evident that this was a staged rehearsal for the big day.

A week later, on August 17, at 4:35 P.M., Ramon appeared for his appointment. Trotsky was alone in his study, as was his custom when he received a visitor on business. The entire visit lasted eleven minutes. Natalia was not at home that afternoon.

Ramon carried his raincoat on his arm, August being the rainy season in Mexico, and he wore a hat. Furthermore, instead of taking a chair, he sat informally on the edge of Trotsky's working table, loaded with books and papers. This was grossly disrespectful behavior, since Trotsky was known as a person with the manners of a grand seigneur who was meticulous about his handling of both people and papers. It was quite an upsetting experience.

"I don't like him," he told his wife after brooding about the episode. "What sort of a fellow is he? One should find out more about him." He then spoke of the proposed article of Ramon's and described it as muddled, commonplace stuff.

"I made some suggestions to him," he added, as he seemed to be subconsciously pondering the visit. "Yesterday he did not resemble a Frenchman at all. Suddenly he sat down on my desk and kept his hat on all the while."

"Yes, it's strange," Natalia, puzzled, chimed in. "He never wears a hat."

"This time he wore a hat," Trotsky emphasized, but pursued the subject no further. Natalia thought that Trotsky had perceived something new in Ramon's character, but was "in no hurry to draw conclusions." Although she, too, had been taken aback by the strange behavior of Sylvia's "husband," she let the doubts sleep in her subconscious mind.

On Tuesday, August 20, 1940, Leon Trotsky awoke at seven. He said to his wife, Natalia:

"You know, I feel very well this morning, better than I have felt for a long time. I took a double dose of sleeping powders last night. I've noticed that it does me good."

Since the Siqueiros mass attack, Trotsky would greet Natalia in the morning, as he flung open the steel shutters that protected their bedroom windows from assassins' bullets with these words: "Well now, no Siqueiros can get us." And sometimes he would say upon waking: "You see, they didn't kill us last night after all; and you are still dissatisfied." One morning he added: "Yes, Natasha, we have received a reprieve."

On this particular day of August 20, Trotsky was filled with energy and was unusually cheerful. It was the rainy season in the valley of the Aztec capital, but that morning the sun shone brightly, while masses of dark clouds hovered at the edges of the twin volcanic peaks, Popocatepetl and Iztaccihuatl.

Trotsky dressed hurriedly after his massage and went to the courtyard which was brilliant with roses and geraniums flowering in the midst of Mexican cactus. He began to feed the rabbits and chickens in their hutches. For security reasons, this had become his most common form of exercise. Trotsky enjoyed caring for animals. He liked physical work and, as with other tasks, he put tremendous energy into it.

After almost two hours of uninterrupted manual work in the patio, Trotsky sat down to breakfast at nine. He told Natalia again how well he felt, and spoke of an article he was planning to dictate that morning.

At the same time, at the Hotel Montejo, Ramon was in a

hurry to leave. He had been feeling ill all week in Room 113 which he occupied with his American "wife." To the manager, Miss Noriega, he was known as Frank Jacson, Canadian.

"Jacson" was very withdrawn, spoke to none of the other guests, and stayed by preference in the hotel garden where he had his breakfast and other meals. The "Jacsons" obviously wanted to be left alone. They dressed simply. Miss Noriega thought that "Mrs. Jacson" was a rather disorderly person.

On the morning of August 20, "Jacson" left the hotel early. Miss Noriega saw him leave with a raincoat tucked under his arm although the sun was shining. On the other hand, there were those storm clouds clustering around the volcanic peak of Popocatepetl. He told Sylvia he was going to the United States Embassy to take care of his visa before their planned departure for New York. He returned about noon in an angry mood.

At that very moment Trotsky stepped out of his study into the patio. "The whole day was one of the most tranquil," his wife Natalia recalled afterwards. "I saw him standing there bareheaded under the scorching sun, and I hastened to bring him his white cap to protect his head against the merciless hot rays."

Trotsky started to work on an essay dealing with the issue of conscription in the United States. He was interrupted by the arrival of his attorney Rigault, who brandished a defamatory article in *El Popular*, Lombardo Toledano's newspaper which served as a thinly disguised mouthpiece of the Comintern. Rigault represented Trotsky in the case of the attack of May 24 which was still pending while the search was going on for its organizer, David Siqueiros.

It was one o'clock. The young German Trotskyite, Otto Schuessler, one of the guards, was off duty that day and went downtown to join his fiancée for the afternoon and evening. He ran into Sylvia and her "husband" in front of the white, gleaming Palace of Fine Arts, an ornate marble structure which dominates the business center of Mexico City. The "Jacsons," as they were known in the Trotsky establishment, said they were returning to the United States the next day and that they would come to bid good-by to "the Old Man" around four or five that afternoon. They invited Otto to bring his fiancée to a restaurant for dinner with them at seven-thirty.

Sylvia was pleasant and smiling. The usually voluble Ramon was pale, uneasy and almost tongue-tied. Suddenly he excused himself, saying he had an appointment, and departed.

Sylvia told Otto she was worried. Her "husband" was in delicate health even though he was an athlete. No doubt, it was the altitude of Mexico City and the sort of food he insisted on eating. She went back to the hotel and nervously waited for a message from him. Throughout the early afternoon, she bothered Miss Noriega with questions about her husband, and whether he had left some message for her.

In the meantime, after the departure of Mr. Rigault, Trotsky looked into his wife's room to tell her that he and the attorney had decided that it was necessary to answer the defamation in *El Popular*. "And I will take the offensive and will charge them with brazen slander," he observed with vehemence. And once more he assured Natalia, "I feel fine."

"After a brief siesta," she wrote afterwards, "I saw him sitting at his desk, which was already covered with items relating to the *El Popular* case. He continued to be in good spirits. And it made me feel more cheerful. Lev Davidovich had of late been complaining of general enervation to which he succumbed occasionally. He knew that it was a passing condition, but lately he seemed to be in greater doubt about it than ever before; today seemed to us to mark the beginning of improvement in his physical condition. He looked well too. Every now and then I opened the door to his room just a trifle, so as not to disturb him, and saw him in his usual position, bent over his desk, pen in hand. I recalled the line, 'One more and final story and my scroll is at an end.' Thus speaks the ancient monk-scribe Pimen in Pushkin's drama *Boris Godounov,* as he recorded the evil deeds of Czar Boris."

Trotsky worked until five in the afternoon, and had dictated about fifty short pages of his exposé of Stalin's machinations and of the attack on him in *El Popular.*

"I went back to Sylvia," the assassin stated when he recounted his movements of the early afternoon of that fatal day, "and we went to the Salon Don Quixote where we had an aperitif and afterwards I took her to the hotel and left her there."

Later that afternoon Ramon wandered about the city, according to his account. It is a fact that he showed up at the Wells Fargo office where he collected his mail.

All the preparations had been made and, for the moment, there was nothing for him to do. In one pocket of the raincoat was the article he had written to submit to Trotsky for his criticism. It was to serve as the pretext for entering Trotsky's study and being alone with his victim.

Inside the khaki raincoat, sewn into the lining of the right-hand pocket, there was a dagger with a brown sheath embroidered with silver threads. This weapon was 13¾ inches long. As a murder instrument, it was not particularly suitable because of its excessive length. Mercader bought it, perhaps on impulse, in anticipation of the crime, in La Lagunilla, the great Mexico City market for second-hand goods.

He also carried an ice-axe, or *piolet,* the handle of which had been cut down for easy concealment. Its heavy wooden stock was about a foot long. Its steel head was about 7 inches long from tip to tip and symmetrically balanced at the haft. One edge was sharp like an ice-pick. This was normally used to get a purchase in ice and rock while climbing beyond the snow line. The other edge was a forked hammer claw, used by mountaineers to detach and split blocks of ice. This weapon was in a pocket of the brown raincoat, and attached to it by a cord.

In his back trousers' pocket, Ramon carried a third weapon—a .45 caliber Star automatic pistol with eight bullets in the magazine and one in the firing chamber. The automatic was of Spanish manufacture. Because of its large caliber, it would have enough impact to knock a man off his feet if he were hit any place on his body.

Ramon also carried on his person a letter which purported to explain to the world the motives for the crime he was about to commit. In this purported "confession," he claimed to be a disillusioned follower of Trotsky who had been ordered by the latter to go to the Soviet Union and kill Stalin, and had recoiled with horror from the proposal. This letter was in French, probably translated by "Jacson" himself. He had all along pretended to the Trotskyists to be a Belgian travelling on a false Canadian passport, and that French was his native language. The French version had been typed a few days before. Now he took out a pencil and wrote in at the bottom of the letter, "JAC, August 20, 1940."

An unusual procedure. When one types a letter, it is customary to type in the date at the top right-hand corner of the first page. The fact that the letter was dated in pencil obviously meant that it had been prepared in advance and that Ramon had probably had it in his possession for some time. It was equally remarkable that the letter of "confession" and the article for Trotsky's perusal had been typed on different machines.

Later, Ramon would assert that, after leaving Wells Fargo, he drove to a deserted lot near the new highway into the capital and close to the railway crossing. There he claimed to have burned his forged passport and other papers. Whether this was true or false, no documents revealing his true identity or role in the conspiracy against Trotsky would be found after the murder either on his person or in his hotel room.

He had now crossed his private Rubicon. Ramon went back to where the Buick was parked and took the road to Coyoacan. He did not worry about the possibility that Sylvia would go to the Trotskys independently to look for him or meet him there. Theirs was a relationship of long standing and he knew that she was submissive, dependent on him and perhaps a little afraid of him. She was the sort of woman who worries and frets and is easily driven to tears, but she was not in the habit of acting independently.

As he approached Coyoacan, Ramon was moving consciously towards the accomplishment of two enormously difficult tasks: First, to carry out what he would later call "my great historic act." Second, to escape from the fortified house with his life.

All the provisions for the assassin's escape had been made and everything was in readiness. He would see Trotsky alone in his study. He would kill him with a single crushing blow of his ice-axe, without attracting attention. He would then leave the study, walk out of the house and make his way through the patio to the exit. Once out on the street, he would get into his car and drive around the corner. (There another car, with his mother in it, was waiting for him with a chauffeur at the wheel. One block away Eitingon, the field director of the operation, was stationed in still another car, with the engine idling.)

No one had anticipated that Trotsky would be able to make an outcry. It was assumed that he would not have an opportunity to seize and fire either of the two loaded pistols normally on his desk, or to reach the switch which set off the alarm system. It was also assumed that the assassin would be able to get out of the building before anybody else entered the study or before either Natalia or the guards happened to look through the window and notice that Trotsky was not seated at his desk in a natural position.

If any of these mishaps should occur, Ramon had his automatic and he could try to shoot his way out of the walled house and garden guarded by a contingent of heavily armed men on the inside and by Mexican police on the outside. Thus, the chances of escape depended altogether upon the perfect handling of the murder weapon behind the closed door of the study, allowing time for the assassin to get out of the villa.

If he succeeded in leaving the place alive in his Buick, he would quickly abandon it to avoid a possible chase and get into one of the cars waiting for him nearby. He would be driven immediately to the airport where a private plane, with its pilot at the controls, was ready to take off. A brand new false passport had been prepared for him and validated through special liaison arrangements with certain persons in the Mexican Foreign Office. Barring mishaps, "Jacson" would be in a different country with a new name and a new nationality before midnight of the day of the murder.

Trotsky, Natalia and some of his staff had tea as usual about five o'clock. After tea, Trotsky went out in the garden to feed his rabbits again.

Joseph Hansen, his chief secretary, was on the roof near the main tower when Ramon arrived. With Hansen were C. Cornell, secretary and guard, and Melquiades Benitez, handyman. These three were connecting a siren with the alarm system so that, in the event of another mass assault, warning could be given simultaneously to the entire guard detachment and to the Mexican police stationed outside the walls.

At about 5:20 in the afternoon, Hansen saw Ramon approaching in his Buick sedan. Usually he parked with his front bumper against the wall of the compound. This time, however, he made a complete turn so that his car was parallel to the wall and facing the city from which he came. Hansen noticed this fact, but he did not suspect Ramon's purpose behind it.

Ramon got out of his car and waved to the three men working on the roof. "Has Sylvia arrived yet?" Hansen was surprised. He had not known of any appointment with Sylvia and her "husband," but then Trotsky often forgot to tell his guards about such matters.

"No," Hansen replied. "Wait a moment." Cornell pressed the switch and the double electric doors opened. Inside the patio, Harold Robins, another guard, received "Jacson" and brought him to the rabbit hutch where Trotsky was feeding his animals. "Damp grass swells the bellies of the rabbits," Trotsky explained as he selected dry forage.

Looking down from the balcony of the house, Natalia saw her husband feeding the animals. At first, she did not recognize the man with him, but then he raised his hat and approached the balcony to greet her. She now recognized Sylvia's "husband." "There he is again," Natalia thought. "Why is it that he has started coming so often?"

"I'm frightfully thirsty," he said after his greeting. "May I have a glass of water?"

"Perhaps you would like a cup of tea?" she suggested.

"No, no," he said. "I ate late and I can still feel my meal up here." He pointed to his throat. "It's choking me."

His face was gray-green, Natalia thought, and he was even more nervous than usual. She drew no sinister inference, nor did the others, from his refusal of the invitation to have tea.

"Why are you wearing your hat and topcoat?" Natalia asked. "It's so sunny today."

"Yes, but you know it won't last long, it might rain," he replied. Actually, he had the raincoat pressed hard against his body.

She wanted to contradict him. The thought flashed through her mind that "Jacson" was always boasting about his ability to go around bareheaded and without a coat in the foulest weather. But she decided not to pursue the subject.

"And how is Sylvia feeling?"

He did not seem to understand the question. Interrupted in

his thoughts, he repeated the name stupidly, as if he were coming out of the ether. "Sylvia? . . . Sylvia . . . She's always well," he replied finally.

Now he began to retrace his steps toward the rabbit hutch where Trotsky was still working. As he did so, Natalia asked him whether his article was ready and if it was typed. Ramon made a clumsy movement with his left hand, the hand that was also pressing his raincoat against his body, and extracted a few typewritten pages.

"It's good that your manuscript is not written by hand," Natalia said. "Lev Davidovich dislikes illegible manuscripts."

"Jacson" and Natalia approached Trotsky.

"You know he is expecting Sylvia to call on us," Trotsky explained to her in Russian. "They are leaving tomorrow."

Natalia said she had not known that.

"Yes . . . Yes . . . I forgot to mention it to you."

She said that was too bad, as he could have taken things to New York for Trotsky. Ramon said he could call tomorrow at one, but Natalia replied: "No, no, thank you. It would inconvenience both of us."

She turned to Trotsky, replying to his hint that they should invite "Jacson" and Sylvia for tea or dinner as a farewell gesture. She explained that he had already refused tea on the grounds that he felt sick.

Trotsky looked at him attentively:

"Your health is poor again. You look ill . . . That is not good."

There was a pause. Trotsky obviously did not want to tear himself away from the rabbits. He had gone over the outline of "Jacson's" article a few days before and thought very little of it. Then there had been that hat episode in the study, which had struck Trotsky as bizarre, particularly in a man who always went around bareheaded. Natalia felt that her husband had observed something about Sylvia's friend that was changing his evaluation of the man. On August 20, she believes, he was in the process of digesting these new impressions and reaching a conclusion.

"Well, what do you say, shall we go over your article?" Trotsky, shaking off his hesitation, at last turned to Ramon.

"He fastened the hutches methodically, and removed his working gloves," Natalia described the scene. "He took good care of his hands, or rather his fingers, inasmuch as the slightest scratch irritated him, interfered with his writing. He always kept his pen, like his fingers, in order. He brushed off his blue blouse and slowly, silently started walking towards the house accompanied by 'Jacson' and myself. I came with them to the door of Lev Davidovich's study."

As Trotsky closed the door behind his visitor, the thought crossed his mind, as he soon recalled on his death-bed: "This man could kill me."

But he did not listen to the voice of his subconscious.

Trotsky sat in his chair with the broad, rough-hewn table which he used as a desk in front of him. It was piled with magazines and books. Pens and pencils were in a jar. There was an old-fashioned blotter, an ivory paper-cutter, a gooseneck lamp, the dictaphone with its disks. A few inches from Trotsky's hand was his .25 caliber automatic, which had been oiled and reloaded only a few days before. There was also a Colt .38 in the study. Each weapon had six cartridges in its magazine. The switch that would turn on the alarm system was also within Trotsky's reach. It was in this room that the leader of the Opposition to Stalin spent most of his waking hours. There was even a couch in the room on which he took his daily siestas.

Ramon stood at Trotsky's left side where he could prevent his victim from turning on the alarm switch. Then, as the assassin later told the police:

"I put my raincoat on the table on purpose so that I could

take out the ice-axe which I had in the pocket. I decided not to lose the brilliant opportunity which was offered me and at the exact moment when Trotsky started to read my article, which served as my pretext, I took the *piolet* out of my raincoat, took it in my fist and, closing my eyes, I gave him a tremendous blow on the head. . . .

"The man screamed in such a way that I will never forget it as long as I live. His scream was A*aaa* . . . very long, infinitely long and it still seems to me as if that scream were piercing my brain. I saw Trotsky get up like a madman. He threw himself at me and bit my hand . . . Look, you can still see the marks of his teeth . . . Then I pushed him, so that he fell to the floor. He lifted himself as best he could and then, running or stumbling, I don't know how, he got out of the room."

The three guards were still at work up at the main tower. One of them, Joseph Hansen, recorded what transpired next:

"A fearful cry rent the afternoon calm—a cry prolonged and agonized, half scream, half sob. It dragged me to my feet, chilled to the bone. I ran from the guard-house out onto the roof. An accident to one of the ten workers who were remodeling the house? Sounds of violent struggle came from the Old Man's study, and Melquiades was pointing a rifle at the window below. Trotsky, in his blue work jacket became visible there for a moment, fighting body to body with someone.

" 'Don't shoot!' " I shouted to Melquiades, " 'you might hit the Old Man!' " Melquiades and Cornell stayed on the roof, covering the exits from the study. Switching on the general alarm, I slid down the ladder into the library. As I entered the door connecting the library with the dining room the Old Man stumbled out of his study a few feet away, blood streaming down his face.

" 'See what they have done to me!' " he said.

At the same moment Harold Robins came through the north door of the dining room with Natalia following. Throwing her arms frantically about him, Natalia took Trotsky out onto the balcony.

Three or four minutes after she had left Trotsky and Ramon at the door, Natalia heard "a terrible, soul-shaking cry," and, without recognizing it as coming from her husband, she rushed toward the agonizing sound. Trotsky was leaning against the post of the door between the dining-room and the balcony, his face covered with blood, his hands limp, his sharp blue eyes naked, without their glasses (they had been smashed in the death struggle).

"What happened? What happened?" Natalia cried.

"I flung my arms about him, but he did not immediately answer," she recalled. "It flashed through my mind: perhaps something had fallen from the ceiling—some repair work was being done there—but *why was he here*?

"And he said to me calmly, without any indignation, bitterness or irritation: 'Jacson.' Lev Davidovich said it as if he wished to say, 'It has happened.' We took a few steps and Lev Davidovich, with my help, slumped to the floor on the little carpet lying there."

Hansen relates what went on at this moment:

"Harold and I had made for 'Jacson,' who stood in the study gasping, face knotted, arms limp, automatic pistol dangling in his hand. Harold was closer to him. 'You take care of him,' I said, 'I'll see what's happened to the Old Man.' Even as I turned, Robins brought the assassin down to the floor.

"Trotsky staggered back into the dining room, Natalia sobbing, trying to help him. 'See what they have done,' she said. As I put my arm about him, the Old Man collapsed near the dining room table.

"The wound on his head appeared at first glance to be superficial. I had heard no shot. 'Jacson' must have struck with some instrument. 'What happened?' I asked the Old Man.

" 'Jacson shot me with a revolver; I am seriously wounded . . . I feel that this time it is the end.' "

" 'It's only a surface wound. You will recover,' " I tried to reassure him.

" 'We talked about French statistics,' " responded the Old Man.

" 'Did he hit you from behind?' " I asked.

Trotsky did not answer.

" 'No, he did not shoot you,' " I said, " 'we didn't hear any shot. He struck you with something.' "

"Trotsky looked doubtful; pressed my hand. Between the sentences we exchanged, he talked with Natalia in Russian. He touched her hand continually to his lips."

"Natasha, I love you," he said, and then added: "Oh . . . Oh . . . No one, no one must be allowed to see you without being searched."

Natalia's account continues:

"Carefully placing a pillow under his broken head, I held a piece of ice to his wound and wiped the blood from his face with cotton. . . .

"Seva must be taken away from all this," Trotsky said, referring to his eleven-year-old grandson. Speaking with increasing difficulty, but quietly, his voice breaking, he went on:

"You know, in *there*"—his eyes moved toward the door of his study—"I sensed . . . understood what *he wanted to do* . . . He wanted to strike me . . . once more . . . But I didn't let him."

There was a note of satisfaction in those words: "But I didn't let him." Just then, Natalia saw one of the guards, Charles Cornell, his face chalk-white, revolver in hand, rush into the study.

"What about *that one*?" she asked the stricken Trotsky. "They will kill him."

"No . . . impermissible to kill, he must be *forced to talk*," Trotsky uttered the words slowly.

It was 5:50. Hansen climbed up to the roof and called to the police outside to get an ambulance at once. A neighborhood physician was sent for.

As Hansen entered the study, he saw that Robins had cornered the assassin whose pistol lay on the table, his blood-splashed axe on the floor. Robins was hitting him with the butt end of his pistol. Hansen advanced on the terrified "Jacson," hitting him on the mouth and behind the ear, and breaking his hand in the process. Then Robins clubbed him down with his pistol.

As Hansen recalled the event eighteen years later:

"As he stood in the doorway of Trotsky's study, stained with blood, pistol hanging from limp arm, he looked wrung out. My first impulse was to shoot him. But I decided better not. I felt sure he would talk if we could keep at him a little while. So I kept the police out while Harold, then the two of us, and then Harold alone, worked him over. But he wouldn't talk. I think he went unconscious twice or so, and I again became afraid that, giving way to impulse, we might kill him. That was the first I realized how hard this person really was. He would sooner die than talk . . ."

Years later, political analysts and novelists would weave a fantasy of speculation around the assassin's conflicting and ambiguous utterances at that time, such as, "they made me do it" and "they have imprisoned my mother." But as the years went on, even the eyewitnesses began to think that the killer was speaking the lines of his well-rehearsed part in the great criminal drama he had helped stage.

A search of the prisoner revealed all the weapons he had concealed and $890 in bills, a sum large enough to enable him to get out of the country in a hurry. It was evident that he had hoped to kill Trotsky silently with a single blow, leave the house without attracting attention, but if necessary, shoot his way out of the place.

Back at Trotsky's side, Hansen told the "Old Man" that he had been hit by a pick and that the wound was superficial.

"No," Trotsky said. He pointed to his heart. "I feel here that this time they have succeeded." He smiled faintly with his eyes. "Take care of Natalia. She has been with me many, many years."

Soon his reflexes began to fail on the left side. The ambulance came and took him to the Green Cross Emergency Hospital. Natalia and Hansen rode with the dying man to the hospital.

Pulling Hansen's head toward his lips, Trotsky whispered with great effort: "He was a political assassin. 'Jacson' was a member of the GPU or a fascist. Most likely the GPU."

About two and a half hours later, Stalin's revolutionary enemy lapsed into unconsciousness from which he would never emerge. X-rays showed that an immediate operation was necessary, and leading Mexican brain specialists trepanned the skull. They discovered that "Jacson's" ice-axe had penetrated almost three inches and had caused massive destruction of brain tissue. Trotsky was nearly sixty-two and had been in ill health for the past few months. Nevertheless, he survived for 26 hours after the operation, a tribute to his immense natural vigor.

Meanwhile at 7:45 P.M., some two hours after the assassination, Sylvia arrived a quarter of an hour late to her dinner appointment with Otto Schuessler and his fiancée. She was upset at finding that her "husband" was not there:

"It's funny. I don't know what is the matter with him, but there is something wrong. When he is late, he always phones the hotel. He told me that he would come to fetch me at half-past four to say good-by to the Trotskys and he neither came nor phoned. I hoped to find him here."

She telephoned the Hotel Montejo and other places where he might be. Shortly after eight, Schuessler proposed phoning the Trotskys, but Sylvia objected: "It is impossible for 'Jacson' to be there. He never goes without me."

Schuessler phoned anyhow. The person who picked up the receiver told him:

"Come at once. 'Jacson' has just tried to kill the Old Man."

In the taxi, Schuessler told Sylvia what he had just heard. In the course of a few minutes, her entire world disintegrated.

The three arrived at the Trotsky house where Sylvia was briefed on what had happened and then asked to go to Police Headquarters. On her arrival there, she was arrested. The secret service men, under Colonel Salazar, regarded her as an accomplice.

As they eyed the suspect, they found before them a small, slight young woman, frail to the point of looking childlike. Sylvia Ageloff was a dark blonde, her hair soft, loosely waved and fine textured. The face was heart-shaped, with a small pointed chin. The eyebrows were heavily marked, the eyes large in proportion to the face. The nose was short and straight, the forehead very broad and the cheeks faintly hollowed. She was very nearsighted and wore thick-lensed glasses. She was several years older than her beau who, however, looked like a man in his thirties. She seemed to be disinterested and careless in her dress and, while she had a soft, childlike appeal, she lacked distinction of any sort.

She was now in a state of near-hysteria, and burst into tears whenever Trotsky's name was mentioned. She demanded that the police kill her lover. The investigators were puzzled how it was possible for her to have lived with the prisoner for two years without having any idea of what he was really up to. She said that she now realized that "Jacques Mornard" which she believed to be his real name, was a GPU agent, and that he had made love to her solely to get access to Trotsky and kill him. They thought she was being melodramatic and confined her in the Green Cross Hospital where the badly-mauled 'Jacson' was imprisoned and where Trotsky was dying.

"Kill him! Kill him!" she kept screaming between spasms of sobs.

In the late afternoon of August 20, around six o'clock, when the police alarm was sounded and a commotion stirred up in the neighborhood, Caridad Mercader and her paramour Eitingon, stationed in their separate cars, knew that something had gone wrong. Instantly cries echoed down the street that Trotsky was dead or wounded. And when the Green Cross emergency ambulance came rushing to the scene of the crime, Caridad and Eitingon lost no time in getting away. Both headed by separate routes for foreign lands. There was danger that the assassin's identity might be discovered within a matter of hours, that Caridad's complicity in the affair would be presumed, and that all the resources of the Mexican police would be marshalled in a search for her.

Through its special connections, the apparat had managed to get for Caridad Mercader a new false passport under a different name, to replace the papers with which she had entered the country. Before the night of the attack had passed, Caridad reached a neighboring Latin American country.

Eitingon as General "Leonov" took off at the same time for the Pacific port of Acapulco where a Soviet freighter, anchored off shore, was getting ready to depart. Driven by a chauffeur who was a trusted member of the party's underground, the Soviet officer, after an all-night ride, found himself under the Soviet flag on board ship. That very day he was out of the jurisdiction of Mexico.

Caridad and Eitingon met again in Moscow some weeks later. Caridad had been preceded there by Angelica Arenal, wife of Siqueiros. Angelica with her two children had been given refuge in Russia after the abortive assault, and remained there for two years. Siqueiros was at this time a fugitive in Chile.

Great honors awaited Caridad. She was taken by Lavrenti

Beria himself to be presented to Stalin in the Kremlin. She was decorated with the Order of Lenin for her part in the liquidation of that "dangerous enemy of the people," and promised that everything would be done to rescue her son as soon as the war permitted. It was during the Blitz of London and the expected German invasion of England.

Stalin then announced his government's award to Ramon Mercader of the Order of the Hero of the Soviet Union for his "valorous act," and entrusted the medal to his mother for safekeeping until his release. Enrique Castro Delgado, the author of the undisputed chronicle *J'ai Perdu la Foi à Moscou,* who was the representative of the Spanish Communist Party at the headquarters of the Comintern, vouches for this fact. Delgado saw a great deal of Caridad in Moscow where she proudly exhibited to him her son's decoration.

7

The False Autobiography

President Lazaro Cardenas of Mexico was a convinced revolutionary socialist and was sympathetic toward the Soviet Union. Nevertheless, he reacted to the challenge posed by the assassination of Trotsky with characteristic courage. When the news first reached him, he pronounced it "the dirtiest crime committed in Mexico for a long time." On August 30, Cardenas commented on the role of the Mexican communists in the murder:

"If they have considered it expedient to abandon cooperation with Mexican organized labor in its struggle for continuing improvement and have instead allied themselves with a foreign power in the organization of armed assaults that dishonor civilization, then the result has been the recent crime, which will be censured throughout all time by history as dishonorable for those who inspired it and foul for those who actually perpetrated it."

The President and Mrs. Cardenas called on Trotsky's widow to express their condolences. Cardenas considered that the honor of Mexico was at stake. He made it plain to the authorities that he wanted a thoroughgoing investigation and that no guilty person, regardless of his position, was to be shielded. His administration, however, was thoroughly infiltrated by communist elements. Moscow's network had acquired considerable power to execute or short-circuit policy decisions, to spread fear, to inflict punishment, to grant rewards, to disseminate lies and to suppress the truth. Stalin's followers were prepared to do everything in their power to prevent the identity of the assassin and his relationship to the NKVD from being disclosed. Moreover, President Cardenas' presidential term ended in 1940—that is to say, within a few months of the murder.

A few minutes after six on the afternoon of August 20, General Jose Manuel Nunez, Chief of the Mexican Police, proceeded to Coyoacan where he arrested the bruised and bleeding "Jacson." Taken to the Green Cross Emergency Hospital, he was guarded there by ten policemen to prevent him from being killed or committing suicide. On August 26, "Jacson" was moved to a so-called armored cell in the Sixth Precinct Police Station located in the same building as the hospital.

The man primarily in charge of the investigation was Colonel Leandro A. Sanchez Salazar, Chief of the Mexican Secret Service. Salazar, a professional soldier, who had been appointed by President Cardenas, was neither a communist nor a fellow-traveller, and he had some understanding of the political background of the case as he had been investigating the May 24th mass attack on Trotsky's house and was still busy searching for Siqueiros and his accomplices charged with the murder of Sheldon Harte.

Because of the world importance of the Trotsky assassination, two other organizations were competing with Salazar. These were the regular police under General Nunez and the Confidential Service (*Servicio Confidencial*) of the Ministry of Interior, a department which had been deeply infiltrated by communist elements.

Upon the arrest of "Jacson," the police found on him the letter of "confesssion" which he had signed and dated in pencil immediately before committing the crime. Written in French and filling three sheets of paper in single space typing, it contained the request that it be made public in case anything happened to the purported author "Jac."

In this open letter, the prisoner stated that he came from an old Belgian family. As a student of journalism in Paris, he had become interested in "social injustice," had joined the Trotskyist organization and had been ready "to give even the last drop of my blood for the cause."

A representative of the (Trotskyite) Bureau of the Fourth International had approached him in Paris with the request that he go to Mexico to meet Trotsky face to face, according to the letter. He agreed to this plan enthusiastically. Since wartime mobilization was in effect, he had to be provided with false papers, as well as money, by the organization.

It was made clear to him, the "confession" continued, that "more was expected of me than of an ordinary party militant, but nothing was spelled out. . . ." He was instructed to stay away from Coyoacan at first and to approach Trotsky only little by little, "so as not to attract attention to myself. . . ."

The rest of the letter described his alleged progressive disenchantment. After several conversations, Trotsky proposed to him that he proceed to Soviet Russia "to organize there a series of attempts against various people and, in particular, against Stalin." This, the assassin maintained, was "contrary to all of my principles," but he concealed his true feelings in order to plumb the baseness of Trotsky.

For the author of the letter "the drop of water that overfilled the glass" was Trotsky's alleged statement to him "that he counted not merely on the support of a great nation, but also on the backing of a certain parliamentary committee." The references are to the United States and to the Dies Committee. He now realized, the letter went on, that "perhaps the Stalinists were not so far from the truth when they accused Trotsky of looking at the working class as if it were a dirty sock."

The letter continued with charge after charge against Trotsky. He had nothing but contempt for the Mexican Revolution. He was probably plotting the murder of Mexico's chief political leaders. He hated and distrusted even the members of his own Party. How had he been able to afford the transformation of the Coyoacan house into a fortress? "Perhaps the consul of a great foreign power, who visited him frequently, could answer that question." Another hint at the United States. The statement concluded on a sentimental note:

". . . I add that, being engaged to a young woman whom I love with all my soul because she is good and loyal, when I told him I could not go to Russia because I wished to marry first and after that would go only with my wife, he became nervous and told me that I must break with her because I could not marry a member of 'that minority rabble' (the dissident Trotskyites). Yet, it is probable that after my act, she may not want to see me any more; nevertheless, it is also because of her that I have decided to sacrifice myself utterly in order to rid the labor movement of a leader who can only harm it, and I am sure later, not only she, but also history will vindicate me when it is seen that the implacable enemy of the working class has disappeared."

This letter had been intended for use in the event of Ramon's death or escape; it was to have been found on his corpse or left on the scene of the crime. The only autobiographical statements it contained were that he had studied journalism in Paris and came from "an old Belgian family." In wartime, with Belgium and Paris both under Nazi occupation, neither of these generalities could have been readily refuted. Experts would have recognized the letter as characteristic, both in style and content, of other known fabrications of the NKVD. However, this fact could not have been easily established had the assassin perished at the scene of the crime or escaped from it. Without being available for examination, the NKVD would have been enabled to make the Trotsky murder seem like an insoluble mystery. Yet the internal evidence that the letter was of NKVD manufacture was conclusive.

It was particularly interesting that the letter contained no breath of criticism of the communist movement, of the Soviet Union, or of Stalin. Yet if Mercader had really decided to join the puny Trotskyite movement rather than the powerful mass organizations of Stalin's vast communist camp, the only possible reason would be that he had felt disillusionment with and repugnance for Stalinism. The absence of any such implication in the "confession" of a disenchanted Trotskyite was psychologically false. The NKVD, however, never inserted criticisms of Stalin in fabricated documents of this sort, as its minions had no appetite for anything which could possibly be misconstrued by their all-suspicious leader.

It was also curious that the letter charged Trotsky with being in the pay of a great power and one of its "parliamentary committees." Here again the ponderous hand of Moscow was visible. During the Soviet purge trials, Trotsky had been branded as a Nazi agent. But in 1940, Soviet Russia and Nazi Germany were leagued in the Stalin-Hitler pact, and the legend was accordingly changed to make Trotsky a tool of "American imperialism." After the Nazi attack on the USSR, the Trotskyites would again be branded as fascist agents. The rigmarole about unnamed foreign powers, congressional committees and consuls was typical jargon of the Moscow variety.

It was also characteristic of the NKVD to accuse Trotsky, not of a wrong-headed policy, but of the most heinous personal defects and common crimes. The letter piled these charges one on top of the other without any subtlety or regard for the plausible. According to the "confession," Ramon, when he met Trotsky face to face, saw a man animated solely "by hate and the desire for vengeance," a person saturated with contempt for others, a man both paltry and venal, who was treacherous to his friends, supporters and benefactors. He was a tyrant in his personal relations; he took money from foreign governments, and had no hesitation in plotting the murder of his Mexican hosts.

If all this were true, why had nobody else, among the hundreds of persons who knew Trotsky well, noticed it? Not all of them were Trotsky's supporters. If Ramon had said that he found Trotsky a supreme egoist, a political zealot, a man without personal warmth or ease in human relations, a disciplinarian and something of a pedant, the portrait, while harsh and one-sided, would have been recognizable. Max Eastman and Louis Fischer had made criticisms of this sort. But these critics agreed in recognizing Trotsky's personal integrity, his intellectual eminence, his consuming faith in his own Marxist conception of socialism. The picture of Trotsky in the "confession" bore no resemblance to the reality. It was rather a copy of the familiar caricature of Trotsky that had been drawn by Stalin's NKVD during the Moscow trials and tirelessly parroted by all the communist parties of the world since then.

The immediate problems of the police were to investigate the statements made in "Jacson's" letter, to establish his true identity, and to find out who his accomplices and superiors were.

As Colonel Salazar proceeded to question the prisoner, he began to make certain appraisals. Salazar saw his antagonist as a consummate actor with a highly agile mind. Under interrogation, this nervous man, a chain smoker, was guarded and evasive. When the questions touched on the crime itself, he became disturbed. The police chief sensed "great internal torment." He also concluded that only a man of unusual strength of character could have carried out a crime of this sort in the given circumstances.

Within a few hours of his arrest, "Jacson" made statements to the police which amplified his letter of "confession." He now asserted that his real name was Jacques Mornard Vandendreschd, that he was the son of a literary man and Belgian diplomat, and that he had been born in Teheran in 1904 when his father was Belgian minister to Iran.

He said his parents had returned to Belgium when he was two years old. Eight years later, according to his amplified imaginary autobiography, the family had moved to Paris, his father having retired. He graduated from a Jesuit college in Brussels in 1920, then spent four years in Belgian military schools. He was an anti-militarist and attended those schools unwillingly at his father's insistence.

In 1924, he left the Royal Academy at Dixmude and later went to Paris to study journalism at the Sorbonne. He became the assistant to a French sports writer named Paul de Lacourt who wrote for *Le Soir*. His earnings were supplemented by a family income which was quite ample as his father had died in 1926, leaving four million Belgian francs.

In 1934, he claimed to have married a Belgian girl, but they could not get along, and were separated. He was divorced five years later. He said he had an older brother, Robert, who was forty and a diplomat. To these invented items he added certain data which could be verified.

He declared that he had met Sylvia in Paris in 1938 at a time when he was still studying journalism at the Sorbonne. Through her, he became interested in Trotskyism.

He described his sojourn in Mexico and added details to the brief statements in his letter about attempts on the lives of Soviet leaders:

"On a certain occasion, Trotsky was going to send me to

Russia with the object of organizing a new state of things in the USSR. He told me that I must go to Shanghai on the China Clipper where I would meet other agents in some ships, and together we would cross Manchukuo (Manchuria) and arrive in Russia. Our mission was to bring demoralization to the Red Army, commit different acts of sabotage in armament plants and other factories."

But when he argued with Trotsky against the assignment, he claimed:

". . . Trotsky crushed me as if I had been paper in his hands. It was then that there was born in my brain the idea of killing him. I thought for a week and then came to the conclusion that there was no way out except to kill him and then commit suicide. I hoped that if I could get to him and give him one blow, I would have time to escape, and that is why I took the *piolet.* I bought the pistol from an individual who deals in arms and paid about 160 or 170 pesos for it, and in addition I gave him a typewriter on Saturday, the 17th. On the 20th, I wrote a letter on that machine. . . .

"I was skilled in the use of the *piolet;* two blows were sufficient to break an enormous block of ice. That is why I thought that a single blow would suffice to kill Mr. Trotsky. . . . If this failed, I thought I would have time to shoot myself. Therefore, I decided to carry the pistol and, as a precaution, the dagger, which I had bought in the Lagunilla and which I sewed into the pocket of my overcoat. If I had succeeded in getting away from the Trotsky house, I would have gone to the National Park to take my own life."

Aided by members of the Trotsky secretariat, the Mexican Secret Service rapidly began to puncture this story. On even the most cursory examination, the assassin's statement began to fall apart at the seams.

(1) In his letter, he described himself as a dedicated member of the Trotsky organization. But in his statement to the police,

he was merely a sympathizer. Sylvia Ageloff declared that, when they were in Paris together, he had shown no interest in Trotskyism and had not even bothered to read the political news in the papers. Under these circumstances, it was hard to believe that the Bureau of the Fourth International, its secret governing body, had chosen him for a mission of such extraordinary importance. Moreover, to identify a member of the organization as belonging to the Bureau would have been a breach of conspiratorial practice. The necessity of this rule had been enhanced by recent murders of leading Trotskyite personnel.

(2) The Trotsky guards had kept a record of the comings and goings of all visitors since May 24. The entries in the guards' book showed that "Jacson" could have seen Trotsky alone in his study on not more than three occasions and for a total of not more than 20 minutes. It was impossible for the prisoner to have had the conversations he claimed in such a short period of time. He claimed that he had decided to kill Trotsky a week before the actual murder, but at that time he had had only one private talk with the Soviet exile and that had lasted not more than five minutes.

(3) According to the Moscow trials, Trotsky had entrusted such resourceful veteran Russian revolutionaries as Zinoviev, Kamenev, Bukharin and Rykov with the task of killing Stalin and overthrowing the Soviet regime, but all had been caught red-handed, induced to confess and brought to punishment. One was now to believe that Trotsky had concluded that "Jacson" could succeed where these men had failed. By the prisoner's own statement, he was a dilettante and perennial student who had no particular skill at anything. He was not a native of Russia and had given no indication that he had ever been in Russia or spoke the language. Yet he was to sabotage war plants, demoralize the Red Army, murder Stalin and help set up a new government in the USSR. Trotsky, moreover, had decided he

was the right man for this stupendous job after a private conference lasting only five minutes.

The prisoner's statement that his name was Jacques Mornard Vandendreschd did not stand up very long. On August 31, eleven days after the murder, Walter Loridan, the Belgian Charge d'Affaires in Mexico, visited the prisoner to find out whether he was really a Belgian national. His findings were an overwhelming refutation of the claim.

First, the assassin alleged that his father had been Belgian ambassador to Persia in 1904 and that his brother was a diplomat, but no person named Mornard was ever in the Belgian diplomatic corps.

Second, the prisoner could not name a single other diplomatic post his father had filled.

Third, Mercader alleged he had studied in a military school at Dixmude, but none existed there.

Fourth, he claimed to have been a student at the University of Brussels. Loridan, who was an alumnus of that institution, found him unable to name any of the professors.

Fifth, he said that the Jesuit College of St. Ignatius of Loyola in Brussels was another of his alma maters. No such institution existed.

Sixth, the address he gave for his mother's house in the suburbs of Brussels was that of a large store in the center of the city.

Seventh, he claimed to have lived as a student in the Flemish part of Belgium, but he was totally ignorant of the Flemish tongue.

Whatever else he was, it was established that he was no Belgian. The name Mornard was falsely assumed by him. The real Jacques Mornard cabled the Mexican authorities. He was a Belgian newspaperman on *La Nation Belge,* in good health and with convincing documentation.

In his statement to the police, "Mornard" claimed to have been born in 1904. This would have made him 36 years old.

Since he appeared to be in his mid-thirties, none of the investigators ever challenged this statement. Yet there were at least three points in Mercader's initial declaration to the police that indicated he was lying about the matter.

He had said that he left military school in 1924 and later began to study journalism at the Sorbonne. When he met Sylvia Ageloff in Paris in 1938, he was still studying journalism. There was obviously something wrong in this chronology.

Similarly, in his statements, his formal college education began in 1919 and was still continuing in 1938. Since he was neither very scholarly nor abnormally stupid, this was also not credible.

He claimed to have been attracted toward Trotskyism by Sylvia. That could only have been in 1938 or 1939. It was then, he said in his letter, that he met "youth of my age" in various leftist organizations. In Europe, a man of 34 or 35 does not consider himself a youth.

Actually, the prisoner had already revealed much. As later psychological tests would show, he had a strong tendency to tell much that was truthful about himself. Hence, his subsequent statements to the police often involved a minimum of invention. All that was needed to bring out the truth in many of his accounts was to substitute the NKVD for the Fourth International.

Mercader falsely alleged that Trotsky had ordered him to go to the Soviet Union to kill Stalin. Speaking to the police about this murder assignment, did he not have in mind the NKVD when he said:

"Trotsky was the destroyer of my being, of my future and of all my emotions. He changed me into a man without a name, without a country, into an instrument of Trotsky which stood in an alley with no way out. It was then that I thought of killing him and afterwards committing suicide."

This statement was made shortly after his arrest, at a time

when the prisoner was alternating between a manic state of incessant, compulsive talking, one might even say repetitious babbling, and a lethargic stupor in which he seemed unable to hold his head straight and in which his main desire was to bury himself in his bed covers. Again, speaking in this state of shock and anxiety, he told the police:

"For me that was total destruction. I was a man thrown into illegal life. I, who might well have died on the battlefield in France, found myself in a blind alley and I had no other remedy than to die against a wall with a bullet in my back and not as a patriot."

When this statement is analyzed, the question arises: How could Ramon have imagined that Trotsky prevented him from dying on the battlefield as a patriot? By his own "confession," he had been an "anti-militarist" as early as 1924. He had told Sylvia that he had been put under military arrest in 1938 for dodging Belgian army service. When his country mobilized against the Nazis, he had acquired a false passport and fled to the United States to avoid fighting for it. Or at least so he claimed.

Yet was he actually opposed to war? Everything known about his character seemed to point in the opposite direction—to a man of action, a risk taker, an adventurer, a man who placed a very high valuation on the soldierly qualities of audacity and discipline.

"For me that was total destruction. I was a man thrown into illegal life." This statement, blurted out under great psychic stress, was entirely plausible if the accusation was directed, not against Trotsky, but against the NKVD. As the police soon discovered, the prisoner was intelligent, had the manner of a gentleman, and it was reasonable to suppose that he dreamed of occupying some day a recognized niche in society. But once his NKVD superiors had ordered him to undertake the murder of Trotsky, he had necessarily become a man without a name, without a family, without a past, without a country. He was now identifiable only as a symbol of betrayal on a vast scale: both political betrayal and betrayal of his mistress. Was it unreasonable to characterize this transformation as "total destruction"?

There was more: "I had no other remedy than to die against a wall with a bullet in my back, and not as a patriot." Again, this accusation, nominally directed against Trotsky, was actually a revelation of the lot and experience of men in the service of the NKVD. "To die against a wall with a bullet in my back." How so? As a deserter from the Belgian Army, he might have been shot by a firing squad, but he would have died facing it. The method of death envisaged pointed to one, and only one, political system, for the NKVD routine is to execute traitors, defectors and other victims by shooting. The bullet is fired into the back of the neck, severing the spinal cord and causing instant death.

What the prisoner was doing in this strange, inverted emotionally charged "confession" was to seek to mitigate and explain his personal betrayal by hinting at something that he could not directly reveal. Once he had been set on his course of murder, he had moved down a blind alley, without choice, his identity destroyed, knowing that defection on his part would be punished by execution at the hands of his superiors.

Thus, within a week of the crime, the prisoner had dropped certain important clues to his identity which seemed superficially to have been the result of carelessness, but which could be attributed to the unconscious surging through barriers of self-control and calculated deceit imposed by his superego. Moreover, it appeared that under the ideological carapace of a communist zealot there cropped out a deeply-felt resentment at having been manipulated and destroyed by his Soviet superiors.

Under excellent medical treatment and inoffensive if not considerate handling by the police, the assassin quickly drew back into his shell. At first Colonel Salazar had urged him to make a clean breast of it, and tell the whole truth about himself and his backers. But that was all in vain. Finally, Salazar had brought up Sylvia and raised the question as to what she would think of his deed.

"I am completely sure that for Sylvia it would be better if I were dead than alive," he answered. "I begged Trotsky's secretaries on that day to kill me, but they didn't wish to. I wanted to die. . . ."

But this was a momentary lapse. Salazar then arranged a confrontation of the couple. Unsuspecting, the bandaged prisoner, supported under the arms by two policemen, was brought into the room where Sylvia was lying in bed, sobbing.

"Colonel, what have you done? Take me out of here!" the surprised Ramon began to cry, as he tried to break loose and leave.

"Take that murderer away! Kill him! Kill him!" Sylvia screamed hysterically at the sight of her lover.

Colonel Salazar endeavored to calm her, and urge her to talk to her "husband" for the sake of getting at the truth.

"A thousand times no!" she cried. "He is a hypocrite and assassin! I want to see him killed the way Trotsky died. He is a *canaille*."

"Colonel, colonel, why did you bring me here?" Ramon pleaded.

Salazar asked Sylvia if it was true that her "husband" had become disillusioned in Trotsky. "Rubbish!" she exclaimed and turned upon Ramon: "Don't lie, traitor! Tell the truth even if you pay with your life!"

When questioned about Ramon's story that he had received $5,000 from his mother and had left $3,000 with her for safekeeping, Sylvia insisted that the money must have come from the GPU, but admitted it was true that he had entrusted her with $3,000.

"Were you sure of his affection?" she was asked.

"I was sure of it. But when he killed Trotsky I saw that he had been deceiving me."

On all other points of Ramon's "confession," Sylvia had the same response: "Lies! Lies! He's a liar! A *canaille*!"

Salazar used all his powers of persuasion on the prisoner without any effect. He appealed to him to think of Sylvia who might become the chief witness against him, but he remained unmoved. Salazar then changed his tone. "Up to now we have treated you with every consideration," he warned. "It will be very disagreeable for us to have to change our methods."

"I have understood you perfectly," Ramon replied without batting an eye. "Oh, I am greatly distressed that you do not wish to believe me, but, truthfully, I have no other motive than that outlined in my letter. I have much respect for justice and have no desire to deceive you. My 'act,' not my crime, is serious indeed and I am ready to suffer the consequences whatever they may be. . . ."

The prisoner insisted, however, that he would continue to reiterate the explanation given in his letter, adding: "Even if you should cut the skin off me centimeter by centimeter."

Having killed the Old Man, Trotsky, the symbol of his father whom he had disowned and hated, the assassin nevertheless could not entirely suppress within him a sense of remorse or anxiety. He subconsciously betrayed it in a dream, real or concocted, which he submitted in writing in the course of his subsequent psychological tests. The internal evidence of this little composition points to its being the record of a true and unforgettable dream which may have occurred before the crime. Translated from the French, it reads as follows:

"There was a funnel in the shape of a cone. Formidable,

enormous, like Popocatepetl; very brilliant as though it were made of chrome steel. It had great resonance, it amplified sound. I was standing on top of the cone, the wide base of which pointed upward and below there was my friend, the pharmacist. I was circling around, on top. My friend said to me: 'Throw yourself down, I have chloroform.'

"And then waves of color appeared. Behind me there was an old man, could it be a doctor? The old man said: 'No, there is no chloroform.' I was worried because I thought my eardrums would burst.

"It was like that all night. I woke very tired, like someone who had been beaten."

Now there are those who would interpret this dream in the obvious and now standardized sexual terms. Yet the profound anxiety in the midst of a dangerous situation which it reflects, together with certain otherwise baffling features, indicate its real significance. The dream mirrors the ideological conflict in the assassin's mind on the eve of his great leap.

The formidable steel cone suggests the pyramid of power built by Stalin—the man of steel. And its amplified resonance stands for its enormous appeal to the masses of the world.

Standing on its inverted base shows the dreamer's uneasy life in the environment of the Opposition to Stalin's Comintern—the Trotskyite Fourth International. And his aimless circling around may very well represent his inner floundering between the Stalin and Trotsky brands of communism.

The pharmacist could be Eitingon who invites him to take the jump in the assurance that the chloroform of forgetfulness and a new life represented by the waves of color awaited him below.

But then the Old Man, Trotsky, appears and warns him: "No, there is no chloroform." And all night long, "like someone who had been beaten," anxiety pervades his entire being, foreboding a future filled with unrelieved fear.

8

Prisoner against Psychologist

On September 3, 1940, Raoul Carranca y Trujillo, the examining magistrate in the case against "Jacques Mornard" and Sylvia Ageloff, appointed two psychologists, who were also specialists in criminology, to make a study of the assassin. One was Dr. Jose Gomez Robleda, the head of the Department of Social Medicine at the National University of Mexico. The other expert was Alfonso Quiroz Cuaron, Professor of Criminology in the School of Law and Social Sciences at the University of Mexico and Director of the Mexican Reformatory for Boys at Tlalpan. Dr. Quiroz became more deeply engrossed in the case than his senior colleague, and has continued throughout the years to study and inquire into the unsolved aspects of the singular crime and of the character of its perpetrator.

The psychologists functioned as officers of the court. Their examination of the prisoner was an integral part of the Mexican judicial process, separate from police or other legal investigations, and chiefly as an aid to the judge in his decision as to sentence and place of confinement. This investigation was nontherapeutic; it involved no confidential relationship of doctor and patient; it was virtually unlimited in its scope.

In the case of the Trotsky murder, the judiciary was faced with mounting public pressure for an early trial. President Cardenas and his government were outraged by the fact that Trotsky had been killed while under the protection of the state as a political refugee. The fact that a foreigner had come to Mexico to kill an internationally known revolutionary who enjoyed the right of asylum seemed to the Mexican public particularly reprehensible. There were demands of swift justice for the assassin.

In spite of this public demand, Judge Trujillo insisted that ample time be allowed for an adequate psycho-social study of the prisoner. The two criminologists spent six hours a day, six days a week for the next six months—a total of 972 hours—with the inmate. They were given every possible help by the prison authorities, the police, other law enforcement officers and various medical specialists. In addition, the two professors used their students for the leg-work aspects of the investigation. The completed report, including the conclusions of the psychologists, was submitted to the court as an "Organic-Functional and Social Study of the Assassin of Leon Trotsky." It is 1,359 pages long, and formed slightly more than half of the entire court record of the case.

The examiners were tireless and unusually diligent in their work. They gave literally dozens of physical and mental tests, checked and rechecked them, and incorporated both the test material itself and their interpretations of it in the report to the court. No psychological study of comparable magnitude has ever been made of a political assassin.

Ramon was in an infirmary cell in the Green Cross Hospital when the two experts appointed by the court first went to see him. The prisoner was recovering from the severe beating at the hands of Trotsky's guards. He had already been interrogated by the three separate police organizations concerned with the crime and was negative in the extreme toward any new group of interrogators. Gomez Robleda and Quiroz explained their plans and the authority given them by the court. They stated that they were interested exclusively in the technical and psychological aspects of the case and that they had no concern with its political implications. They explained that they were impartial experts appointed by the court and that their function was not to assist the police in gathering evidence or to entrap the prisoner.

The prisoner was evidently unconvinced by this and stated flatly:

"You are not going to get anything out of me."

If his lawyer showed him the Mexican statute defining the scope of the psycho-social study, Ramon had every reason for his attitude of suspicion and mistrust. The court was directed to take into consideration the background, social milieu, education, upbringing and motives of the offender. This broad area obviously included piercing his identity, exposing his intricate and almost life-long relationship to the NKVD and revealing that he had been motivated by implicit and total obedience to the Soviet state. While the psychologists were, as they stated, independent, the scope of their investigation coincided with the main problems the police were attempting to solve. It was impossible for Ramon Mercader to cooperate wholeheartedly without giving away precisely those secrets that he was pledged to keep.

At the same time, he was in the unenviable situation of a man formally charged with murder and awaiting trial and sentence. He had no way of knowing how long he might have to wait before trial. At the time, Mexico had on the books a law providing the death penalty for homicide under exceptionally atrocious conditions, and it was possible that the trial judge might view the Trotsky assassination in this light.

Considering the matter, therefore, the prisoner realized that it was to his interest to cooperate with the psychologists at least as far as possible without revealing those secrets he was determined to keep. A favorable report might reduce his punishment. Like the vast majority of prisoners in similar situations, he was on his best behavior with Gomez Robleda and Quiroz; he showed the more attractive side of his personality, was patient, courteous and even managed to curb his quick and violent temper.

There was also the matter of Sylvia Ageloff. She had been arrested and was being held as his accomplice. However impersonal his original attitude toward her may have been, he had lived with her, with many interruptions, for over two years. He had deceived her profoundly and his sense of guilt toward her (which was nonexistent toward Trotsky) manifested itself during his interrogation. He stated on numerous occasions that she was completely innocent, but his protests and his obvious fear that she would be mistreated and unjustly convicted merely convinced the police that Sylvia was his accomplice. He was afraid she would turn state's evidence and as a witness incriminate him further. A man of enormous self-control and determination, he wept openly and buried his head in the pillow on his cot when newspapermen had told him that Sylvia was having a severe nervous breakdown. His concern about Sylvia was evidently one of the considerations that made him decide to cooperate with the psychologists.

Moreover, Ramon was lonely. A gregarious person, he enjoyed talk, liked an audience, was a good raconteur and was confident of his ability to dominate or deceive the psychologists. They would provide relief from the solitude and restrictions of prison confinement with their interest in his personality, and that was a topic which he found absorbing.

The prisoner decided to answer most questions freely. He treated the interviews and tests as a battle of the mind in which he set for himself a number of tasks: to elaborate a consistent false autobiography; to prevent the psychologists from finding out who he really was; to conceal his NKVD connections, and to convince them that Sylvia Ageloff was not implicated. He was slowly emerging from the stupor, the anxiety neurosis and preoccupation with pain which had characterized his condition after his arrest. He threw himself enthusiastically into the running encounters with his examiners.

The psychologists began with physical measurements, a complete medical examination and the various laboratory tests that went with it. They took encephalograms, tests of skill, coordination and dexterity. Then they proceeded to various examinations bearing on his intelligence, memory and reasoning ability. Simultaneously, they started a series of interviews which dealt with his childhood, family recollections, early schooling, adolescence and awakening interest in sex.

If there is an ordained psychiatric pattern to a magnicide, the childhood and youth of Ramon Mercader as they appear in his own self-revelations, recorded in the medical reports, provide a classical model of it. Perhaps the decisive experience in his infancy was an acute infantile trauma. There can be no doubt that Ramon was a very sick baby. His mother was unable or perhaps unwilling to breast-feed him and fourteen wet nurses were tried, but without any success. He believed that he was finally kept alive by being given minced horsemeat mixed with cognac.

At the time of his birth, more than half of all deaths of children in Spain in the first year of life were caused by a baffling disease known as marasmus. The name derives from the Greek and means "wasting away." Marasmus is the result of depriving the infant of his natural relationship with his mother, or with some mother substitute.

Ramon's other statements about his early childhood, derived no doubt from family reminiscences, included the item that he had had an umbilical hernia which eventually cured itself, that he had suffered from anemia and that he was extremely weak, frail and thin. All of this again suggests marasmus. For that matter, the fact that he was able to take horsemeat doused in brandy indicates that his constitution was organically strong and that his troubles were probably psychosomatic.

When he was finally able to eat regularly, Ramon was given physical therapy to strengthen his abdominal muscles, but he remained small for his age until adolescence. He told the examining psychologists that he began to walk and to talk at a very early age. He said that relatives told him that even as a very small boy he was proud and taciturn. He liked to try out his accomplishments in private before showing them to the family, as he was unwilling to fail at anything in public.

As a boy, he was willful. Although smaller than his schoolmates, he got into incessant fights with them. He was particularly concerned with proving his bravery and never hesitated to fight boys much bigger than he was. He believed that he was something of a child prodigy, but in school he was not studious and relied on his native intelligence to get good marks. In spite of his neglect of his school work, he did well.

He had learned French, he lied to Dr. Alberto Lozano Garza, the examining physician, because it was spoken in his home and had learned English in a kindergarten run by Englishwomen. He had gone to primary school, then to military school, he claimed once.

The medical report of Dr. Garza showed that as a child Ramon had suffered from stomach swellings and congenital phimosis, which was however not sufficiently troublesome to require an operation until the age of 21 when he had it corrected by circumcision. It also disclosed that he had masturbated as a child, but that it had never been a problem for him later.

The physical examination revealed a number of scars on Ramon which marked him as an accident-prone personality, and were consistent with his explanations of their origin. There was a large, deep scar far back on the tongue which he said he had received while climbing a tree; two scars on the upper lip which he claimed were the result of being hit by a stone and the recoil of a rifle. Scars on his scrotum he attributed to medical treatment for a kick received during a football game. He claimed that the scar on his right forearm had been caused by a fencing wound (actually, he had received it during combat on the Aragon front). His other scars were finger wounds, inflicted by a dog bite when he was a child and by Trotsky during the latter's death struggle.

In addition to the visible scars, there were reminiscences of acts of self-injury. Once, while playing a game, he made a bad play and kicked himself so hard that he injured his knee. He recollected that, when he was a soldier, he had had a disagreement with a subordinate and had taken out his anger by kicking the ground and severely injuring his ankle. Again, he had a disagreeable encounter with a superior officer. Finding this man's impertinence almost unbearable, he went away and "took the anger out" on himself. This practice of kicking and wounding himself when angry with others is similar to the behavior of three-year-olds who are frustrated in their attempts to express their rage by kicking or otherwise injuring the omnipotent adults who restrain them, and therefore indulge in temper tantrums in which they scream and kick the floor. The difference is, of course, that the toddler is restrained from harming adults by physical impotence; the self-punishing adult—by his superego and sense of guilt.

In the mass of material concerning Ramon's childhood and

in his reminiscences of later life, the consistent pattern of self-punishment followed situations in which he was treated with a severity that he had considered excessive and unjust.

Ramon told the psychologists that the Jesuits who ran the school to which he was sent as a child (which contradicted his statement to Dr. Garza that he had attended a military school) were extremely strict and punished him constantly for the slightest infraction. He felt they were unjust and hated them. He added that he became one of the worst and most unruly pupils in the school. He said that he had been sent to the Jesuit school against his will by his father. Yet, when his knowledge of Catholicism was tested, he failed to give the correct answers.

Ramon remembered his paternal grandmother as a devout, austere and physically healthy person. He spoke fondly of his father's father, describing him as a tall, strong man with a sweet disposition who liked to humor his grandchildren. The old gentleman would pretend to go to sleep and let the children draw pictures on his bald head. Ramon remembered doing this on a number of occasions, and recalled that Grandpa also used to hide gold coins in his pockets and let the children climb over him to search for them.

Another game Ramon remembered playing as a child was driving nails into the floor. He was allowed to do this in the nursery and he recalled it with great pleasure. Drs. Quiroz and Gomez Robleda have suggested that the nail-driving and drawing of pictures on the grandfather's skull were expressions of Oedipal hostility toward Ramon's father. In these two operations, they saw the assassination of Trotsky as the re-enactment of a murder which the child had already committed symbolically.

Ramon spoke of his father with undisguised dislike. He once remarked that his father was always preoccupied with cleanliness and that he carried his fear of disease to such extreme lengths that he always had his vegetables washed in potassium permanganate before they were cooked. On another occasion he referred to his father as "a bourgeois sure of the interests of his class."

Yet, despite this undisguised attitude of hatred and contempt for Pablo Mercader, there were some respects in which the son followed in his footsteps. The prisoner was also extremely clean. Although he referred with contempt to the business of washing vegetables to avoid contamination, Ramon himself reacted in a somewhat similar way. When he was placed in a dark and dirty cell in the penitentiary, one of the first things he did was to buy whitewash and hire a fellow prisoner to help him clean and paint the cell. He was equally concerned with bodily cleanliness. Although there was only cold water available in the prison, he requested permission to shower daily. Similarly, when he was taken to a private clinic for tests, he asked to take a hot bath. In prison, he shaved every day, was scrupulously clean and dressed neatly and somewhat formally. Like Pablo Mercader, his allegedly dead father, he was something of a food faddist.

Ramon's unbounded admiration for his mother was evident in all of the examinations. He depicted her as a strong, active and fearless person. He said she had gone to a Catholic college, where she had studied sculpture, silver-working and other "feminine things." She was a happy, cheerful person, agreeable in society, very direct in her manner toward other people and with a great interest in strenuous sports. At home, she treated the servants with great kindness and, when the children were small, cared for them with affection. It is evident from another incident that this affection was accompanied by discipline. Ramon recalled that she would tell him in advance what punishments would be inflicted for various offenses. He accepted these punishments and characterized her as a just person.

In a brief statement which he prepared for the psychologists in answer to the "Question of Punishments," Ramon completely absolves his mother of any fault:

"When I was small, I never refused a punishment if it was just, but I rebelled if it was unjust," he wrote. "For example, once when my mother scolded me for having eaten some apples, she told me that next time I would be punished and that she would stand me facing the wall. One day when she was not at home I ate some apples and then put myself facing the wall. When my mother arrived, she found me standing there."

The active sports his mother had enjoyed, Ramon recollected, included horseback riding, swimming and hunting. She was habitually reckless and had a number of accidents, of which the most serious were an automobile smash-up and several falls from horses. In the course of years, she commenced to develop a spirit of rebellion against the social conventions; she turned to reading Voltaire; she broke off some of her friendships with people in the family milieu whom she considered stuffy; she began to be regarded as eccentric by her husband's friends and relatives.

Ramon's admiration for his mother was revealed by the fact that he habitually presented her as almost exactly similar to himself. The point at which the degree of self-identification with his mother became apparent was when the prisoner was asked to describe her, having already been asked to do the same for himself on a previous and entirely unrelated occasion.

He saw his mother as "tall, slender, green-eyed, muscular, ample hair, light olive complexion, physically agile, interested in sports, interested in revolutionary reading, has had lots of accidents, has arteriosclerosis, is jovial and cheerful, was educated as a Catholic, is amiable and considerate to the servant class, dislikes aristocrats."

The description of himself was, with a very few exceptions, identical with this characterization of his mother. Thus he characterized his mother as being reckless and interested in sports, and revealed himself as courting danger in such sports as mountain climbing, fast driving, boat racing, flying, and hammer and javelin throwing. He stated that his mother was interested in revolutionary reading and, in speaking of himself, said more specifically that he read Marx and Lenin. She was amiable to servants; he loved the working class. She disliked aristocrats; he hated aristocrats and capitalists. She had unusual arteries which made it impossible to control her high blood pressure by medication; he described himself as sclerotic.

This last identification was particularly interesting since it was clearly a product of the prisoner's imagination. The physical examination showed that his heart was strong and steady and his blood pressure normal. There was no evidence of arteriosclerosis. The prisoner claimed that he had become "sclerotic" because he had once been given an injection of calcium chloride. Even if this injection had been administered, it would not have had the effect he imagined. Patently, Ramon identified himself completely with his mother, even inventing non-existent similarities.

On the subject of the assassination, he assured the medical examiner that he had not believed that he had killed Trotsky since the latter stood up after the attack, fought back and had then gone into the other room; that he had not realized that he had been successful in his attack until much later when he was told that Trotsky was dead. In describing this scene and the beating he got from the guards, the assassin's face grew red, he broke into a sweat, his fingers and lips trembled uncontrollably.

"There is nothing of major importance wrong with him," concluded Dr. Garza in his medical report on the prisoner. "He smokes very heavily, he is a regular drinker, but says that he has never in his life been drunk; that he has always satisfied his sexual appetites, which were never excessive, whenever the occasion offered."

While Ramon was careful to be polite to the two examining psychologists, his true attitude of amused contempt occasionally broke through the veneer. He told anecdotes about couples which he would palpably invent for the benefit of his interrogators. These couples were usually men and, in every instance, they did or said something incredibly stupid.

As a communist, Ramon had no use for Freud and, as a matter of fact, knew nothing about his theories. In the course of the discussions with the psychologists, his contempt for them visibly increased. He told a great deal of truth about himself, almost as an open expression of his sense of intellectual superiority, taking care, however, to lie about those particular aspects of his life which bore directly on his false statements to the police.

It must have come as a shock to the prisoner to learn the findings of the examiners when their report was submitted as part of the trial docket. The accusation of weakness and latent homosexuality was a blow at his manhood. The most bitter part of the matter was his subsequent discovery that the judge relied on the psychologists' study in fixing the length of the prisoner's sentence.

This study is of extraordinary value because of the massive data it contains; as for the authors' conclusions, there is room for controversy. The examinations began only two weeks after the murder when the direct emotional impact of the crime on the mind of the assassin was still fresh. The industrious examiners collected mountains of interview material and test results. Hence, judicious selection of these data does without question reveal the character structure and motivational patterns of the killer. Much is still hidden in the Moscow archives about the training of Ramon for the Trotsky assassination. But the character of the man, both on the conscious and unconscious level, is laid bare by his own statements. In this sense, we perhaps know more about the psychological drives and personality of Ramon than of any other magnicide in history.

Ramon was five feet ten inches tall, with a slender, light-boned body. His shoulders were broad and slightly stooped, his arms long in proportion. His hands and feet were attenuated and slender. His hair was abundant and curly, his eyes large, green and myopic. The prisoner was astigmatic and generally wore glasses. His nose was narrow and straight, his teeth strong and regular, the mouth wide, the brows heavily marked, the forehead broad, high and deeply furrowed. Dr. Quiroz observed in his report that Ramon's skin was "a light olive over his entire body which is extremely even in tone and without variation on any part of his body."

At the time of arrest, Ramon's body had the slightness of a very young man. The psychologists noted the lack of body hair and the youthful pattern of the prisoner's beard. They observed that he was left-handed and stressed in their report as abnormal these three factors—body structure, hair distribution and left-handedness.

The encephalograms showed no physical abnormalities of the brain, but the frequency of the brain waves was somewhat more rapid than average. The heart was strong with a regular beat, the pulse slow and steady. The assassin's metabolism was normal and no glandular disturbances were indicated.

Without glasses, Ramon was myopic and astigmatic. With glasses, he could not only see accurately and observe with precision, but could detect by eye variations in level as slight as three-tenths of a millimeter. His taste and sense of smell were normal, though smoking had apparently reduced his sensitivity to unpleasant odors. His physical strength was not unusual, but was that of a man in good training and wiry by nature.

Tests of skin sensitivity yielded unexpected results. Ramon's skin was hypersensitive over his entire body, particularly in the areas of tongue, head, arms, hands, fingers and feet. This extreme sensitivity to pain made his willingness to submit to very painful tests, imposed by the psychologists, remarkable.

The psychologists noticed that Ramon did not seem to hear well and they were therefore particularly careful in checking his hearing. He had complained of pains in the ears and, since he had been beaten about the head by Trotsky's guards, there was good reason to suspect physical injury. However, no such impairment or abnormality was revealed. Moreover, tests of his hearing showed that he could recognize differences of a tenth of a tone. Yet he affected deafness on occasion.

The prisoner soon emerged from the protective cocoon of stupor into which he had fallen at the time of his arrest. He no longer sought refuge by remaining in bed and covering his head with the sheets as he had done during the first month of his imprisonment. Nevertheless, he continued to insulate himself from the condemnatory outside world by not hearing.

The tests continued. Ramon's sense of time was found to be unusually accurate. The psychologists also discovered that he could walk a chalk line blindfolded for six yards without any change in direction. His reaction time was unusually swift. His perceptions were accurate and detailed. When tested for manual sensitivity, he could, while blindfolded, detect differences in level in objects over which he passed his hands of less than three hundredths of a millimeter. This is the range of sensitivity of a highly skilled watchmaker. In view of this surprising discovery, the prisoner was given a series of metal engravings only one centimeter square to identify. He was able to draw all major shapes while blindfolded. He identified one object by name as a hammer. In the other cases, he drew the outlines and surfaces of that which he had discerned by touch in the form of mirror images. Awareness and recognition of form to this extent is most unusual.

Memory tests related to his past life yielded meaningless results since Ramon was bound by his false autobiography. His memory for objects in photographs which were shown him was unusually accurate, detailed and complete. Nor was he easily misled by questions designed to confuse him. In a series of such photographic tests, he was trapped into giving false responses only once or twice. This served to confirm a more general picture of the assassin as a person with great confidence in his judgments who was not easily swayed by the suggestions of others.

His ability to memorize was also tested. He learned and remembered accurately whole series of numbers, nonsense syllables and words in foreign languages. He was told to decipher a code message but failed. However, he grasped the theory of the code very quickly, devised a code for himself and proceeded to write a message for his examiners in his own cipher. He gave them the key and then deciphered the message for them.

He was given wooden puzzles to solve. These were of the Japanese type, very intricate, consisting of pieces of wood which had to be fitted together in a precise fashion in order to make the puzzle whole again. The method followed was to allow Mercader to examine the puzzle and then take it apart. It was then removed. On the following day, the pieces were brought to him and he was asked to reassemble it blindfolded. On one of these tests, known as the devil's cross, he performed the blindfold assembly in seven seconds. The most complicated of the puzzles consisted of 24 pieces with 348 facets when assembled. The prisoner was allowed to study this for three days. He then reassembled it blindfolded in the presence of the examiners in ten minutes and 20 seconds.

Interestingly enough, the only test of this sort which he fumbled consisted of a large sphere, about the size of a human head. Ramon's extraordinary awkwardness in handling this object was attributed by the psychologists to traumatic association with his crime in killing Trotsky by a blow on the head.

While these tests were being administered, the psychologists were examining the prisoner's behavior closely. He seemed to be always restless and in motion. Since his limbs were long and slender and his physical movements active and agile, his gestures seemed to have a theatrical, exaggerated quality. When angry, he repressed all motion except for the trembling of his finger-tips. The lines of his face deepened; the eyes became fixed and staring, penetrating and very brilliant; the lips were pressed closely together and the nostrils would flare. The sudden access of anger was accompanied by involuntary trembling and extreme pallor. When profoundly disturbed by questioning in any area which Mercader felt very dangerous to him, he would fumble with his cigarette, burn his fingers, drop ashes or sparks on his clothing or papers. This state of anxiety was accompanied by a tendency to compulsive talking so that the words seemed to pour from his mouth without volition, there was frequent repetition of phrases and often the sense was lost. Ramon would put an end to this reaction by a strong effort of will accompanied by some distracting move such as brushing off ashes or stamping out a small fire caused by his cigarette.

The pattern of anger was shown to a lesser extent when the prisoner was preoccupied or withdrawn. This was apparent in prison and had been observed previously by a number of members of the Trotsky household. When preoccupied, he would tend to fumble with his coat or anything that he held in his hand; he seemed almost unaware that he was being spoken to; he would emerge from his unresponsive state only with great effort and without remembering what he had just said.

In spite of his growing antagonism to the examiners, he poured out to them purported reminiscences of his childhood and youth; talked about his interest in sports and physical activity, revealed his political beliefs, discussed his sexual attitudes and experiences. He did card tricks for the psychologists. When he was cheerful, he sang revolutionary songs. Once, when the psychologists were recording his voice, he performed an impromptu satire, a comic pantomime in which he played all the parts, changing his voice and manner as he shifted from one character to another.

In addition to the play-acting involved in his efforts to maintain his false autobiography, Ramon gave other evidences of his interest in deception. To perpetuate the fiction that he was the Belgian, Jacques Mornard, he insisted on speaking French with the examining psychologists and police, but didn't bother with the other prisoners. He persisted in his claim that he was a newspaperman though he couldn't write a story, dictate either to a stenographer or a dictaphone, or answer simple questions about how a newspaper is put together and printed.

The subject of art came up only twice. He commented on the beauty of a pre-Cortesian mask which had been unearthed by archaeologists in Mexico and reproduced in the newspapers. He also discussed a painting by Frida Kahlo, the wife of Diego Rivera. Mercader was fond of this particular painting. It was of psychological interest because it represented a dual personality. It is called *The Two Fridas* and shows the artist as two women seated side by side on a bench with hands clasped. Superimposed on the breasts of both women are anatomical drawings of the human heart. These hearts are linked by blood vessels which wind between the two figures, and blood drips slowly from the end of a vein which is held by a doctor's clamp. The choice of this portrait for discussion was both part of the prisoner's tactic of taunting and mocking his examiners and a genuine expression of his preoccupation with the split personality.

The prisoner throughout was prepared to give his examiners any information they wished which did not endanger him or his Soviet superiors. He was interested in the tests and in the apparatus used. He was anxious to prove his ability to perform any task or succeed in any test set before him. Yet his respect for the two psychologists was evidently slight. This was revealed particularly by the anecdotes concerning the two stupid yokels, who invariably did things inadequately and came to a bad end, with which he would greet the criminologists each morning. Having discharged this small accumulation of hostility, Ramon would be more at ease in continuing the tests. He was in fact reluctant to lose his audience and often thought up stories or bits of information with which to detain them when they were about to leave. On one occasion, he remarked ironically: "Don't leave. This is your home."

Ramon talked freely about his activities as a sportsman. He told stories of mountain climbing in the Alps and the Pyrenees. He spoke of his interest in old sports cars and racing, and said that in Paris he had been a member of a club of owners of antique cars. He claimed to be skilled at javelin and hammer throwing. He spoke of sailing small craft out of French harbors and wondered wistfully what had happened to his own sailboat. He reminisced of happier days when he had taken part in a regatta.

In order to find out whether or not he had really been a mountain climber, a soldier and a newspaperman, as he alleged, the psychologists asked him to prepare questionnaires on these three subjects. He did so and his efforts were shown to experts who concluded that he knew very little about journalism or the military profession, but that he was an expert alpinist.

The psychological and physiological tests had revealed several things. The NKVD obviously had chosen its man wisely and well, for he combined a very large number of aptitudes that could be turned to espionage and murder. He was fluent in several languages, he could pass for a gentleman anywhere, he was attractive to women and could be ingratiating to men when he chose. He was a skilled athlete. His reaction time was fast; he had a photographic memory; he could follow a chosen path in the dark; he could detect the slightest sound; he could learn highly complicated instructions quickly and recall them accurately; he could recognize complex objects by touch in the dark, take them apart and put them together again. His nerves were steady, his health was reasonably good, his self-control was almost perfect. He had a gift for acting and enjoyed deceit.

It is true that he was caught and that the actual murder was a bungled job, as far as his escape was concerned. But he was more than a person trained to commit the perfect murder. He had the ability to follow the long road which led through seduction of Sylvia Ageloff to acceptance by the Trotsky household and to the creation of a situation enabling him to deal with his victim alone in the privacy of his study.

The men who had selected him for the perilous assignment made a highly astute choice in another respect. For though the prisoner unwittingly did reveal many things about himself, he never directly betrayed either the NKVD which he served or those who helped him in his crime. And he has persisted in remaining behind the façade of "Jacques Mornard."

9

Portrait of an Assassin

During the first month of his imprisonment, Ramon Mercader spent almost all of his time in bed. He had collapsed after the beating at the hands of Trotsky's guards. He collapsed again after the formal reenactment of the crime. His examiners, puzzled by the fact that he occasionally emerged from almost total unawareness of the surrounding world to an alert and defiant defense of his act, decided that he must be faking.

Even if there was an element of shamming in his behavior, it was clear that Ramon was going through a phase of massive repression. He spent almost the entire time in bed, often with his face down and the sheet pulled over his head. He wept when he was told that Sylvia Ageloff had also been made prisoner and that she was ill from shock. One of his examiners, impressed by this behavior, was led to philosophize about the bed:

"The bed has an ambivalent meaning; it represents life, death, pleasure and pain. One is born there and sleeps there. The bed of the prisoner, since he sleeps there, is a symbol of freedom; at night, when he goes to sleep, he achieves freedom. The prisoner spends much of his time in bed, he takes 'refuge' there."

And it was while he was there that his poor tolerance of pain was commented upon by all the newspapermen and hospital personnel who saw him shortly after his arrest. Though he had been severely beaten, the observers felt that the expression of profound suffering on his face was out of proportion to the physical injuries inflicted on him. He seemed unusually apprehensive of pain and shrank away each time his head wounds were to be dressed. A number of photographs taken at this time show him with a look of agony. Medical tests revealed that he actually was hypersensitive to touch of any kind in almost every part of his body, but particularly so on the head, arms, hands, fingers, feet and tongue.

At the moment of the attack, Trotsky succeeded in getting hold of the assassin's hand and biting his finger. On a number of occasions, Ramon referred to this bite with indignation. When he was arrested, his coat was covered with blood. The police took a small piece of the lapel for analysis. Weeks later, he showed the jacket to the psychologists and complained angrily that the police had destroyed his clothing.

This interest in his personal appearance was not a casual matter. The prisoner had come to Mexico on an assassination assignment. Yet he is known to have brought with him a large trunk and a number of suitcases filled with clothing. According to his own statements, he shipped a trunk to New York through the Wells Fargo agency around June 13, 1940, which contained: dinner clothes, two suits, a pair of riding breeches, a pair of slacks, hunting boots, spurs, two overcoats, three or four pairs of pajamas, a cane and a number of shirts.

Ramon informed the authorities that his other clothes were in Room 113 of the Hotel Montejo. The police went there and found one dozen shirts, four pairs of pajamas, two sweaters, bathing trunks, two silk scarves, two belts, four ties, nine pairs of underpants, two undershirts, 21 pairs of socks, gloves, a jacket, two pairs of drill slacks, a dozen handkerchiefs, a pair of brown and white shoes, a blue bathrobe, two hats.

This preoccupation with clothing continued while in prison. The examiners referred to him as dressing meticulously "with a studied, careless elegance." Photographs of him taken in his cell show him wearing a well-tailored suit, including the vest, and with a hat. In a test, where he was asked to define words, he wrote:

"Elegance is that quality which makes it possible for those who know how to do so to dress well, but it is very difficult to be elegant."

The fastidiousness in dress was patently related to a type of male whose sex pattern is altogether too familiar. It is the type that divorces or separates with ease, that is casual about extra-marital affairs, and which abounds in Don Juans. It is also noted for the care in avoiding venereal disease or causing pregnancy. Ramon's history disclosed frivolous sexual relationships with women. By his own statement, his sex life was "prophylactic." While he said that he wanted a son, he was in fact childless. Nor had he ever had a venereal infection.

When questioned insistently about his sexual attitudes, his answers showed superficiality and emotional dissociation. Thus, the sort of information that he volunteered was that he liked slim, Nordic women, that he had thought of Sylvia as a possible mother of his son. He gave no indications of currently unsatisfied sexual needs.

The prisoner described himself as irascible, impulsive, vengeful, excitable, rebellious and dominating, in a long questionnaire of self-appraisal. On another occasion, he made a great point of his alleged ability to control his emotions completely. While he showed remarkable self-possession and great powers of dissimulation, this was attained only at the cost of a tremendous exercise of will. His extreme pallor and the involuntary trembling of his fingertips when in a rage indicated the extent of the effort necessary. Even when simply in a preoccupied or daydreaming mood, Ramon seemed to withdraw beyond reach of human contact. He would emerge from these moods by an exercise of willpower and swiftly reassume his usual attitude of gentlemanly courtesy and detailed awareness of all that was going on around him.

In the course of their examination, the psychologists gave Ramon a Rorschach test which consists fundamentally of having the subject examine patterns made by ink blots on standardized cards and state what they look like. The data resulting from this test, regarded as one of the most valuable tools of diagnosis of personality, provided material for an outline of Ramon's character structure.

The picture that emerges is that of an intelligent and sensitive person, who has withdrawn emotionally from intense relationships. There is an element of laziness and passivity about him, due to his detached attitude. He gives the external impression of a rather well-adjusted, banal person who is ready to do the "accepted" thing at the risk of over-committing himself. He is shown to be fearful and self-destructive in his inner self. But to conceal from the world that self he builds a façade to protect himself from his own attitudes: he drives himself, he disciplines himself, he is compulsive, and he takes great risks.

The tests showed that Ramon had excellent coordination, very swift reaction time and the intelligence of a "superior adult." He displayed a marked interest in competitive sports, in gambling and in machinery. Actually, he was an enthusiastic sportsman. As for gambling, he spent much of his leisure time in prison playing cards or dominoes. In tests of mechanical aptitude, he exhibited great skill. For example, he was able to take a Mauser rifle apart in the dark and put it together again in three minutes and 46 seconds.

Found to belong to the type of person who makes up his mind quickly and definitely, Ramon told his examiners: "It is ridiculous for a man to spend his days thinking about what he is going to do. I do not do this. I like to act and to solve my difficulties while I am acting."

This self-analysis is borne out by the many specimens of the prisoner's handwriting. All of the writing tests were given in Spanish, but Ramon insisted on replying in French, as demanded by his false autobiography. Since the examiners were uncertain of their command of French, they arranged for all of Ramon's answers to be in writing, even the quick word-reaction tests. We therefore have specimens of the prisoner's handwriting in many different moods. They range from the violent, half-mad, manic-depressive to samples evidencing integrated and concentrated thought. But they nearly always show a man of great energy in a tremendous hurry, possessing little concern for form.

A few weeks after the examinations started, the prisoner evidently reached the conclusion that there was no point in hiding his real political views. He insisted that he had not committed an ordinary murder, but had performed "a political act" which history would justify. He said that he had done the working-class of the world an immense service by destroying one of its false leaders. He described himself as a soldier of the world revolution who had carried out an important political task. Soon he progressed from these generalities to the statement that he had studied Marx, Engels and Lenin. He added that his examiners would do well to read Lenin whom he characterized as "a true revolutionary genius" and an expert at clear exposition of complex ideas.

A series of tests were prepared by the examiners to determine whether or not Ramon was, as he claimed to be, a student of Marxism-Leninism. He was given a questionnaire based on a book by Friedrich Engels. His answers were sent for evaluation to an expert who concluded that they were those of "a person very well trained in these matters." The prisoner was asked his opinion of the test and replied:

"The questionnaire is well organized in its coverage of the development of the proletariat through time, but I believe that questions concerning the problems of the petit bourgeoisie should have been included and also the questionnaire completely omits the peasants and the intellectuals." He was also given 75 questions concerning dialectical materialism, obviously a much more difficult subject, taken from a standard book by Bukharin. On this test, Ramon's performance was only moderately good. His extreme competitiveness and desire to succeed at everything he attempted made him make wild guesses when he obviously did not know the right answers.

He claimed that he had studied social science, philosophy and anatomy himself by assiduous reading. He said he had learned enough about it to write a children's primer on anatomy (the physicians considered this presumptuous and untrue). He listed his reading as having consisted primarily of the following authors: Marx, Engels, Cruveilhier, J. J. Rousseau, Voltaire, Proudhon, Pascal, Lenin, Tolstoi, Gorki, Plekhanov, Kropotkin and Gogol. That he should have mentioned the relatively unknown Cruveilhier, an authority on pathological anatomy, among literary and political figures, was evidence that his statement about studying anatomy with the aid of various friendly surgeons in Paris was no idle play of his imagination.

So deeply had the clichés of communism been drilled into Ramon that many of his responses to word-association tests lacked spontaneity and failed to give deep insight into his personality structure. Whenever the stimulus word was one about which communists held strong views, his response was the stereotyped answer right out of the Kremlin's orthodox textbook.

His characteristic political reactions can be seen from his definitions of certain terms. He described the *GPU* as "a police organization like the Deuxiéme Bureau, Intelligence Service, etc."; *commerce* as "legal theft"; *wealth* as that which "will soon belong to the oppressed classes." *Prostitution* he defined as "one of the ulcers of capitalist society," *delinquency* as "one of the evils of social injustice," while *liberty* and *justice* were to him "expressions of social balance" (that is to say, ideological reflections of the class structure of society). *Religion* he branded as "the opium of the people" and *Jesuits* as "lackeys of the capitalist class." *Bukharin* was to him "a type of traitor caused by the death agonies of Russian capitalism." Since the word-association test was given during the period of the Nazi-Soviet pact, Ramon described Hitler as a "politically astute visionary," rather than with the old phrase of "a reactionary beast." But when he was given the word *Trotsky*, he did not reply with the expected cliché of counter-revolutionary or agent of Wall Street, but with an original description: "*a self-centered egotist.*"

The extent to which communism completely absorbed his life was also revealed by the songs which he sang in prison: the *Marseillaise* (which had become more popular than the *Internationale* since the Popular Front had been decreed); *La Carmagnole*, both in its original version and as sung in Spain during the civil war; and *The Young Guard* were his favorites. In the last of these, Ramon laid stress on the line: "We work for a great cause."

When asked for his opinion of the Russo-German war a few days after Hitler's attack, before the collapse of the Red armies, he said that Stalin had organized a great army and that the Russian people would follow him with love to the last drop of their blood. As for Mussolini, he characterized him as a mere buffoon. Churchill was to him an aristocrat who assumed leadership to profess principles in which he did not believe, because if he had, he would not have vacillated about taking the side of the Spanish Republic, instead of stating as he did that "all of Spain is not worth one drop of the blood of English seamen." It was the prisoner's opinion that these men should not dare to judge Stalin who was labelled by them a Russian imperialist because of Trotsky's intrigues abroad.

He showed great familiarity with anything relating to Spain, as in the remark on Churchill. He expressed the view that the defense of Madrid proved that powerful modern armies can be stopped by the valiant resistance of the people. But when asked about the military aspects of the Spanish civil war, he quickly retreated from the subject, saying that he knew almost nothing about it, having only been once in Santander when he went there on a short trip from Biarritz.

The examiners did not follow up on other indications of the apparent Spanish background of their subject. Having claimed that he had studied art, Ramon was asked by the psychologists to name some Renaissance painters. "Velasquez," the prisoner began, then became tongue-tied and visibly embarrassed. The only painter he could name was a Spaniard, even though he placed him a century too late.

Equally revealing was his remark, during another talk with the psychologists, about having seen a remarkable bullfight in which no less than nine bulls were killed and the toreadors and some of the spectators were dressed in costumes of the time of Goya. It is a fact that bullfights in costume had occurred in both Madrid and Barcelona in 1928—the centenary of the death of Francisco Goya. And Ramon had been employed as an attendant at the Goya Exposition that year, a fact which was, of course, missing from his false autobiography.

Then there was the occasion when he spotted a pattern made by water stains on the plastered ceiling of his cell. He remarked to some inmates who were present that it reminded him of the profile of Franco. "See, there is his big nose," he commented. And proceeded to trace the rest of Franco's features.

While he was not quizzed about his allusions to Spain, he was pressed to talk about repentance for his crime. He replied that he had nothing to repent or expiate personally. On the other hand, he admitted that the law required him to serve a prison term as punishment for the murder and stated that he would accept the decision of the court in his case as just. Nor did he make any protest at the legal requirement that he pay the widow, Natalia Trotsky, a cash indemnity.

When asked how he expected to rehabilitate himself, he replied that he was not in need of rehabilitation. He told his examiners that he was not concerned with plans for his future life. Once past the first shock of capture and imprisonment, he decided to behave in a manner calculated to win the approval of his fellow-convicts and of the prison authorities. This has been the unvaried and consistent pattern of his conduct throughout the nineteen years of his life in prison.

But not once during this long period has he evinced any interest in the fate of Sylvia Ageloff, the victim of his seduction. When the charges against her were dropped early in the proceedings and she was allowed to return to the United States, where she later married and made a new start in life, she passed out of his existence without leaving the slightest psychological scar on his inner being.

The prisoner showed his scorn, as time went on, for his examiners' inability to pierce his mask. Once he dropped the remark: "Psychologists as a rule cannot see further than the points of their own noses." This was characteristic of the cocksure trained communist who felt in those days perhaps more than now that the Western mind is not instructed in the psychology and mentality of the Stalinist school. The Mexican authorities of the period were not unique in their lack of equipment to gauge a professional communist operative like Ramon. Their American intellectual peers let the documentary disclosures by Whittaker Chambers of the Alger Hiss spy ring gather dust in the Washington files at that very time. And six years later the alert editors of the leading newspaper in the capital of Canada would not even look at his world-shaking secret documents nor listen to the desperate pleas of Igor Gouzenko, the Soviet code clerk, when he was in imminent danger of being kidnaped by Stalin's gunmen in Ottawa.

Ramon's attitude of superiority, however, inevitably led him into traps. He betrayed himself and his Moscow training—for the record at least—on several occasions. Such an occasion was the time when he described for the psychologists one of his memorable dreams. Penned by the prisoner in his own hand, it purported to be the story of a dream in which he had gone sailing in a regatta held, of all places, at Royan.

Now Royan was the hideout of Trotsky in France when he arrived there from Turkey in 1933. Royan then became the object of intensive espionage by Stalin's agents and the subject of numerous reports to headquarters in Moscow. By the selection of Royan as the locale of his dream, the assassin showed a great familiarity with the history of Trotsky's life and activities in exile, a familiarity that may very well have come from his briefing days in Moscow under Eitingon's tutelage. Such a briefing includes a thorough perusal of the confidential files in the NKVD archives, in this case, the files on Trotsky.

In addition, the very contents of the dream betrayed Ramon's obsession with the image of Trotsky, if the story is not interpreted according to the usual sexual lexicon of psychoanalysis. Here is the text, translated from the French:

"At the harbor exit of Royan, we were on a two-motored Diesel outboard boat that was very racy. After we had passed the sand bar, I don't know why, we were on board a 15-meter sailboat with a very high sail, two jibs and a wooden rudder. In the stern as well as in the bow, there were respectively two and three other men. During my dream they were people who were known to me, but I cannot remember having been able to give a name to them. And I cannot now identify them. We returned to the race at a place which vaguely reminds me of the roadstead of Cannes or Villefranche. The race was taking place between several other sailboats and also the outboard. This last was not able to pass us because the buoys were so close to the edge of the deck that they did not leave enough free space when we were tacking and listing—and listing, the mast almost touched the water and prevented him from cutting in close to us. We made some tacks in which we listed so far that the large sail touched the water. During one of these tacks, we saw a boat which had sunk and the men were swimming. We had tacked so sharply that we had almost touched bottom and when the boat tipped the keel was in the air. To our great astonishment, it regained its normal position. The race had disappeared and we were sailing in a circle, the men who were swimming did not wish to come on board . . ."

Allowing for the fact that the author of the story of the dream was at the same time a virtuoso actor in a grand masquerade, it still does not matter whether the dream had actually occurred or was but an imaginative bit of satire. If we are correct in believing that dreams are simply a "continuation of thinking by other means," as Dr. H. J. Eysenck, the British psychologist, puts it in his *Sense and Nonsense in Psychology*, then they should be able to tell us something about the problems, wishes, and fears of the dreamer.

Would it not be plausible to visualize the Diesel-powered boat in Ramon's composition as Stalin's ship of state? The strange transfer from that boat to the 15-meter sailboat may very well represent the author's passing from the powerful overt Communist Party into the precarious underground of the NKVD in its hunt for Trotsky. The boat which had sunk would seemingly represent Trotsky's organization, and the men who "were swimming" would fittingly describe the floundering Trotskyites in the international regatta of communism. But as opponents of the prevailing Red establishment, they "did not wish to come on board" the Stalin vessel. To a faithful Kremlin follower this pattern of behavior was clearly characteristic of the Opposition—the official name assumed by the Trotsky movement in the Soviet Union.

After submitting to his examiners his account of the regatta dream, Ramon said that it reminded him that he had once been on a yacht that had been sailing into strong head winds for three days. He mused that he had had no sense of danger at the time, but realized later that he had been in very real peril.

In this reminiscent mood, he went on to say that whenever he had been in difficulties he had had a recurrent dream that he was swimming in the water in a very special manner. His body was unable to penetrate the water; the water touched only his chest and abdomen. This dream was accompanied by an odd taste, like champagne.

The complete inability to make close human contacts, which is revealed here, is aggravated by the sense of frustration which the recurrence of the dream suggests. Water is an accepted female symbol, representing both the mother and woman as a sexual partner. The prisoner's sense of isolation is shown in this repetitious dream of the lonely swimmer, trying in vain to force his limbs into the resistant surface of the water. He openly avowed his loneliness when Dr. Quiroz asked him a question about his watch, to which he replied: "It is my only companion."

That Ramon took refuge in self-isolation was evidenced by the fact that for a long time after the assassination he ate almost nothing. Then he shifted to warm milk and bread, which he had both for breakfast and dinner. With this self-imposed diet, champagne must indeed have been on his mind as the symbol of the high life to which he had aspired in his adolescent years and which he later abjured when he took the vow of a knight in Stalin's corps.

The assassin gave away another clue to his having been trained in Moscow, of all things, in the field of behavior as an accomplished dissembler. In one of his more hostile moments during his examination by the psychologists, he told them that their knowledge was of no value in coping with a man who knew how to control his emotions. He then made a passing reference to Kamo as such a man, and printed the name in large letters in a box drawn by him over that of Lenin.

Now the history of Kamo, virtually unknown in the West, forms part of the course of studies in the Soviet schools for infiltration and sabotage. Kamo is held up as the model of a revolutionary who was able to pretend for three years that he was insane, and in this way had completely deceived the attending physicians and saved thereby his own life. Ramon's underlying thought, that he too could fool the psychologists and that any Marxist revolutionary was mentally superior to a bourgeois scientist did not escape Drs. Quiroz Cuaron and Robleda Gomez. But, being totally unfamiliar with the name and character of Kamo, they gave the matter but brief mention. It was equally clear that Ramon admired Kamo immensely and that he seemed to draw a parallel between his own life and that of his hero. And it also showed that Ramon had chosen as an ideal a revolutionary who had turned criminal for the revolution's sake.

Who was Kamo? In 1907, the Bolshevik Party was near its nadir. Its political influence was evaporating and it had no money. To get funds, Lenin resorted to the methods of banditry. Particularly in the Caucasus organization, the Party financed itself by armed robberies, of which the most famous was the bombing of a stage coach carrying money under heavy guard for the Tiflis state bank. Through this operation, the Bolshevik treasury acquired a quarter of a million rubles; dozens of people, some soldiers, others merely bystanders, were killed.

The field organizer of this crime was Ter-Petrosian, whose undercover name was Kamo. In the Soviet lore, Stalin was credited with being the planning genius of this daring hold-up. Kamo fled to Berlin. Here he planned another "expropriation" for Lenin, this time an attack on the head of the famous Berlin banking house of Mendelssohn. The banker, Kamo naively imagined, kept his hoard somewhere in his house, no doubt in gold coins, perhaps hidden in a closet.

Kamo was arrested by the German police carrying a suitcase packed with explosives and an infernal machine. The Imperial Russian Government now demanded his extradition as a common assassin. The German socialist press, it must be mentioned, rushed in to defend this "class war victim."

Leonid Krassin, one of the secret Bolshevik leaders, then employed in Germany as an engineer (who after the Soviet Revolution served as Soviet ambassador to the Court of St. James) told Kamo that his only chance to survive was to pretend to be insane. Kamo obliged. He howled, rolled on the floor, attacked his guards. He was thrown naked into an ice-cold underground cell and kept there for days. Then, for four months, he remained standing, never sitting down. This was followed by a hunger strike. When forced feeding was attempted, he resisted until his teeth were broken. He tore out half of his hair and arranged it in patterns on a blanket. He simulated a realistic attempt to hang himself.

With incredible courage (or, if one prefers, an insatiable need for self-mutilation), Kamo continued to torture and abuse himself. After a year and a half, the German doctors finally ruled that he was fit to stand trial. Now Kamo simulated a new form of insanity, one of the symptoms of which was total anaesthesia of the skin. To test him and to amuse themselves, the German doctors applied hot irons to his epidermis and pricked him with needles. But the terrorist remained stoically impassive.

He was turned over to the Czarist government simply because the German authorities got tired of feeding him. He faced certain death, but was saved by a vast howl of indignation from the liberal press of Western Europe. The Russian authorities reluctantly pretended to believe that he was mad and threw him into the psychopathic ward of a mental hospital.

From this hospital, Kamo escaped, made his way to Paris and presented himself to his hero, Lenin. David Shub, in his biography of Lenin, gives us a picture of him as swarthy, half-blinded in one eye by a bomb fragment, uncouth, naive, with the terrible childishness of a man who kills for a cause he was too stupid to understand. With Krupskaya, Lenin's wife, he cracked almonds and monologued about his revolutionary exploits.

The figure of Kamo, as outlined to Ramon and other students in the Moscow school for murder, was that of a shining knight who had been a close associate of Stalin, and who was an incarnation of the creed that treachery, robbery and assassination can also gloriously serve the cause of social revolution.

In the idealized portrait of Kamo engraved upon the mind of Ramon we have a striking likeness of the mentality of the man who assassinated Trotsky and who all these many years has unremittingly played the role of a man of mystery. Moreover, to Ramon the story of Kamo is, as he told Dr. Quiroz, "an historic document which serves to show how 'revolutionaries' are able to deceive 'psychiatrists' and make them look ridiculous." In this role, Ramon saw himself as a revolutionary hero looming large in future history books.

A large number of word tests of various kinds were given Ramon during the first months of his imprisonment. One of these tests consisted of requesting the prisoner to write down the first 100 words which occurred to him. He supplied banal responses, consisting largely of objects in his cell. Of these, the most significant words, virgin and corpse, according to the psychologists, suggested an addiction to his mother and a wish to kill his father. (Ramon had once remarked that the medical students in Paris called corpses sandwiches because they were spread out on slabs and sliced up by the students.)

Another word, cat, represented Ramon himself. This deduction was based on the fact that he had once told the psychologists that he could see in the dark and that he had claimed that he used to write articles under the name of Catzu, and that he was taciturn and secretive like a cat.

Ramon was then given the Word Response Test, consisting of stimulus words and responses with an associated term. When given the word *sing*, his first reply was the conventional *music*, but, when tested a second time, he paused for a very long time, 13 seconds, then said *talk*. Here he treated *sing* in the underworld sense of confession to the police. (The reply was in French, of course, but *chanter* has exactly the same connotation.)

His reaction to *flight* was first *to run*, which tells us nothing, then *road*, given quickly. Before giving this response, he lit his cigarette hurriedly, then almost immediately put it out, and started to go through all his papers. This is part of his characteristic behavior pattern when something disturbs him.

When he was given the word *deception*, he waited 12 seconds, then said *theatre*. He smiled and said: "Oh yes, yes," an admission that he was playing a role, and enjoying it. In another test, consisting of questions which can be answered "yes" or "no," and designed to determine the extent to which the subject is introverted, he was asked whether he always did the same kind of work. He replied affirmatively. This was a direct statement that he was a professional revolutionary. When asked whether he abandoned difficult or tedious work, he said, No.

The data collected by the psychologists convinced them that Ramon's psychic difficulties sprang chiefly from his nursing difficulties in infancy which made for emotional insecurity. This insecurity was later translated into an Oedipus Complex of an unusual sort, involving unrepressed hatred of the father and complete identification with an aggressive, domineering mother. They considered that his initial rebellion against his father had been projected to society at large. In other words, he had become a revolutionist because he was still caught in the neurotic prison of childhood struggle against paternal authority and was acting out that struggle in a different and larger arena.

Struck by the combination of stories which Ramon gave about his childhood, by the unusual people whom he said he had known and by his defiant claim that the assassination of Trotsky was a great deed which would be acclaimed by history, the examiners attempted to fit the assassin's image of himself into Otto Rank's theory of *The Myth of the Birth of the Hero*, (Vienna, 1909) a hypothesis that the early lives of the folk heroes of great civilizations are woven of fantastic events which are essentially uniform throughout space and time. As Rank reconstructs the "average myth":

"The hero is the son of parents of the highest station, most often the son of the king.

"His conception is impeded by difficulties, such as abstinence or temporary sterility; or else his parents practice intercourse in secret because of prohibitions or other external obstacles. During his mother's pregnancy or earlier an oracle or a dream warns the father of the child's birth as containing grave danger for his safety.

"In consequence the father (or a person representing him) gives orders for the new-born babe to be killed or exposed to extreme danger; in most cases the babe is placed in a casket and delivered to the waves.

"The child is then saved by animals or poor people, such as

shepherds, and suckled by a female animal or a woman of humble birth.

"When full grown he rediscovers his noble parents after many strange adventures, wreaks vengeance on his father, and, recognized by his people, attains fame and greatness."

Freud refers to a number of heroes whose birth myths correspond to this pattern, among them Sargon, Oedipus, Karna, Paris, Telephos, Perseus, Heracles, Gilgamesh, Amphion and Zethos.

As for Ramon, on the basis of his own autobiographical statements, there were certain similarities which intrigued the psychologists. He claimed to be the son of a Belgian diplomat of noble origin associated with the Belgian court (the hero as the son of the king). He was frail and near death as an infant. He was suckled by humble wetnurses and his life was spared by feeding him horsemeat and cognac (the hero rescued by animals or poor people). He loved his mother. He had killed the "evil father" in the form of Trotsky. Finally, he believed that he would be acclaimed by history as a hero who had saved the working-class from a false leader. Ramon's willingness to accept the assassination mission, involving the risk of his own death, argues—in Freudian terminology—a greater than average death wish, i.e., a willingness to sacrifice himself for an impersonal goal. His rebelliousness toward authority went with this readiness to sacrifice himself for some cause. The conflict between an acquired aggressiveness and a deep-seated passivity made the Soviet order a natural home for him. The Communist Party gave him a moral and ideological justification for acting out his central conflict.

Totalitarian political ideologies provide an almost tailor-made impersonal arena onto which a person can vent his conflicting feelings of love or hate for his parents, according to a recent study made by Dr. Norbert Bromberg and detailed before the American Psychoanalytic Association. He cited the case of a man who openly vented his feelings of anger against the capitalistic system, which he identified with his father, the real object of his hate.

"Capitalism, like his father, he considered wholly cruel, avaricious, tyrannical, unjust, hypocritical and dishonest," Dr. Bromberg reported. "The communist movement, and its leaders like himself, were full of brotherly love, beneficent, freedom-loving, just, forthright, wise and honest."

When the deified "Father of Nations," Stalin himself, awarded to Ramon the highest decoration in the Kremlin's possession—the Order of the Hero of the Soviet Union—the assassin achieved the glory of his dreams. The terrorist made his peace with his inner self, the rebel in him was stilled forever, and there emerged the philosophical executioner.

10

The Mask Is Off

Nearly twenty months had elapsed from the day of the assassination of Trotsky until the assassin, under his assumed name of Jacques Mornard, was brought to trial in Mexico City. There were those who believed that he would be acquitted, so sharp was the change that had been wrought in the political climate of the war-torn world during this time. Stalin, who had been an ally of Hitler, was now an ally of Hitler's powerful enemies. In the course of these twenty months Mexican justice showed its adaptability in the case of Siqueiros, which involved complicity in the slaying of Robert Sheldon Harte.

The enterprising Colonel Salazar of the Mexican Secret Service, galvanized into action by the murder of Trotsky whom he had once suspected of staging the abortive attack of May 24, now caught up with the fugitive David Alfaro Siqueiros. He had him tracked to his hideout among the miners of the western state of Jalisco where he was arrested towards the end of September, 1940. Siqueiros and his accomplices were indicted on nine counts and were charged with organizing the first massive assault and with responsibility for the murder of Harte.

Then matters took a strange turn. The lawyers for the defendants requested two *amparos*. This is a Mexican legal device designed to protect individuals against unjust prosecutions and to safeguard their constitutional rights. As a result, Siqueiros found himself freed of the charges of homicide, attempted homicide, use of firearms, criminal conspiracy and usurpation of official functions. This was hailed as an acquittal.

The charges that remained against the prisoners were the comparatively minor offenses of housebreaking, unlawful use of police uniforms, robbery and damage to property. The robbery referred to the seizure at Trotsky's villa of the two getaway cars; the damage to property was that caused by the machine-gunning of the Coyoacan house.

New indictments were supposed to be drawn up covering these lesser charges. Meanwhile, Siqueiros was out on bail. Petitions of "independent intellectuals and artists" urged the President that justice be administered to Siqueiros in the light of the fact that "artists and men of science are considered as the bulwarks of culture and progress."

The court accepted Siqueiros' allegation that the firing of over 300 bullets inside the Trotsky house, riddling the bedrooms and wounding Trotsky's grandson, had been for "psychological purposes" only. There had been no intention of killing or hurting anybody. The testimony of the two chauffeurs that Siqueiros, when he heard Trotsky had escaped the hail of bullets, had exclaimed, "all the work in vain," was disregarded by the court. This *amparo* corresponded to throwing out several counts of an indictment on insufficient evidence.

An *amparo* was also granted against charging the Arenal brothers and the other conspirators with the murder of Sheldon

Harte. The evidence before the court was that Harte had been taken by the defendants to a house rented and equipped by them. He had then been murdered by gunfire; his corpse had been buried; the bloody cot and blanket had been burned. The Arenal brothers, who were the last people seen alive with him, had taken flight.

The court decided that this did not provide a *prima facie* case for trial of the defendants for murder. As Siqueiros' lawyer stated, Harte could have been killed by a "fifth column" organized by Trotsky or murdered for purposes of robbery. The defense suggested to Judge Emilio Cesar that robbery might be the "simple" explanation of the case.

Judge Cesar also denied that the assailants formed a "criminal conspiracy." Such a conspiracy must, according to Mexican law, be organized to commit crimes "in general terms." It cannot be directed against one individual or only one family. It must be characterized by "stability and permanence."

The charge of impersonating public officials was thrown out because, while the assailants had disguised themselves as policemen, it was not proved that they "had tried to exercise some of the corresponding functions of a public officer without being one . . ." That is, they were disguised as officers, but had not fraudulently usurped police functions.

Siqueiros made light of his share in the abortive attempt to liquidate Trotsky. "An unfortunate bit of political sniping on my part," is the way he described it. And to illustrate before the examining magistrate how far he had once gone with his sniping, he regaled the court with an account of his conference with President Cardenas on the subject of Trotsky. He told how, in the last stage of the civil war in Spain, he had flown back to Mexico for a three-day visit for the sole purpose of calling on Cardenas to impress him that Trotsky must be expelled from the country and Trotskyism must be destroyed in Mexico.

"President Cardenas has given arms to the Spanish people to

fight for the revolution, but at the same time he has armed Leon Trotsky so that, from his base in revolutionary Mexico, he can fight against the revolution," was what the Mexican volunteers in Spain had been saying, according to Siqueiros. He claimed that by attacking the Soviet Union as a police state the Trotskyites were subverting the revolutionary forces everywhere. The Mexican Communist Party leaders had advised Siqueiros to handle Cardenas with tact and not to offend him by speaking of his inviting Trotsky to Mexico as a blunder. After the interview, Siqueiros was convinced that he had made no real impression on the President.

While Siqueiros was still out on bail, arrangements were made to let him go to Chile to paint some murals. At a banquet in Mexico City to celebrate Mexican-Chilean cultural relations, the Mexican ambassador to Chile, Reyes Spindola, casually told the Chilean ambassador to Mexico about it. There was a to-do when it was discovered that the poet Pablo Neruda, Chilean consul and a leading communist, had been instrumental in the matter. But Ambassador Spindola persisted in his efforts on behalf of Siqueiros, and officially requested the foreign office of Chile to admit the indicted artist, in spite of the fact that by jumping bail he would still be a fugitive from Mexican justice. Siqueiros turned up in Chile.

If the lot of Siqueiros gave comfort and hope to Ramon in the expectation that he would escape with a light sentence, he was due for a rude shock. Yet the assassin's expectation was shared in the circles closest to his victim. As Natalia Trotsky put the matter:

"If there had not been judges to maintain that Siqueiros assaulted our house only to steal two automobiles which he abandoned a few hundred meters away . . . if there had not been judges to maintain that the gangsters of the GPU were not members of a gang but 'co-thinkers' and that the shots fired over our heads were only for 'psychological' effect, we would say beforehand: the GPU will fail in its attempt. But Siqueiros, assailant, assassin, incendiary and agent in the services of the GPU, is free. Why not Jacson?"

Mrs. Trotsky guessed wrong. The conviction of Siqueiros, one of Mexico's greatest living painters, on a charge of murder, would have been embarrassing to the Mexican government. Moreover, the conspiracy indictment threatened, not only him, but a large segment of the Mexican communist leadership. Under the usual rules of criminal conspiracy, all of the plotters would have been equally culpable in the murder of Harte. Thus, the stakes were such that the entire communist apparat and its influential network of fellow-travelers were massed and mobilized to thwart justice. Another factor was that by this time the Soviet forces were battling successfully the Nazi invaders and the USSR was gaining general popularity. And who was the victim of the famous Siqueiros? Sheldon Harte, an unknown American youth, an admitted Trotskyite.

It was the reverse with the assassin. He was an unknown who would not even disclose his identity. And his victim was a world-famous revolutionary leader, whose murder constituted a historic event. The crime, moreover, was a direct and personal affront to President Lazaro Cardenas who, in granting Trotsky asylum, considered himself responsible for his protection. It was an affront to the Mexican nation that a foreigner had dared to come to the country with forged papers to stain by his assassination the principle of political asylum.

Under Mexican law, the trial judge must hand down a verdict within a year. Ramon's lawyer waited until the last moment legally available to him to charge the trial judge with prejudice against the prisoner, and then appealed to a higher court to have him removed from sitting in the case. At the same time, the assassin withdrew his previous carefully prepared story of his motives and preparations for the crime. The reason for this was that this earlier statement admitted premeditation and virtually invited a stiff sentence.

He now contended that he had been in no condition to speak with a clear mind immediately after the crime. His head had been bandaged and he had been unable to read the documents he had signed. He had been in a state of moral depression during the interrogations so that he did not care what he said and alleged that he had been physically mistreated by the police. In his particular case the latter charge was found to be untrue, as special orders had been issued from above to treat the prisoner with the utmost propriety.

What really happened, Ramon now said, was that he had called on Trotsky with his article only to be told, "you are nothing but a military idiot." This wounded his pride and, then, to make matters worse, Trotsky began to attack him physically. Ramon asserted:

"I want to note that Leon Trotsky began to fight and shout before the blow, in order to free himself from the pressure of my left hand on his coat, no doubt so as to draw his revolver, but I was faster than he . . ."

This change in his story from premeditated murder to self-defense did not explain the letter of confession found on his person or the fact that he had entered Trotsky's study armed with pistol, knife and ice-axe.

The other major change was that Trotsky was no longer represented as an agent of the Dies Committee and of Wall Street imperialists. He was now an agent of the Nazis. This alteration of the record was made by the prisoner and his attorneys with a perfectly straight face for the simple reason that Soviet foreign policy had gone through a diplomatic somersault.

The same man who had characterized Hitler as "a visionary" in his discussions with Dr. Quiroz now affected the true voice of a Belgian patriot:

"I have always considered it an honor to die on the battlefield against the forces representative of the greatest barbarism typified by the Nazi hordes."

He was asked:

"You came to believe that Trotsky was an agent of Hitler, as the communists say?"

"Absolutely," he answered firmly.

At that time President Franklin Delano Roosevelt, at the suggestion of his good friend Dan Tobin, czar of the Teamsters' Union, had authorized prosecution under the Smith Act of certain Trotskyites in the Middle West who were a thorn in the flesh of the union leadership. They were convicted and sent to jail on charges of seditious conspiracy. Ramon found here some handy ammunition for his defense, in line with the then prevailing Communist Party support of the prosecution of the Trotskyites under the Smith Act. Those were the days of superpatriotism for *The Daily Worker*, which called for a purge by the Department of Justice of all known anti-communists. Ramon's brief stated:

"Several of the persons who have filed through this trial, such as Jake Cooper, Albert Goldman, etc., many days before the events of Pearl Harbor in the United States, were summoned to court to answer charges of two crimes: one of conspiracy, and the other of crimes of sabotage and treason . . ."

The implication that some of the witnesses against him at his trial were themselves held guilty of conspiracy and treason, Ramon argued, showed that he deserved special consideration from the court.

However, the attitude of the prisoner both before and since the murder, the court held, had been one of "falseness and artifice." The assassin had not come to Mexico to work as a follower of Trotsky, but rather "with the sole object of killing Trotsky."

There is no capital punishment in Mexico for ordinary homicide. The prosecution asked for a 23-year sentence: 20 years for premeditated murder, two for assault with weapons, one for illegal possession of arms.

On April 17, 1943, two years and eight months after the crime, the prisoner was brought to court to hear sentence passed upon him. He was immaculate, clean-shaven and manicured. His attitude was defiant and when he learned the second half of the proceedings was being broadcast, he threw his hat over the microphone to stop the broadcast.

The court sentenced him to 19 years and six months for premeditated murder and six months for illegal bearing of arms. Upset by the verdict, Ramon filed an appeal but on May 19, 1944, the Court of Appeals upheld the sentence.

Even before Ramon had gone on trial, the Soviet underground operating from New York began to organize a very cautious attempt to rescue him. During the war years, especially when Hitler's armies were cutting deep into Russia and when the Kremlin depended so much upon American aid, Stalin was careful not to offend the United States by rash acts of abduction and terror. In 1942 and 1943, numerous letters of a suspicious character passing between New York City and the Mexican capital were intercepted by the U. S. wartime office of mail censorship. Laboratory examination disclosed that these letters contained secret cipher messages written in invisible ink, that they related to a conspiracy to "spring" Trotsky's assassin from prison, and that a number of "letter-drops" had been set up both in the United States and in Mexico to handle communications in this operation.

Jacob Epstein, a veteran of the communist-controlled Lincoln Brigade in Spain, received ciphered correspondence concerning this plan from Spanish and Mexican comrades. He continued this correspondence until November, 1943. Shortly thereafter, Pavel Klarin, Soviet vice consul in New York and an aide of General Vassili Zubilin, the former head of the NKVD in the

United States, proceeded to Mexico. Epstein followed him there. He was charged on the witness stand with being in communication with Klarin on at least eight occasions.[17]

An American woman named Helen Levi Simon Travis, who had once been employed as a writer by *The Daily Worker*, transferred $3,700 to a certain Enrique de los Rios in Mexico City. This transfer was made in response to an urgent appeal for funds by the conspirators in Mexico.

A woman named Anna Vogel Colloms, a New York City high school teacher, was accused of serving as a "letter-drop" and as a courier in this operation. On August 12, 1943, she left for Mexico carrying in her baggage an apparently new box of personal stationery. At the border, American officials found at the bottom of the box five sheets of paper completely covered with writing in code. Mrs. Colloms was allowed to proceed to Mexico without the box. She made a half-hearted attempt there to get in touch with Epstein. In the meantime, five fresh sheets of paper had been substituted by government agents for the original ones bearing the secret messages. On the way back to the United States, Mrs. Colloms collected the box from the customs officials who had retained the original sheets and returned their fresh replacements to the underground courier.

When interrogated by the House Committee on Un-American Activities in 1950, Epstein, Travis, Colloms and half a dozen other persons accused of belonging to the conspiracy were asked if they were communists and if the charges against them were true or false. They all refused to answer these questions, invoking the guarantees of the Fifth Amendment.

This first known effort to rescue Ramon petered out because the authorities had intercepted the coded correspondence and ferreted out the identities and plans of the conspirators.

In Moscow, Caridad Mercader, the mother of the assassin, was receiving assurances from her lover Eitingon and his superiors in the Kremlin that as soon as the critical period of the war was over, an operation to rescue her son would be launched. Together with the famous La Pasionaria, she was the most privileged person in the underground colony of top Spanish communists who found refuge in Moscow, and enjoyed a life of relative luxury, as described by the untamed Campesino, the guerrilla commander, after his escape from the Soviet Union.

Caridad shared an elegant apartment with her former radio operator, the beautiful Carmen Brufau, one of the schoolteachers whom Caridad had recruited into the apparat. Carmen was blue-eyed, about thirty, and her first husband, now a Mexican citizen, was the "Juan" who had accompanied Caridad on the first mission to Mexico in 1936. In earlier days, Carmen had known Ramon well and, in talking to the psychologists, he had once let her Christian name slip. He covered up rapidly by identifying her as a "champion swimmer" whom, he said, he had known in Paris. On another occasion, in answering a questionnaire, he described his mother's companion as "a very mannish sportswoman."

Caridad was under instructions not to discuss the murder of Trotsky or her son's role in the affair. Now for the first time she had the opportunity to study life in the "Workers' Fatherland" at close hand over a period of several years. She was also able to see how the authorities treated her compatriots who had fought for the establishment of a Soviet Spain. With the exception of a small clique, the majority of the refugees were assigned tasks for which they were physically unequipped, and for which they had no training. They were given starvation rations and many died like flies. Spanish women became prostitutes for a few crusts of bread. The abandoned children of the broken and dispersed Loyalist families formed gangs of homeless teen-agers who survived by begging, stealing and sometimes killing. In accordance with the Soviet criminal code, some of these delinquent children were executed. And they were indicted and sentenced, not as common criminals, but as Spanish Fascists (Falangistas).

Unlike La Pasionaria, who played high politics in the Comintern hierarchy, Caridad was a fighter. She did not close her eyes to the horrors being perpetrated all around her, but very few suspected her true feelings. She was extremely discreet about expressing them, knowing that this discretion was necessary both for her own survival and to enable her to secure Soviet help to free her son. While she shared confidences with an intimate Spanish comrade of independent views, she remained friendly with Carmen Brufau who acted as the Kremlin's watchdog over her. Brufau's unflagging devotion to Moscow was demonstrated when she was expelled from Switzerland in the 1950's as a suspected Soviet spy.

Caridad went to the front, serving as a political commissar of the Spanish battalion that fought shoulder-to-shoulder with the Red troops during World War II. The tide of war had completely turned in favor of the Soviet Union, Russian forces were deep in Poland, and Caridad began to press the Kremlin to redeem its pledge to rescue her son. Stalin's reluctance to undertake an effort in that direction was due to his anxiety not to jeopardize the relations with the United States when he was playing for far greater stakes in the international game.

Consumed with determination to get her son out of the Mexican jail, Caridad addressed letters to Lavrenti Beria demanding authorization for her to go to Mexico to organize an attempt to rescue Ramon. She threatened to go to the Cuban ambassador in Moscow, since she was a native of Cuba, to seek protection unless her request was granted. This action produced results.

Stalin gave his approval. Caridad received from Beria a trove of jewels worth from 50 to 60 thousand dollars to finance a rescue operation. A plan was worked out which called for a Mexican physician, Dr. Carlos D., to inject Ramon with the virus of an infectious disease which would necessitate moving the patient to a hospital for contagious diseases outside the penitentiary. The NKVD plan envisaged it as a simple matter to arrange for his escape from such an institution.

On March 9, 1945, Caridad appeared in Mexico City and rented a flat in the Azteca Apartments in Hamburgo Street. Her inseparable companion, Carmen Brufau, sailed from Odessa and joined her in Mexico where they again shared living quarters. Caridad discovered upon her arrival that other plans to liberate her son were being hatched by the resident chiefs of the communist underground under the direction of Carlos Contreras. And she became suspicious that these plans spelled an operation of the type resorted to by Stalin on similar occasions, which might end in the "accidental" death of Ramon. Caridad learned that Contreras had offered a fund of $100,000 to a leading Spanish refugee to organize, with the aid of a bribed prison warden, the escape of her son. The warden would be an unwitting accomplice, as he would take Ramon out of prison one night solely to accompany him to a house of prostitution in the city. The flight would take place from there. The offer was turned down.

Caridad approached one of her close Spanish friends now in Mexico, whom she had helped during his trying days in Moscow, and told him about her misgivings. She pleaded with him to organize her son's escape. He could use communists or any others he chose in the operation, so long as he alone had full charge of it and saw that only reliable elements were used. He was assured that he could have all the money he needed for the purpose. Although beholden to Caridad, the man refused to have anything to do with the matter. He was grateful to the Mexican government and its ambassador in Moscow for enabling him to find refuge in Mexico, and would not repay the hospitality with a crime against the state.

Ramon himself refused to cooperate in the dubious rescue schemes of his underground comrades. Not once during his mother's postwar stay in Mexico did she visit her son in prison, so ironclad was the regime imposed by the NKVD on all concerned to insure the secrecy of the assassin's identity. She was so full of suspicions that she did not go out alone after dark.

Unable to achieve her objective, Caridad left for her native Cuba. From there she requested permission to take up residence in France where her daughter Montserrat and her son, Jorge, were living. In the application she stated that she had no occupation, but had an income of $950 a month from her Cuban properties.

Montserrat had married and was now Madame Dudouyt. She had been deported to Germany in 1941 and liberated from a concentration camp by Allied forces on April 26, 1945. The Dudouyts, French citizens, live with their two children in a suburb of Paris and own an antique shop on the Left Bank of the capital. Montserrat, seen in March, 1959, looked like the very image of Ramon. Jorge Mercader, a chemical engineer, had also been freed from a concentration camp as a French citizen, and was suffering from osteomyelitis. His brother Luis had remained behind in Russia when their mother left for Mexico and France. The white-haired Caridad occupies alone a modest apartment in Paris where she leads a retired life as a Cuban citizen, paying her rent punctually, receiving no visitors except for her family, and does not mix with her neighbors. When Ramon completes his sentence in 1960, she will be 68 years old.

Perhaps the greatest shock she had to endure in recent years was the news of the fate of Leonid Eitingon, the man she had once hoped to marry. After the downfall of the omnipotent Lavrenti Beria, his entire coterie of lieutenants was purged. Eitingon was arrested as a traitor and plotter against the Soviet regime, and vanished without trace like so many officers of Stalin's terror machine.

Many myths have grown up around the prison life of Trotsky's murderer to which he, "the world's most notorious political assassin," as he has been described in the press, contributed in a large measure with his studied behavior of a "Kamo." Yet the facts are quite ascertainable. He spent the first 18 years of his imprisonment in the old Federal Penitentiary on the outskirts of Mexico City, the so-called "Black Palace" of Lecumberri which houses some 3800 inmates. In the summer of 1958 he was transferred to the newly-constructed ultra-modern reformatory several miles out of the capital on the road to Puebla. "Reformatory" is the only fitting description for this penal establishment sprawling over a vast area, in which all buildings are one story in height, which boasts a full complement of craft shops, a grand cafeteria, as well as a spacious restaurant, and facilities for study and entertainment.

I saw the assassin in both places of confinement. When I made a surprise call on him in the closing days of 1947, he greeted me, in English, with an unfriendly exclamation: "Who are you? What do you want?" When told that the purpose of the call was to discuss the publication of his own true story, he quickly ushered me out of his cell. There was time enough, however, to size up the man and his surroundings. It was visitors' day, and he was fully and fashionably dressed. Being tall and slim, he looked debonair. His cell, spacious and sunny, in the shape of a triangle, with a little open-air patio in front, contained a neat bed and a table loaded with books and magazines.

Late in February, 1959, on an inspection tour of the new reformatory where the best-behaved prisoners of the state of Mexico are serving out their sentences, I had occasion to observe Ramon several times, without attempting to engage him in conversation, and to study his new surroundings, including the shop he operates and the classroom where he teaches the rudiments of electrical engineering. After a lapse of more than eleven years, it was difficult to recognize the once debonair figure in the man with a double chin and tortoise-shell glasses, wearing an open shirt and slacks, and weighing at least thirty pounds more. He left the impression of a sedate bourgeois.

Throughout the years newspapermen have attempted to interview him and some succeeded in exchanging a few phrases with the prisoner. His usual line, characteristic of a communist, has been: "I have nothing to tell you. Do you understand? Absolutely nothing. Do you hear? Nothing. I refuse to discuss it. You are all scandalmongers!"

On occasion, Ramon displays a sense of humor. Once, when he boasted to a visiting reporter that he had many friends among American newspapermen, he was asked to name them. "Oh, my friends are the newspapermen who do not write about me," he shot back, laughing at his own wisecrack.

Another time, when Dr. Quiroz Cuaron visited the penitentiary with a friend, the latter lingered behind for a while in the courtyard. He was approached by a well-mannered man who inquired of the apparently curious visitor if he could be of any service to him.

"There is only one person I'd like to see here," came in answer, "and that is the man who killed Trotsky."

"That's easy. I'm the man," Ramon chuckled.

One of the major features of Mexican penology is that the prison authorities permit convicts to enjoy regular sexual relations in their cells with women, whether they be wives or mistresses. In some instances, this involves the recognition of established "female companions" for each prisoner.

Ramon took advantage of this privilege, and soon acquired a mistress, a pretty young Mexican nightclub performer, one of his alleged friends in the city. She brought him food from outside the prison, and carried messages for him. For many years he kept as far away as possible from the prison fare, fearing that he might be poisoned by some secret Trotskyite. There was the occasion when he had received a present of chocolates from an unknown admirer. He asked the prison laboratory to analyze them and they were found to contain enough poison to kill him. Some of the Mexican newspapers treated this as a real murder attempt; others called it a put-up job.

During the early days in prison he was once found in possession of a hidden razor blade in his pocket. He surrendered it readily, saying: "Don't worry. I don't believe in suicide." The psychologists found this unconvincing. On another occasion, he commented at the sight of a device to measure reaction time, "It looks like a bomb." His examiners got the impression that he wished it were.

Actually, what was troubling him was not any urge towards self-destruction, but fear of assassination at the hands of a Trotsky avenger. In August, 1944, in the course of a legal move to appeal his sentence, Ramon indicated that there was a plan to hustle him off to the Islas Marias, a desolate and dreaded island penal colony in the Pacific. He made a statement that "through newspaper information" he had been made aware of plans to assault him physically. If he should be sent to the Islas Marias, he wanted to point out that the isolation of the penal colony and the fact that prisoners were taken there in a small boat would make it much easier for any such attack to be carried out with impunity.

The assassin was at first treated with a certain amount of severity. Jose Farah, the secretary general of the penitentiary, deposed in connection with the prisoner's subsequent application for parole that, because of the nature of his crime, he had during the first years been the object of special vigilance. He was assigned to work as an ordinary piece worker in the prison toy shop. His conduct in the shop was "exemplary" and he was soon put in charge of it. He was always courteous towards his fellow-prisoners. He played cards and dominoes with them, occasionally he entertained them with card tricks. According to Farah, he was eventually given freedom of movement, as a reward for good behavior, throughout the entire interior of the penitentiary, including the administrative offices.

Ramon decided to use every opportunity to earn his earliest possible release. His first major chance which he exploited to the limit was an anti-illiteracy campaign. President Avila Camacho had offered pardon to prisoners who distinguished themselves in teaching their illiterate fellows how to read and write. Two convicts, Isidro Cortes Piza and "Jacques Mornard," threw themselves into this work with extraordinary enthusiasm.

On August 20, 1946, six years from the day of the assassination—Brigadier General Ricardo Nunez Saenz, the director of the penitentiary, wrote President Camacho to remind him that, although he had promised pardons to prisoners who were outstanding in this field, two of them, national champions, Isidro Cortes Piza and "Jacques Mornard," received no recognition for their performance. He stated that "the inmates made literate in this penitentiary, whose number reaches to more than a thousand," had petitioned him to try to get these two teachers pardoned. Denied pardon or reduction of sentence for political reasons, the two criminals were eventually awarded diplomas by the Undersecretary of Public Education.

It did not take long for Ramon to exert an increasing influence over his fellow convicts. He arranged to have an excellent Mexican painter establish a class in the penitentiary and assumed responsibility for getting the prisoners interested and for seeing to it that they attended classes and took their work seriously.

In December, 1952, Ramon was put in charge of the radio and television repair shop of the penitentiary. He started to build up the shop by teaching a class of apprentices. In time, the class grew into a well-attended regular study course in electrical engineering for which the instructor receives extra pay from the government. He was also made responsible for the maintenance of the entire electrical system of the prison, including lighting systems, motors and refrigeration.

According to a report made to the Crime Prevention Department, dated December 3, 1954, Ramon spent his time reading technical books on electrical engineering, some political and social books, and a good deal of general literature. The report added that he enjoyed writing and sometimes had technical articles published.

In recommending that the prisoner be paroled in 1956, the former Director of the Penitentiary, General Ricardo Nunez Saenz, spoke of his excellent relations with his fellow prisoners and with the administration, claimed he had made no attempts to escape or to proselytize anyone for communism, and characterized him as an extraordinarily responsible worker. "Among the commissions that I knew he carried was that of being in charge of the entire electric lighting system, which is extraordinarily complicated, so much so that even the electric light company is not entirely familiar with it."

Rumors soon spread that Trotsky's assassin became so rich from the radio business that he was wallowing in luxury. Actually he is operating a small but profitable business. The Mexican penal system provides that convicts are permitted to sell the product of their own labor. Where prison shops are cooperatives, the general manager obviously gets a much larger share of the earnings than ordinary apprentices and workmen. But Ramon had made it clear during a 1958 interview with Dr. Jesus Siordia that, as a good communist, he regards profit as dishonest, and avowed that he would not lend himself to the organization of so-called "businesses" in the penitentiary for the purpose of exploiting other prisoners.

This professed philosophy did not prevent him from accumulating enough capital to buy for his present mistress, Roquelia Mendoza, a second-hand Lincoln, a hardtop model. Miss Mendoza, who became its owner on November 13, 1958, drives it to the prison when visiting her lover there, and her license plate No. 88480 has become familiar to the guards. To be sure, it is a Lincoln of 1952 vintage, but it represents, according to the prevailing market in Mexico, a very considerable investment.

On August 20, 1953, the day he became entitled to parole upon the completion of two-thirds of his term, the prisoner was shocked at the news given out by the warden of the Federal Penitentiary, General Florencio A. Loyo. The warden announced that official records received from Spain left no doubt that "Mornard" was really Ramon Mercader. The news caused a sensation in the press and reporters descended upon the penitentiary to interview the prisoner. According to *The New York Times* of August 23, the "newsmen who visited him in his cell said he showed signs of panic . . . He is eligible for parole, but General Loyo said he doubted that he would apply for it."

The following year, in 1954, Ramon engaged the services of Eduardo Ceniceros, a prominent political figure, as his lawyer and started a vigorous fight to obtain parole. The Mexican penal code governing parole, which defines it as a right not a privilege, would have entitled the prisoner to parole in normal circumstances.

The Crime Prevention Division of the Ministry of Interior, entrusted with the consideration of parole petitions, requested Dr. Quiroz to furnish it with a report of his findings concerning the true identity of the prisoner. These findings established with the help of fingerprints, photographs and other documentary evidence, that Jacques Mornard, alias Frank Jacson, was in reality Ramon Mercader.

Dr. Quiroz, in his unfavorable report on the parole petition, seized the occasion to characterize the unreconstructed assassin:

"Our subject has committed a crime of a common type; he believes that he achieved a high purpose by murdering; he believes that he remained a moral man after having assassinated;

. . . he does not feel any repentance for the crime; he believes that the death of Trotsky was of benefit to the working class; he does not consider himself an assassin, or a magnicide, or as morally insane, or abnormal; he admits the possibility of committing crimes against one's personal convictions or ideals, and he believes in the absurd possibility of committing the perfect crime."

Opposing the negative position taken by Dr. Quiroz was the report of Dr. Jose Sol Casao, which had been solicited by the Division of Crime Prevention. The verdict of Dr. Sol Casao was that the assassin constituted a political problem, not a psychiatric one. He was socially dangerous to the extent that all dedicated communists are. To deny him parole on these grounds, he maintained, would be tantamount to proposing that all communist cadres be kept in prison indefinitely.

On January 24, 1956, the Division of Crime Prevention denied the petition for parole. In its opinion, the prisoner had not "expressed any moral regrets for having committed the crime." Furthermore, he considered himself "above and beyond the laws," and not an assassin. He was "proud of his status as an enigmatic man . . ."

Ceniceros, the attorney, complained that "a high official of the Executive Power" was exerting his influence against parole, hinting at ex-President Cardenas, who indeed still felt very strongly about the crime. Other Mexican officials were afraid that, if released, the prisoner could not be deported (because no other country would take him) and that in Mexico he might be murdered, by one side or the other, thus causing another international scandal.

The case was taken on appeal to the three-judge First Circuit Court. The first question raised there was whether a man could be paroled who had not been officially identified. The court found that the prisoner had never been officially identified in the record, and that his continued refusal to state who he was was a negative factor.

The tribunal concluded that the good conduct of the prisoner was alone not sufficient reason for parole, since the law spoke of repentance, while the petitioner had never expressed any regrets for his act. He lost the fight for parole.

The final issue before the court dealt with the provision of the law that any foreigner who enters the country illegally is subject to imprisonment of from six months to two years, and to deportation thereafter. While the fact that Ramon had entered Mexico illegally was established at his trial, he had never been convicted of this offense. There are those in Mexico who predict that, immediately upon completion of his sentence, in 1960, he will be re-indicted for illegal entry, given the maximum sentence of two years, and then deported.

The Mexican government is in the unusual position of having a confessed and convicted murderer on its hands who is adamant in denying his nationality and identity. Having played successfully the parts of Dr. Jekyll and Mr. Hyde—Jacques Mornard and Frank Jacson—in his intimate relationships with Sylvia Ageloff and the Trotsky household, the prisoner has since his arrest in 1940 worn without change the mask of a man of mystery. He has steadfastly refused to furnish data about his schooling, employment, military service, living relatives, and past domiciles, data which are subject to verification, in support of his claimed origin. Throughout the years, he has permitted his identity to be the subject of fanciful speculation in the world press as well as in police and intelligence circles.

Yet from the very beginning of his arrest, clues began to appear that he was of Spanish origin, despite his insistence that French was his native tongue and that he had learned his fluent Spanish in Mexico. There were the tradesmen, hotel employees and garage personnel who had had dealings with the assassin before he committed the crime, and who told the police that he spoke Spanish perfectly, without any accent. There was the American consul, Morris N. Hughes, who obtained recordings of the assassin's speech from the police and forwarded them to Washington for analysis, where experts reported that *he spoke French with indications of a Spanish accent.* There were the French friends of Trotsky, Alfred and Marguerite Rosmer, who thought that he might be a Canadian of mixed origin, but they were sure that he was neither French nor Belgian.

There were two Catalans in the employ of the Mexican police who were present during an interrogation of the prisoner soon after his arrest, when he made an exclamation which convinced them that he came from Catalonia. Other bits of evidence, which had been inadvertently provided by the prisoner, as related earlier, strongly suggested that the prisoner was a native of Spain. One of these came to light in the late summer of 1957 when two letters of his to a new girl-friend, Guadalupe Gómez, employed as secretary in a modern art gallery, accidentally fell into the hands of the proprietor, a well-known lady in Mexico City.

The letters, addressed to Senorita Gómez, were delivered by messenger in her absence to the proprietor who discovered to her dismay that they came from "Jacques Mornard." The letters, in addition to their amorous contents, referred to persons in Brussels, Paris and Rome for the senorita to look up, as she was preparing to go to Europe and had applied for an American visa to go through the United States. A cursory investigation disclosed that the gallery had for some time been used as a "mail-drop" by Ramon for communication with suspicious characters. But more significant was the fact that the letters were written in the kind of Spanish which showed unmistakably elements of the Catalan language.

When the secretary was discharged, she admitted in her fury her activities for the communist organization. And Ramon, from prison and through various mysterious callers over the telephone, threatened the proprietor for months afterwards, demanding that she refrain from publishing the letters and that she return the originals. The latter she flatly refused to do. A photostat of the more important missive has made the rounds of the Spanish refugee colony in Mexico City.

Among these refugees, there were at the time of the assassination and there are now several living witnesses in a position to make a positive identification of the prisoner. But Stalin's machine of terror was for a long time a powerful deterrent. The non-communist veterans of the Spanish civil war, mostly moderate socialists, were attacked in Mexico by Red strong-arm squads wielding pistols, knives and iron bars. In one such raid on a closed meeting, Julian Gorkin, a leading Spanish refugee, was stabbed in the head and another participant critically wounded. To oppose the Soviet apparat, especially in such an affair as the Trotsky murder, was extremely dangerous business. The Spanish refugees knew that public identification of the assassin, which might lead to the unraveling of the complex underground Soviet network in Mexico involved in the Trotsky affair, would invite the vengeance of the NKVD.

The first published identification of Mercader was made by Julian Gorkin in 1948, in a postscript to General Salazar's book, *Murder in Mexico,* of which Gorkin was co-author. Since it was unsupported by any documentary evidence, the House Committee on Un-American Activities in its 1950 report on the "American Aspects of the Assassination of Leon Trotsky" states that the murderer's "true name and identity have never been established." The position of Joseph Hansen, Trotsky's chief secretary and eyewitness to the assassination, has also all along been that the real identity of the killer still had to be demonstrated.

Conclusive proof that the assassin of Trotsky is Ramon Mercader, a native Spaniard, was secured by Dr. Quiroz Cuaron, the criminologist for the Mexican government, in September, 1950, but was not made public until three years later. That month he represented the National University of Mexico at the World Congress of Criminology in Paris. Dr. Quiroz had decided to take advantage of the trip to Europe to establish once and for all the identity of the prisoner. He brought along with him from Mexico several sets of "Mornard-Jacson" fingerprints.

Dr. Quiroz proceeded to Barcelona. At police headquarters there, he was asked which group of prisoners he was interested in—criminal or political. When he answered, "political," he was told:

"How unfortunate! The Reds, when they controlled the city, destroyed all the records of political prisoners."

Continuing his search for positive proof, Dr. Quiroz proceeded to Madrid, where he called on the fingerprint expert at police headquarters. The latter took the set of prints Dr. Quiroz had brought with him, and disappeared in the direction of the room where the files were kept. Prepared for a long wait, Dr. Quiroz looked at his watch. Exactly one minute and forty seconds later, the technician returned with a find.

"These match," he said, as he handed to Dr. Quiroz a yellow and dusty card. It was evident to the Mexican visitor that the card had not been removed from the files for years. It contained the fingerprints of Jaime Ramon Mercader del Rio and had been taken when he was arrested in Barcelona on June 12, 1935, on the charge of secret membership in a communist youth organization.

Together with copies of the fingerprints, Dr. Quiroz obtained photographic material of the Mercaders, including two pictures of the mother and son which show a resemblance between them almost as remarkable as that of a pair of twins. The additional photographs from albums in the hands of members of the Mercader family living in Barcelona, recently found through the efforts of the author, make the proof of the assassin's identity self-evident and irrefutable.

The dissembler's mask had been ripped off the legal face of the magnicide, but underneath there remains the far more baffling psychological mask of the inner man. To what breed of political assassins does Mercader belong? History knows a small band of men, who have risked or given their lives in attempts to assassinate great leaders who symbolized enormous power. This group included fanatics with a hero-complex like John Wilkes Booth, who believed that he would achieve immortality by saving the South when he shot Lincoln; patriotic rebels like Oscar Collazo, a well-adjusted family man, who as a member of the Puerto Rican nationalist conspiracy attempted to assassinate President Truman in order to call attention to the alleged suffering of his country under American rule; idealistic terrorists of the Czarist epoch, like Perovskaya and Kaliayev, who saw in the assassination of the Emperor and his aides the road to human brotherhood and a reign of freedom under which human life was sacred, a species to which Albert Camus has devoted some penetrating pages in his study of nihilistic murder in *The Rebel.*

Ramon Mercader is related to none of these types. Common to them all are passion and individual initiative, the latter quality standing out even in cases where conspiratorial accomplices are found. Not so with Ramon who is a trained, indoctrinated killer with the sense of duty of a professional executioner. Although he has imitated the stoicism of the bomb-throwing Kamo who concealed his identity after the crime, Ramon's crafty insinuation into the affections of Sylvia and into the bosom of Trotsky's household in order to perpetrate the crime is a pattern of behavior of which the tempestuous revolutionary individualist Kamo was incapable.

One of the first to glimpse behind the double mask worn by the assassin was Joseph Hansen who observed him before the crime within the walls of Trotsky's villa and after the assassination, in the course of the penetrating questioning by Trotsky's lawyer.

"At first Jacson cooperated in the cross-examination," Hansen writes, "answering the questions readily and seeming to be amused by this childish game. He took precautions just the same, demanding that the questions be translated into Spanish before he would answer. Jacson had an opportunity to hear the question first in English and this gave him more time for consideration. Later when he began to feel enmeshed, he had to have the questions repeated. The cooperative pose was soon gone. The invalid pose went with it. A different kind of person began to emerge. He seemed to care less for the impression he might make on the audience and more for the damage that might result from his yeses and noes. The pauses for calculation grew longer, the resistance stiffer. At times he became peremptory and towards the end he asserted himself as strongly as if he had the power to dominate the scene and take over. Finally, he refused to have anything more to do with this imposition. I realized then that he had the inner force to run any gang he might be in.

"The impression I had now was in complete contrast to my first impression of him as a neutral character. I no longer wondered that Sylvia had not noticed anything strange about Jacson. He was a person of high ability in the kind of work required in such organizations as the Soviet secret police. He must have been selected for this assignment out of the immense GPU apparatus after the most careful consideration, observation and testing."

Further light on the character of the assassin became available to the Mexican authorities in August, 1958, when Dr. Emma Sanchez, professor of psychology, examined him and gave him a series of fresh tests. In an independent report designed, in the words of Dr. Sanchez, "to provide a better picture of the results of the tests given to Mercader del Rio," the prisoner is officially identified as Mercader instead of the previous "Jacques Mornard."

The report, which completely confirms the conclusions of the earlier tests conducted by Dr. Quiroz, states: "In the drawing test, Mercader del Rio revealed himself as an automatized and rigid personality. . . . The entire test shows a lack of flexibility and of humanity due to unconscious needs." Other drawings by Ramon revealed his family, consisting of only three figures, father, mother and son, as "completely rigid, dehumanized." The son, himself, is made to look "like a man, too small in relation to his mother." A sketch of Paris by the prisoner is "symbolically a representation of the feminine; the image of the mother divided by the River Seine." Dr. Sanchez describes it as "a completely Oedipal drawing of a traumatic infantile fixation." Highly revealing is the inscription made on this drawing by Ramon: "Although they don't want it." With this he clearly betrayed his determination to get to his mother in Paris upon his release from prison, despite the indicated opposition, which could come only from Moscow.

Finally, in a drawing of a floor plan of a house for "a small family of three, papa, mama and son," the assassin gave himself away by writing the last four words not in Spanish, but in the Catalan dialect.

The decisive characteristic which sets Mercader apart from the old, familiar types of political assassin is that the individual in him is totally submerged in a vast organization of colossal power, the Soviet state. He is a product not of a hot-headed or visionary secret society of Utopians, but of Stalin's hard-boiled school of murder which raised a generation of soldiers of the coming communist world revolution. He showed this schooling in a discussion with the examining psychologists when he propounded the theory, in terms of Marxist dialectics, that treason is necessary to achieve the new order.

The key to Mercader, who typifies the modern political assassin, is to be found in the special character of the organization in which he has enlisted for life. The Soviet power is an amalgam of a temporal state and a political religion. It is in the nature of a military order in which the government authorities and the Communist Party priesthood are one supreme source of faith and strength. Mercader became an assassin both as a servant of that government and a missionary of its communist faith, and is beyond redemption.

The code of conduct of a Kremlin myrmidon dictates that morality is a bourgeois heritage, humanity an abstract entity in a materialistic conception of life, murder—a mere mechanical exercise. For him all the eternal questions have been immutably resolved by the "science" of Marxism-Leninism-Stalinism.

The *hombre enigmatico* thus turns out to be the prototype of the coming race as seen from Moscow in her universalist role of the mother of all nations. It is a race in which man and machine alike will be the harnessed twins laboring, to the accompaniment of stimulating joy-cries, to create infinite material wealth for a happy life forever and ever. Beneath the mask of the prisoner in Mexico lurks the Kremlin's happy robot of the future.

11

The Mother Speaks

When the completed manuscript of this book was in the hands of the printers, I received the following unsolicited communication from Enrique Castro Delgado whom I had interviewed last winter in Mexico City. He wrote about "a project on foot" in Mexico, in connection with reports of the publication of this book, to attack its revelations and to confuse the American public by claiming that "the unhappily celebrated assassin of Trotsky" is really a man called Jacques Mornard. If this "new" version were widely accepted, he added, "the crime would be dissociated from its source: Moscow." In sending this memoir, Mr. Castro gave me permission to use it as I saw fit so that the world may have the whole truth about the murder. Mr. Castro had not read my manuscript, nor did he know of the fingerprints or the photographic and other evidence about the assassin's identity presented in this volume.

His communication is a singular document by itself, and it makes a moving sequel to the story of Ramon Mercader. Mr. Castro is no ordinary witness. Born in Madrid in 1907, having gone to work in a metal shop at the age of 12, he grew up to become a journalist. He joined the Communist Party of Spain in 1925, was imprisoned both under the Monarchy and the Republic, and upon the outbreak of the civil war in his country organized and led the famed Fifth Regiment. He became a member of the Central Committee and the Political Bureau of the Spanish Communist Party, held top posts at the front, and escaped to Russia after Franco's victory. In 1944 he broke with the Party in Moscow, was expelled from the Comintern and, after some precarious months, managed to get out of the Soviet Union. He published an outstanding book on his experiences there. He has been living quietly in Mexico, employed in an editorial capacity, and has been working on another book dealing with the psychological metamorphosis of persons turned out by the Soviet mill. In the following text, the explanatory notes in brackets are my own:

> That which I am now going to tell you, friend Levine, I have never told to anyone. And I have not told it because I believed for a long time that the drama of 1940 had ended long ago. It is not so. The drama survives through time. Corpses, which live and speak and feel and suffer, have prolonged its existence until today . . . I know full well that the crime involved these three people: General Leonid [Eitingon Kotov] one of Beria's trusted aides; Caridad Mercader, one of the most trusted agents of Leonid; and Ramon del Rio Mercader, made an assassin by his own mother. And I know, friend Levine, I know because I heard it from the lips of the person who knew it best . . . and it happened this way:
>
> I came to know Caridad Mercader in the summer of 1943 in Moscow. She came to visit me—"because I wished to know you personally"—in my room at the Hotel Lux, after having

seen Jesus Hernandez [formerly Minister of the Spanish Republic], a refugee in Russia. I had expected her call, Hernandez having previously phoned me. When she arrived Esperanza (my wife) went to open the door. For her an embrace; for me a handshake. I remember perfectly that she was wearing a knitted gray dress and that on her breast was displayed the Order of Lenin. She was tall, slender, with white hair, her face angular, with thin lips. She was incredibly attractive, spoke rapidly with a slight Catalan accent . . . She smoked uninterruptedly, lighting one cigarette from the stub of the previous one. She gave the impression of being a great lady, a slightly strange great lady. She spoke. We talked for a long time. And when she left, she invited us to come to her house for lunch or dinner at our convenience. We became great friends.

Time passed.

The day of my trial in the Black House on the Soviet Square came: my expulsion from the Comintern and from the Communist Party of Spain. My tragedy lasted months, when I was between anguish and death. In those terrible days of solitude in a city of millions, Caridad Mercader continued to be our great friend.

"You are right, we have been deceived. This is not Paradise . . . It is the most terrible of hells known to man," she would say. My visits to her house at that time occurred almost daily. I would arrive at eleven in the morning and often I did not leave until very late at night, because I found there a friendship without fear or reserve. There we spent hours and hours sitting on the edge of her bed and talking about everything: of yesterday and of tomorrow. A great talker, she spoke to me of Mexico, of its climate and people, or of Paris, of her days of solitude and exhaustion, or of trips through Europe, although she never told me the reasons for these interminable travels about the world . . . One day Caridad started to speak to me about her anxiousness to leave:

"Here I am doing nothing . . . I merely die bit by bit . . .

Furthermore, Enrique, I can't get used to it, I can't get used to it." This idea began to be an obsession with her. She spoke of nothing else. She didn't wish to talk about anything else. And, as time passed, her nerves were more and more shattered. Until the moment came when Caridad was really a sick person: from insomnia and anxiety to escape. Not a single week passed in which she did not write Beria for permission to leave, or to Merkulov or to Sudoplatov. Sometimes these letters were calm, sometimes they were violent and filled with forebodings. Occasionally, General Leonid appeared there. The two of them would go into the dining-room and talk and talk. When he left, Caridad would return to the alcove and drop on the bed. For several minutes, she would remain silent, staring at the ceiling . . . Afterwards, she paced the floor and smoked and cursed out loud. Only when her son, Luis, appeared did she manage to control herself; or when Brufau, also a Catalan woman, an agent of the N.K.V.D., would come—among other tasks she had that of watching Caridad . . .

Autumn came. Every day, I was filled with uneasiness as I left the Hotel Lux. I would walk slowly toward Caridad's house on Kalujskaia, one of an interminable row of identical houses in which the agents of the N.K.V.D. lived. One entered from the rear, through a narrow door, or from a side entrance, almost hidden. The porter, old and dirty, controlled the coming and going of everybody.

"Hello, Enrique."

"Hello, Caridad."

And I would follow her inside the apartment. And we would sit down on the edge of the bed, smoking for a time in silence.

"Are you ill?"

"I haven't slept . . . Still another night that I have not slept and I am afraid that if I don't get out of here soon I shall go mad."

"Have you talked to Leonid again?"

"Yes."

"What did he say?"

"That I should be patient . . . That I will get out . . ."

"Then you must calm yourself."

"No . . . Leonid is deceiving me . . . He has always deceived me . . . Always . . . He only comes to keep me quiet, to maintain in me the hope that I will get out, knowing all the time that I will not leave here."

And again the silence.

"Did you speak to Beria?"

"I have tried to talk to him . . . But when I sent him a note asking for an interview, he sent me flowers by Leonid and a message, 'Cordial greetings to Comrade Caridad.' What do you advise me to do?"

"That you be patient . . . The same advice that you give me every day."

"I can't!" She screamed it, in a voice without any fear of being heard. A scream which was followed by sobs. And she dropped on the bed to hide her head among the pillows, continuing to sob . . . Bit by bit she calmed herself; afterwards she got up and, going to the kitchen, she returned shortly with two cups of coffee. And she again sat down and smoked while she sipped the coffee little by little.

And then she began to speak again.

"You don't know these people, Enrique. They are people without souls . . . without souls . . . People who, after taking everything from you, kill you either at once or kill you slowly as they are doing to me now . . . As they are doing to you too!"

"My case is different. I have broken . . . You haven't."

"But they no longer have any use for me . . . No, after my last trip to Turkey,[18] they don't need me . . . I am known abroad . . . And it is dangerous to use me . . . But, furthermore, they know that I am no longer the woman I used to be . . . Because even criminals get tired of being criminals and, when they realize what they are, they want to stop being criminals . . . If I told you . . . And, yes, I am going to tell you, I want you to know that which you don't know, who these people are . . ."

"I would prefer that you didn't tell me."

"You must know it. You have to. Because if anything happens to me, because if I am assassinated by those for whom I murdered, by those for whom I made my son into a murderer, my poor Luis into a permanent hostage and my other two children into ruins, I want you to know. Do you understand me? I want you to know so that with this knowledge you can help to see that no more people are fooled by these illusions as you and I were."

"Caridad . . . Don't you think that it is dangerous for you and for me if it became known that I knew that which I should not know?"

"It is no longer important . . . You are doomed . . . I am doomed . . . They will bury us here unless there is a miracle, the miracle of being able to get out . . . But even if we do get out, we will still be under sentence of death . . . You and I are among those people who will never know in what city we shall be buried."

She paused.

"Enrique, I have travelled around Europe from place to place . . ."

"Be quiet, Caridad!"

"I don't want to . . . I want to avenge myself in some way on these swine . . . On these beasts who, blinding us with the illusion of socialism, have torn me to pieces, have broken my family into bits, everything, everything . . . No, Enrique, we have been poisoned by the literature of the October Revolution, by the illusion of our own Revolution, by the idea of socialism and we didn't realize that we had fallen into a world of lies and terror . . . People do not know this, but one day they must be made to know it. They must know it! . . . They must know that Caridad Mercader is not simply Caridad Mercader, but the worst of assassins . . . Yes . . . The worst . . . Because not only did I travel throughout Europe tracking down Chekists [Soviet secret agents] who had defected or diplomats who had abandoned Paradise, so as to assassinate them pitilessly . . . I have done even more! . . .

More! . . . I made—and I did this for them—an assassin of my son, of Ramon, of this son whom I saw one day come out of Trotsky's house bound and bleeding and unable to come to me, and I had to flee in one direction and Leonid in another . . ."

She rose and searched through a drawer of her chest. Then she came back and sat beside me, showing me two decorations: the Order of Hero of the Soviet Union and the Order of Lenin, which I had so often seen on her breast.

"Do you see this . . . ? This is the reward for the assassination of Trotsky . . . Ramon, the condemned man in Lecumberri Prison, is here nothing less than a Hero of the Soviet Union; and I, his mother, who pushed him to this crime, am nothing more or less than the possessor of the Order of Lenin . . . People who know it envy us, but many do not know the high price of these two *merdes*. . . . Yes, for the assassin of Trotsky is my son, Ramon, whom I in the name of the sacred interests of the Revolution and of socialism, drove to this crime; and I am . . . a thing to inspire horror.

"And I want to get out, Enrique, and get to Mexico . . . To see whether I can get Ramon out; and see whether I can cleanse myself of this crime in any way, a greater crime than that of having killed Trotsky."

We looked at each other in silence.

"But did you do this deliberately?"

"No, Enrique, I was crazed by many things: exalted by the Revolution, inflamed by Leonid who stirred up a new hope that I had buried many years before . . . Because we were going to be married! Because they were going to bring Ramon to me here! And also my children from France! Because here my life was going to begin again without the loneliness and bitterness of so many years . . . ! And it was all a lie: They did not free Ramon, nor did they bring my children from France, nor has Leonid married me, nor did they wish me to get out . . . They only want me to die here, in silence, slowly, hiding my tragedy under this Order of Lenin which burns my flesh . . . It burns me, Enrique . . . !"

And there was silence. Late at night I left the house slowly, wishing to forget, I returned to the Hotel Lux.

Months later, Caridad Mercader was allowed to leave and go to Mexico. For about a year, she tried to find a way to free Ramon del Rio Mercader. But around her the agents of the N.K.V.D. had spread a net. She got into Lecumberri only once but did not see her son. Afterward, an automobile almost ran her down . . . And she felt that they wanted to eliminate her in the same way that she had been employed many times to eliminate others. Driven by fear, she went to the French Embassy one day and managed to get a visa to go to Paris. They tell me that she lives there more disturbed than ever.

ENRIQUE CASTRO DELGADO

Mexico City,
June 16, 1959.

Sources and Notes

1. *The Nation*, New York, October 10, 1936.
2. American Aspects of Assassination of Leon Trotsky. Hearings before the Committee on Un-American Activities, House of Representatives. July–December, 1950. Also, Louis F. Budenz, Hearings before the same Committee, November 22, 1946.
3. Jorge, December 14, 1911; Pablo, November 25, 1915; Montserrat, sister, date in question; and Luis, in June or July, 1923; all born in Barcelona.
4. Hearing before the Senate Subcommittee on Internal Security, Scope of Soviet Activity in the United States. Part 87, November 21, 1957.
5. *The Case of Leon Trotsky*. Report of Hearings before Preliminary Commission of Inquiry, John Dewey, Chairman. Harper & Bros., 1937.
6. "The Zborowski Case," by Henry Kasson (*nom de plume* of the recognized authority on the subject). *The New Leader*, November 21, 1955.

7. Hearing before the Senate Subcommittee on Internal Security, Scope of Soviet Activity in the United States. Part 5, March 2, 1956.
8. "Mark Zborowski, Soviet Agent," by David J. Dallin. *The New Leader,* March 19 and 26, 1956.
9. Hearing before the Senate Subcommittee on Internal Security, Scope of Soviet Activity in the United States. Part 51, February 14 and 15, 1957.
10. Hearings before the Senate Subcommittee on Internal Security, Activities of Soviet Secret Service, May 21, 1954; also Part 86, October 1 and 16, 1957.
11. Same as No. 9, listed above.
12. Same as No. 2, listed above.
13. Same as No. 2, listed above, pages 3409–3416.
14. Same as No. 2, listed above, pages 3401–3407.
15. Elizabeth T. Bentley testimony. Hearings before the Committee on Un-American Activities, House of Representatives, July 31, and August 10–11, 1948; Hearings before Senate Subcommittee on Internal Security, Part 2, Institute of Pacific Relations, August, 1951, and Part 13, April–May, 1952.
16. *La Vie et La Mort en U.R.S.S.,* by General "El Campesino," Paris, 1950. *La Grande Trahison,* by Jesus Hernandez, Paris, 1953. *Vie et Mort de Trotsky,* by Victor Serge, Paris, 1951.
17. Same as No. 2, listed above, pages IX–XV.
18. Dispatched by the Kremlin to Hungary during the war to rescue a group of leading Communists, Caridad managed to bring them to Turkey. When the Turkish secret service discovered her identity as a Soviet agent, she eluded them and fled from the country on an American plane. This discovery ended her usefulness to the NKVD abroad.

Deserving of note are three special and little-known works: Enrique Castro Delgado's *J'Ai Perdu La Foi à Moscou,* Paris, 1950; Report of Royal Commission on Espionage, Commonwealth of Australia, Sydney, 1954–55; and *Jacques Mornard,* by Eduardo Ceniceros, Mexico, 1957, 281 pages, the record by the assassin's attorney of his brief for parole.

Special mention should also be made of the Trotskyite publications, the magazine *Fourth International*, the *Bulletin de l'Opposition*, and *The Militant*, containing valuable first-hand accounts by the Trotskys and members of their inner circle.

Those readers of Chapter Two who are interested in Soviet espionage among the Trotskyites long after the assassination of their leader may derive some useful information from the following note:

> The chief of Moscow's major network in the United States was the third secretary of the Soviet Embassy in Washington, "a short, bespectacled, ugly-looking man," who was none other than Major General Vassili M. Zubilin of the NKVD. It was under Zubilin that Soble served upon his arrival, the same Zubilin who master-minded the theft of the atom bomb secrets during the war years.
>
> One of Soble's first assignments was to spy on the Trotskyites. Zubilin informed him that there were three Trotskyite groups in New York City and that each had a Soviet agent planted in it. Although Trotsky had been assassinated, Soble continued his spying on the Trotskyites. "I met the three Trotsky agents, each at different restaurants, to get their reports," Soble confessed, without troubling to identify them. "From them I received the names and addresses of the members, occurrences at meetings, and activities and trends of the Trotskyite movement."
>
> In March, 1944, when Zubilin hastily departed from the United States, Soble was appointed his successor in charge of the major Soviet spy ring. Soble now had supervision over Boris Morros, the Hollywood producer who was to become an undercover agent for the FBI; Martha E. Dodd, the daughter of William E. Dodd, former United States Ambassador to Germany, and her husband, Alfred K. Stern; Jane Foster Zlatovski and her husband George, a former U. S. Army intelligence officer—(the last two couples are fugitives from American justice in Europe)—and, finally, over Mark Zborowski.

Soble had refused the repeated requests, conveyed through Morros, to go back to Moscow for a report. How invaluable Soble was to the Kremlin as late as November, 1954, has been revealed by Morros who was told that Soble possessed detailed knowledge of Trotsky's followers not only in the United States and Western Europe, but also within the Soviet Union itself.

Index